HOW TO INVEST IN GOLD AND SILVER

A Complete Guide with a Focus on Mining Stocks

Don Durrett

www.GoldStockData.com

(Eighth Edition - February 2020)

ISBN: 978-1-4276-5024-5

www.GoldStockData.com

Gold is money. Everything else is credit.

– J. P. Morgan

When paper money systems begin to crack at the seams, the run to gold could be explosive.

– Harry Browne

Gold still represents the ultimate form of payment in the world ... gold is always accepted

– Alan Greenspan,
May 20, 1999.

Love makes the world go 'round. Yeah, the love of gold.

– Gene Hackman,
from the movie *Heist*.

How to Invest in Gold and Silver

Reader Reviews

Whether you are an individual investor or a professional wanting to learn how to invest in the precious metals sector, this is the right book at the right time. Don takes you through the basics of investing in bullion or stocks; from large cap producers to junior exploration companies. *Must reading for those wishing to familiarize themselves with the intricacies of precious metals investing.*

Jim Puplava, Financial Sense Newshour
(www.financialsense.com)

The book, which in my estimation is a Bible-equivalent for junior resource investors, aggregates the small details investors need to know in order to survive in the junior resource market.

Tekoa Da Silva
(www.bullmarketthinking.com)

I would recommend *How to Invest in Gold & Silver* as an excellent, in-depth book that both the novice and seasoned precious metals and mining shares investors can find very helpful.

Peter Grandich
(www.grandich.com)

Reader Reviews (conitnued)

From my perspective, and with over three decades in the investment game, I cannot stress how much I enjoyed this excellent book. As many of you know, we have been in both "reality-based investing" and the "business of gold" for many years. Reality based investing includes physical gold (and silver) ownership, and Don's book adeptly covers precious metals fundamentals like no one else! Everyone who is into gold ownership must read the first half of this book. For those interested in being a successful junior resource investor, the second half of the book covers everything you will ever need to know! Don Durrett offers a blueprint toward individual prosperity in the tough world of gold and silver investing. Don's website: **GoldStockData.com** is also well worth visiting!

Larry Myles
(http://www.larrymylesreports.com)

CONTENTS

INTRODUCTION

I've been investing in gold since 1991 and silver since 2004. I'm not an industry insider or financial analyst, but a real-world investor. My profession has nothing to do with investing. I decided to write this book because, when I started investing in gold and silver Junior mining companies in 2004, I could not find a good book on the subject. Thus, I made mistake after mistake (investing in stocks that went down and stayed down) and had to learn the hard way.

My experience from investing exclusively in gold and silver assets has given me unique knowledge to write a complete investment guide on these precious metals. I feel I have had enough hands-on experience to let you know the secrets. Once you're armed with these secrets of knowing how to invest in gold/silver, you will likely make a lot of money.

While this book is a complete guide, the focus is on investing in mining stocks. Don't despair if you have no intention of buying any stocks. The first few chapters will be very useful for making decisions on how to buy bullion, coins, or ETFs.

I have purchased more than 100 mining stocks, all with the intention of achieving 300% to 500% returns. That has always been my goal. Most of you probably have a lower goal, which is fine. This book will show you how to reach for a specific investment return. Analyzing a stock's value and upside potential is the same method for all stocks. The only difference is the upside potential and risk level, which is different for each stock. If you want to focus on less upside and less risk, then I can show you how to do that.

In a gold bull market, finding large returns is not that difficult. The key, of course, is finding excellent stocks with a lot of upside potential. Most investors are satisfied with a 10% annual return. If you are in that group, then it should be easy to make those returns investing in gold/silver (as long as this gold bull market resumes).

When I started investing in Junior mining companies in 2004, gold was under $500 per ounce and the mining sector was depressed. It was easy, back then, to find excellent stocks that were undervalued. That will always be the case in a bull market, but finding large returns becomes more difficult as the price of gold/silver increases. Thus, it becomes more important to be armed with the knowledge of how to invest in these metals.

I discovered that it is really not that difficult to find excellent stocks if you know what to look for. However, it took me years to figure out how to value them (upside potential and risk level). When I first started, I depended on the views of others, and that is likely what you will do. You will purchase subscriptions to Internet websites or investment newsletters, and buy what "experts" recommend. You might do really well. But trust me, they will also recommend a few dogs. You will look back on those and wonder why they ever recommended them.

When I first started investing, many of the recommended stocks turned out to be dogs. Now that I know what to look for, I realize that I could have easily identified these stocks as "long shots." Being able to manage the risk in your portfolio by knowing which stocks are "long shots" and which are much more likely to be "winners" is why you need to read this book. It's okay to have a few long shots in your portfolio, but you also need to be loaded up on quality stocks that have big upside potential.

You will know which of your stocks are winners. These are the stocks that will react in a very positive manner when the price of gold increases significantly. While not all of your stocks will react (depending on their properties, location, balance sheet, production, and profitability), some will explode in value every time the price rises. You need to have enough of these winners so that your portfolio rises faster than the price of gold. Otherwise, what is the point of investing in mining stocks?

The only way you can get large returns is to invest in Juniors and Mid-Tier Producers. Investing in bullion and Majors will generally only double or triple your money, and that's not where the big returns come from. If you are reading this and silver is still below $30, then that could be an exception. Some savvy silver investors are avoiding mining stocks and buying the metal.

Investing in Juniors and Mid-Tier Producers isn't that difficult, but it requires knowledge, analysis, and constant vigilance. These are volatile markets, and you can't just watch the gold and silver markets once a week for a couple of hours and expect to be as successful as someone who is putting in more time. When you are investing (building an investment portfolio), you have to watch the markets daily.

You have to monitor the price of gold/silver, general market conditions, and watch certain specific stocks. You have to do the work.

Once you are somewhat fully invested and no longer aggressively adding stocks, you can begin monitoring your portfolio. Every stock should have an exit strategy because of the dynamics of the mining business. Never buy a mining stock and think it is a long-term investment that you will hold forever. You will want to exit for a number of reasons: 1) Their story changed, 2) The gold bull market is over, or 3) It's time to take profit. I will have more to say about this in Chapter 9 on "How to Make Money."

While I have focused this introduction on achieving large returns, about one-fifth of my investments are in large-cap mining companies, called Majors. This is where I started investing. And most of them pay an annual dividend, which I can then use to purchase Mid-Tiers, Juniors, or bullion.

Thus, I have included a chapter on Majors. I also cover ETFs (exchange-traded funds), options, bullion, and coins. I'm big on diversity. I think you should have a little bit of everything, as long as it is a gold or silver asset!

This book is strictly a practical how-to guide for investing in gold and silver, with a focus on mining stocks. It's not a high-level guide that helps you understand why to invest in gold/silver, although I do cover that, as well. My focus is more on the what. I will fill you in on what you need to know in order to invest wisely. I want to help people who want to take advantage of a gold bull market and who want to cover all of the angles. Anyone can purchase a gold mutual fund or gold bullion ETF, and then sit back and make a decent return if gold prices are trending higher. But how much are you leaving on the table? Do you want to do the work and make the most of this one-time opportunity to make much more?

When I purchased stocks like Fortuna Silver at 80 cents and First Majestic Silver at $1.30 after the stock market crash in 2008, I was excited. I knew these stocks were going to roar like tigers and far surpass my silver bullion ETF and gold mutual fund holdings. This allowed me to own relatively low-risk companies that offered a big upside potential, and I wouldn't be locked into minimal returns when gold/silver rose. Showing you how to pick those stocks and build a balanced portfolio is the main reason I wrote this book.

Now, I am not a professional mining stock analyst, but I have spent thousands of hours analyzing mining stocks, and I trust my analysis over that of any expert. I feel that I know enough to help beginners become competent amateurs like myself. If you have already been investing in the gold/silver mining sector for several years, you probably already know everything I'm going to suggest. Moreover, I won't be going into great detail on how to value a company. I will include my simple valuation methods, which I think are perfectly adequate for gold/silver mining stocks.

This book is for beginners/amateurs who want to learn how to invest in gold/silver. It is for people who want to get educated on how to invest in these sectors. It's a short book, so I can't include everything. But once you begin investing, you will quickly pick up any additional information that you may be missing. You will have everything that you need to know to build a portfolio and get started. This is the book I wish I'd had when I was learning how to invest in gold/silver, especially Junior mining stocks.

Ninety percent of the books out there on investing in gold/silver are total junk. I know, because I have bought several of them and learned very little. It's especially hard to learn how to invest in Juniors. While my fifteen years of investing in Juniors does not designate me as an expert in this field, I feel my knowledge is sufficient.

I've tried to make this book extremely readable. I have been writing books since 1991, and this was my eleventh. The good news is that you found this book and that a writer took up investing in gold and silver. In other words, this book wasn't written by a professional investor who doesn't know how to write or a writer who doesn't know how to invest. For that reason, you should find it a very valuable guide.

This is the eighth edition of this book. When I wrote the first edition in 2010, someone told me to keep it fresh because when the mania into gold stocks arrives, investors are going to want to buy books that are fresh. I took that advice to heart and have updated it regularly.

When I was writing the second edition in 2011, I got the idea of analyzing every gold and silver mining company. That turned into my website: www.goldstockdata.com. It is perhaps the best database on the Internet for gold and silver mining stocks. It currently has over 800 companies, including nearly every gold or silver miner in the world with a market cap over $3 million. What makes the website so valuable is that it combines data and analysis. You can quickly search the database to identify companies that match your risk level, and then read my analysis of the stock.

In the third edition, I added a new chapter called "How to Value Mining Stocks." I subsequently added this chapter to my website under the link "Mining 101" along with two YouTube videos. I created this chapter and videos to help investors pick mining stocks. After you finish reading the book, I recommend that you view these videos.

One final disclaimer. Investing in gold and silver mining stocks is extremely high risk due to its volatility. For example, from 2011 to 2015, the HUI index fell 83% (628 to 105), while gold prices fell 45% ($1923 to $1062). The HUI is an index of the 30 largest gold mining stocks, with market caps averaging over $1 billion in value. Many junior and mid-tier stocks fell more than 90% during this period. And even during periods of rising gold prices, mining stocks can fall out of favor with investors and crash quite suddenly. This high-risk level is the reason why the vast majority of investors will never own a gold or silver mining stock. It is one of the highest risk asset classes one can own.

Don Durrett
January 8, 2021

CHAPTER 1

WHY INVEST IN SILVER?

Silver presents an interesting investment opportunity. Why? Because there isn't much left. In 1945, there were approximately 10 billion ounces (bullion and coins) of silver inventory worldwide[1] Today, there are approximately 3 billion ounces (bullion and coins). The total value of silver bullion and coins above ground is about $75 billion, with silver at $25 per ounce. That contrasts with the value of gold bullion and coins above ground, which is estimated to be about 3 billion ounces or about $6 trillion at $1,900 per ounce. Thus, there is about 80 times more gold inventory above ground than silver on a valuation basis

This does not count all of the silver and gold used for jewelry, artwork, and silverware that could be recycled. There are about 15 billion ounces of silver and about 2 billion ounces of gold that could be recycled. Most of this will never be recycled, but perhaps 10% will be as prices go higher.

About 50 billion ounces of silver have been mined, but most of it is gone. Where did all of the silver bullion go? Mostly into landfills. Silver is used in such small quantities in manufactured goods that most silver is not recycled. Thus, it is used and discarded into a waste dump.

Silver is used in thousands of products: TVs, appliances, computers, cell phones, iPads, iPods, radios, transportation vehicles (automobiles, motorcycles, airplanes, ships, trains), jewelry, silverware, medical equipment, electrical connectors, mirrors, door handles, CD-ROMs, DVDs, film, cameras, batteries, solar panels, water purification, anti-bacterial products, etc. It is the second most used ingredient for manufactured items after oil. Moreover, its usage is expanding. Every year, companies are finding new ways to use this versatile metal. For instance, manufacturers recently started putting silver in clothing to keep it smelling fresh.[2] And there was a recent study that confirmed it enhances the effect of antibiotics.

If this list of uses does not get your attention, consider this: China has plans to build enough solar panels by 2030 to consume hundreds of millions of ounces of silver. Where is this large increase in supply going to come from? Increased silver production? Unlikely. Production has been declining in recent years, peaking in 2015 at 895 million oz. Moreover, most of the high-grade silver has already been mined, and grades have been plummeting for decades.

In 2017, silver demand was 1 billion ounces.[3] Most of this was used in the list of products cited above. And since most of these products will never be recycled, this silver is gone forever. This is where the billions of ounces of silver have gone.

Total mine production in 2017 was 852 million ounces.[4] Fortunately, a significant amount of silver is recycled every year (mostly from industrial waste, old jewelry, photography, and X-rays). Without this recycled silver, there would be a large supply shortage.

Silver mine production has not changed much since 2017 and remains around 850 million ounces. However, demand increased substantially in 2020. In 2017, investor demand was around 150 million ounces (see chart one next page). In 2020, it jumped to around 350 million ounces. The final numbers are not out yet, bet we know that silver bullion ETF demand was up more than 65% in 2020.

In December 2019, the SLV silver bullion ETF held 362 million ounces. In December 2020, it held about 550 million ounces. That is an increase in demand of about 200 million ounces. SLV is only one of several silver ETFs and does include demand for silver bars and coins. I would estimate that investor demand was at least 350 million ounces in 2020, which is about 35% of supply. This means that above ground inventory for sale is shrinking.

Even with recycled silver, there is an annual deficit. This deficit is overcome with government sales and from bullion banks. In 2017, the deficit was 27 million ounces (see chart below).[5] Without these third-party sales, there would have been a physical shortage.

Silver Supply & Demand

Since 1945, there has been a consistent annual deficit of silver supply versus silver demand. The deficit has been made up by using existing government inventory and bullion bank inventory. Thus, the global excess inventory continues to wither away, and it's almost gone.

In 1945, the U.S. Government held 4 billion ounces of silver bullion.[6] Today, it has none. Where did it go? It was sold to manufacturers because of supply deficits.

Supply 2017		Demand 2017	
Mine Production	852	Industrial/Fabrication	599
Recycled Scrap	138	Jewelry	209
Total Supply	990	Silverware	58
		Coins & Medals	151
		Total Demand	1017

Without these sales, the economy would have suffered from a shortage, and the price of silver would have soared.

Today, the Chinese Government is the only government with a significant silver inventory. China has been selling it to their manufacturers, but this won't last much longer. Soon, the Chinese will also be out.

Looking at the silver supply and demand chart above, notice the data for Coins & Medals. This is the investor total, and it represented about 15% of sales in 2017. In 2020, that more than doubled. Soon there could be a bidding war between investors and fabricators for silver as supply becomes overwhelmed by investors.

Already most of the silver that comes out of the ground is immediately purchased by someone. There is very little excess inventory for sale worldwide. Of the approximate 3 billion ounces above ground, nearly all of it is held by investors. In 2010, Eric Sprott started a silver bullion ETF (PSLV), and it took him three months to acquire 22 million ounces.[7] Why did it take so long to accumulate? The inventory did not exist. He stated in an interview that some of the silver he received was minted after his order was made.

Silver Shortage Possibility

The main difference between gold and silver is that silver is primarily an industrial metal. More than half of annual silver demand (about 60%) is used for industrial fabrication, whereas only about 14% of gold production has industrial demand. Because of the reliance on silver by so many consumer products, it will likely one day go into a shortage (considering the disappearing inventories and increasing investor demand).

In 1997, the precious metal palladium (used in automobile catalytic converters) was $100 an ounce. Then it suddenly started rising and kept rising all the way to $1,100 by 2001. This breakout occurred when manufacturers began hoarding the metal from fear of a shortage. This same scenario could happen with silver. If you are a manufacturer, and silver inventories begin to shrink at the COMEX (New York Commodity Exchange), you are likely going to begin accumulating your own inventory. Manufacturers won't have a choice. Without inventory, they will have to stop production. Note that this includes just about all of the large international corporations that require electronics in their products.

The question I like to ask is, how high will the price of silver go if we have a shortage? Moreover, since there is no cheap alternative for silver, how desperate will manufacturers like Apple, HP, Sony, Panasonic, Samsung, GE, Nokia, LG, etc., become? You can also add all of the automobile manufacturers to that list. Desperation plus shortages always mean rapidly rising prices.

As mentioned earlier, most of the silver bullion above ground is not for sale. Perhaps less than 50 million ounces are available for purchase globally for physical delivery on any given day. These 50 million ounces are spread out to retailers and wholesalers throughout the world. In 1997, Warren Buffett accumulated 130 million ounces at approximately $5 per ounce. (He sold at a nice profit, but regrets selling early.) It would be very difficult (likely impossible) to accumulate that much silver today in a short period of time.

In January 2017, estimates of the silver inventory showed:

Silver Inventory

Silver Coins and Bullion

Custodial Vaults .... 1750 million oz.
ETFs .... 671 million oz.
Exchanges .... 254 million oz.
Governments .... 89 million oz.
Industry .... 14 million oz.
Total .... 2.7 billion oz.[8]

When I wrote the first edition of this book, there was only 1.5 billion oz. of silver bullion inventory. Today that has nearly doubled. Investors have been taking advantage of low silver prices and have been accumulating silver. The amount of silver held in warehouse vaults has increased substantially in the past decade. While this seems like a large inventory, most of it is not for sale and already has established owners.

There simply is not that much physical silver available for delivery. In dollar terms, we are talking about small amounts of money on a daily basis (millions instead of billions). In other words, it doesn't matter if you have the money (and are willing to pay above market prices); the silver is just not available. The total physical silver market for investors in 2017 was less than $5 billion (new production plus existing physical inventory switching hands). That is a tiny amount when you compare it to the $100 trillion bond market, or the amount of money that is put into CDs every month at neighborhood banks.

Many precious metal investors have been forced to focus on gold. If you have a billion dollars that you want to invest in physical silver, it's not going to happen overnight. It could take months to find that much silver. For this reason, one large hedge fund could double the price of silver if they started hoarding silver with a few billion dollars.

Silver ETFs

In addition to the low amounts of physical silver available for sale, inventories owned by ETFs are increasing quite rapidly. These are exchange-traded funds, such as SLV, SIVR, PSLV, and CEF, which trade like a stock on the major stock exchanges.

These ETFs are backed by physical silver, which is stored in warehouses. SLV, the largest ETF, had 325 million ounces as of 2015, and in January 2020, it was up to 562 million ounces. The total amount of physical silver held by ETFs was slightly over 1 billion ounces in January 2020.

These ETFs are popping up all around the world: England, Canada, Switzerland, Australia, Dubai, etc. (see 2010 chart below).[9] This will shrink inventory levels significantly of physical silver available for purchase. It is my opinion that these ETFs will consume the remaining inventory until a shortage emerges. This is very bullish for the silver price.

Chart showing growth of silver held by silver exchange traded funds.

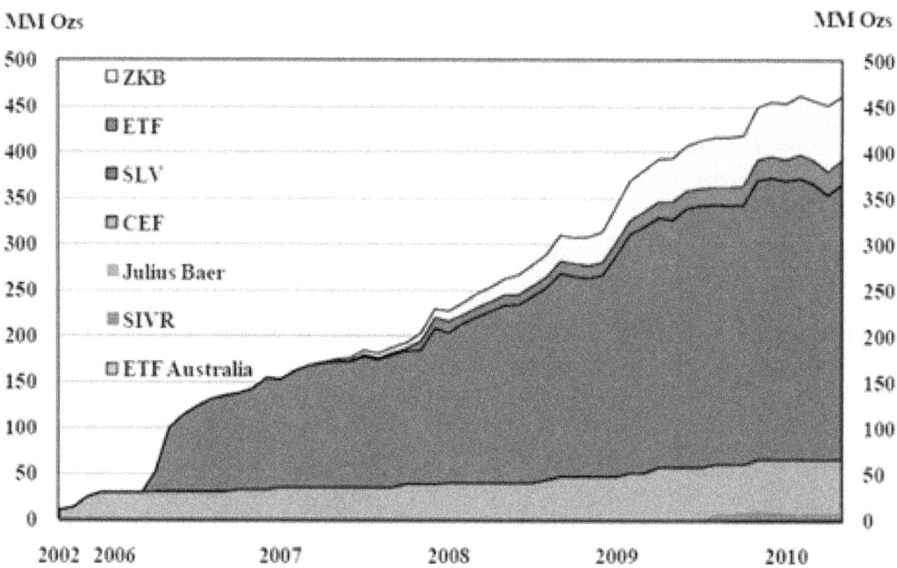

And if the ETFs do not force a shortage, then surely investors who are buying more and more bullion and coins will do so. (Over 500 million Silver Eagle 1 ounce coins have been purchased from the U.S. Mint since 1986.)[10] Once this shortage emerges, the price is going to skyrocket. It's not inconceivable for silver to reach $150 per ounce, and $100 is likely. I used to think that $150 silver was too high a long-term target, but now I think it's possible. If palladium can rise 10x from $100 to $1,000, then silver can rise 10x too if a shortage emerges.

Silver Paper

There is another factor that could drive prices substantially higher. Investors have purchased silver paper certificates to the tune of approximately 1 billion ounces of silver. Since banks do not have this much physical silver, they are exposed to huge losses if silver prices rise. The only thing they can do to hedge against additional losses is to purchase silver (either physical metal or an ETF) or silver futures contracts. If they begin to hedge, this will also drive prices up.

There are two types of silver paper certificates. One is backed by silver, also called allocated, and requires storage fees. The other is paper only and is settled in cash. Most allocated silver certificates backed by silver are in fact "naked." These certificates are not backed by real silver, but instead by promises made by banks and other financial institutions to deliver silver.

I call this a paper charade because the banks and institutions do not have enough physical silver to back up their promises of allocated silver. Instead, they use "pooled" silver accounts that hold a small portion of silver inventory for physical settlements (a form of fractional banking). However, what happens if investors get nervous and begin requesting their physical silver? If that happens, we will see huge shortages, and silver prices will explode.

If you're wondering why banks would sell naked silver certificates, it is free money as long as silver remains cheap and no one redeems their certificates. Investors gave banks billions of dollars, and all banks had to do was promise to pay them back at the current price of silver. This was a risky gambit that is about to be played out.

Gold/Silver Ratio

Originally, I started out as a gold investor, but I began adding silver investments in 2004 when I learned about the explosive upside potential of silver. I expect silver bullion to increase by a multiple of 20 or 30 before this bull market is finished (starting from $6 per ounce in 2001). That would result in a final price of $120 to $180 per ounce. This is not inconceivable. If we have a shortage, there should be a big move into silver by investors. In fact, my forecast is on the low side by many silver analysts. I've seen estimates that silver will reach four figures, and many analysts are expecting silver to reach $300 per ounce.

Another amazing thing about silver is that, even if we don't encounter a shortage, the ratio of gold to silver is in our favor. Today the ratio is $1,850 / $25 = 74. The historical average is around 30. However, if you go back to the 18th and 19th centuries, when silver was considered money, the average ratio was 16. Thus, as silver is perceived more and more as money, the ratio will drop substantially. If gold goes to $2,500 and the ratio is squeezed to 33, then silver will rise to $75.

Another factor that will squeeze this ratio is the ratio of silver to gold in the ground, which is approximately 16 to 1. Moreover, the ratio of mined silver to gold in 2017 was about 8 to 1 (852 million oz. / 101 million oz.).[11] For this reason, if silver is ever again considered money, the gold/silver ratio is likely to narrow significantly.

Some people think that because of silver's usefulness versus that of gold, the ratio could go as low as 10 to 1. While I don't expect that to happen, I do think that the ratio will shrink quite a bit. Today's ratio of 74 is inconsistent with the rarity of silver versus gold. My expectation is that we will see at least a 30 to 1 ratio.

If you are reading between the lines, you will have noticed that silver currently is approximately 100% undervalued versus gold, because of this ratio imbalance. If the ratio was more in line with silver's true intrinsic value, silver should outperform gold by at least 100% in the long term.

COMEX Futures Contracts

When you look at silver future contracts, there is yet another built-in slingshot for the price of silver. Currently, there is a large number of future contracts betting that the silver price will rise (about 200,000 contracts at 5,000 oz. each).[12] If 10% of those contracts decided to take delivery (which is something a holder of a contract can do), they would demand delivery of 20,000 x 5,000 = 100 million oz. That would cause the COMEX to likely default on delivery. In 2019, the COMEX registered silver inventory was 86 million oz.[13]

I think there is a good chance that investors will use the COMEX as a means of obtaining large quantities of physical silver. If this occurs, then there is a good chance of a default on delivery.

Silver: A Smart Investment

With such a low inventory of available physical silver for purchase, it appears to me that investing in silver is a smart investment and also a hedge against uncertainty. With the global economy in turmoil and global debt exploding, it seems inevitable that investors will seek out precious metals as a hedge. It won't take much to create a silver shortage and make the price soar. Already it is becoming difficult to obtain physical silver at local coin shops, although it is still widely available on the Internet.

The question you might be asking yourself about silver: Will it increase substantially in value? I think so. I see only two possible outcomes for long-term silver investors, both of which are positive:

1. The economy does not collapse, and the above ground silver inventory withers down to nothing, creating severe shortages (although this will take several years).
2. We experience an economic crisis and investors pour into silver as a hedge against the uncertainty of fiat currencies.

I expect the global debt bubble (Europe, Japan, and the U.S.A.) to pop and impact our economy and the financial system. So the second outcome seems more likely. This outcome should push silver prices up dramatically.

The first option is possible, but I think it is a long shot. I can't imagine going through this global debt crisis without any pain. And that pain is likely going to translate into much higher silver prices.

Silver-Producing Countries

Whereas gold is mined all over the world in dozens of countries, silver is primarily mined in only ten countries. Here they are, listed in order of production:

Peru

Mexico

China

Australia

Chile

Poland

Russia

U.S.A.

Bolivia

Canada

These top ten countries produce approximately 85% of all silver.[14] To give you an idea of production, the top country (Peru) produces about 100 million ounces per year; while Canada, the last entry, produces about 20 million ounces annually.

Silver as a Byproduct

One of the things I like about silver is that there are not that many pure silver mining companies. Only about 20% of silver production comes from companies called silver miners, and most of these companies are not pure silver miners (they also mine other metals). The other 80% of silver production comes from gold, copper, nickel, and zinc mining, where silver is mined as a byproduct.

What does this mean? Well, if the price of silver ever takes off and there is a mania, there are not that many silver mining stocks to choose from. In my database, there are currently only 18 silver miners with more than 1 million oz. of production. All you have to do is own the good ones, and you are going to do very well. Investors will have no choice but to bid up these stocks, and since this market is so tiny, the possibility for upside is tremendous.

				Rating									
Name	Main Symbol	Last Checked	Type	Upside	Downside	Risk	Your Summary		Current	$ USD	Category	FD Shares	FD Mkt. Cap
Americas Gold & Silver Corp.	USA.TO	02/05/2020	Silver	3.5	3.0	Moderate		CAD	3.840	3.026	MP	99.80M	$301.96M
Avino Silver & Gold Mines Ltd	ASM.TO	03/02/2020	Silver	3.5	3.0	Moderate		CAD	1.600	1.261	J-EM	90.00M	$113.46M
Coeur Mining Inc	CDE	06/01/2020	Silver	2.5	3.0	Moderate		USD	9.590	9.590	MP	245.00M	$2,349.55M
Endeavour Silver Corp	EXK	02/04/2020	Silver	2.5	3.0	High		USD	4.910	4.910	MP	148.05M	$726.93M
Excellon Resources Inc.	EXN.TO	10/12/2020	Silver	2.5	3.0	High		CAD	3.930	3.097	J-EM	39.90M	$123.55M
First Majestic Silver Corp	AG	10/14/2020	Silver	2.5	3.0	High		USD	13.030	13.030	EM	228.41M	$2,976.23M
Fortuna Silver Mines Inc	FSM	01/09/2021	Silver	2.0	3.0	Moderate		USD	8.650	8.650	MP	187.60M	$1,622.74M
Fresnillo Plc	FRES.L	06/22/2020	Silver	2.0	3.0	Moderate		GBX	1,205.500	16.383	M	736.89M	$12,072.83M
Gatos Silver Inc.	GATO.TO	12/12/2020	Silver	2.5	3.0	Moderate		CAD	17.420	13.726	MP	89.00M	$1,221.59M
Gogold Resources	GGD.TO	07/29/2020	Silver	3.0	3.0	Moderate		CAD	2.600	2.049	J-EM	278.00M	$569.51M
Hecla Mining Company	HL	01/09/2021	Silver	2.5	3.0	High		USD	6.080	6.080	EM	541.00M	$3,289.28M
Hochschild Mining Plc	HOC.L	11/18/2020	Silver	3.0	3.0	Moderate		GBX	218.200	2.965	MP	518.00M	$1,536.11M
MAG Silver Corp	MAG.TO	01/01/2020	Silver	2.0	4.0	Moderate		CAD	26.590	20.951	MP	88.60M	$1,856.26M
Pan American Silver Corp.	PAAS	06/04/2020	Silver	2.5	3.0	Moderate		USD	35.410	35.410	M	227.00M	$8,038.07M
Santacruz Silver Mining Ltd	SCZ.V	11/16/2020	Silver	2.0	2.5	High		CAD	0.450	0.355	J-SP	275.00M	$97.51M
Sierra Metals Inc	SMT.TO	01/20/2020	Silver	2.0	3.0	Moderate		CAD	4.200	3.309	MP	164.64M	$544.83M
Silver Bear Resources Plc	SBR.TO	04/21/2020	Silver	3.0	2.0	Extreme		CAD	0.145	0.114	J-EM	697.40M	$79.68M
Silvercorp Metals Inc	SVM.TO	06/15/2020	Silver	2.0	3.0	Moderate		CAD	7.810	6.154	MP	176.25M	$1,084.58M

The Risk Factor

The biggest threat for silver investors is lower prices. We could experience low prices under two scenarios. The first is a strong economy, where investors have little appetite for precious metals. The second is if excessive silver inventory builds, and a supply glut emerges. If this happens, prices could drop substantially and quickly. Mining shares could collapse under this scenario. One way this could happen is if the economy collapses and the manufacturing sector grinds to a halt, thereby reducing industrial silver demand.

On a positive note, if this happens, investor demand could very well exceed the lost industrial demand due to uncertainty in the economy. I think any potential over-supply issues will come after silver prices soar, so over-supply risk does not concern me in the near-term. That is my personal opinion, and it does not reduce the risk of investing in silver. One way to anticipate this potential supply glut is to sell as the price of silver rises. I will be discussing this with my exit strategy in Chapter 9.

Because silver is not considered a monetary metal, it is much riskier than investing in gold. Gold is simple to understand. Gold is a store of value and investors want it for that reason. End of story. Also, gold production is very limited, with only about 3,000 tons mined each year. Thus, gold is a rare commodity that is very liquid.

Silver isn't so simple. This is both a curse and an opportunity. The upside can be substantial, as well as the downside. The volatility is not for the weak of heart. I have seen silver drop from $21 down to $9 in less than one year, and from $49 to $14 over a four year period. Also, during this bull market, there has been a significant correction every single year in the silver market. Often it feels like a roller coaster. So you have to have nerves of steel and believe in the long-term trend.

When silver dropped to $9 in 2008, and to $14 in 2015, I didn't give up on this bull market. I didn't believe for a second that the bull market was over. Instead, I kept buying. I treated it as an opportunity. I don't think this bull market is going to end until we have a final blowoff. So, be aware that the silver market is extremely volatile, and there will be buying opportunities. Below is the price chart for silver from 2004 to 2020 (see chart below).[15]

From September 2013 until 2020, the silver price was in a prolonged correction. Then in July 2020, it finally broke out. I believe strongly that it will now trend higher and reach a new ATH (all-time high) above $50.

Other Potential Threats

There are a few other potential threats that silver investors should be aware of, although they all have a low probability of occurring. There is a very small likelihood that governments could appropriate silver from the ETFs and force liquidation. For instance, if there is a silver shortage because investors are competing with manufacturers for physical silver, governments might be tempted to shut down an ETF, such as SLV (which has about 550 million ounces). This could have the effect of creating a price collapse overnight.

Another possibility is that the U.S. government decides to limit silver investing by increasing taxation to prohibitive levels. If a silver shortage does arise, it is not inconceivable that it could be considered a strategic resource for the economy.

The last threat that I can think of is silver confiscation by the government and the illegality of owning it. This is a long shot that likely will not happen. However, buyer beware. Silver is a risky investment. If you want a true safe haven, then your metal is gold.

CHAPTER 2

WHY INVEST IN GOLD?

I opened the book with silver because it has a much higher potential return than gold. I wanted to get your attention and see if you were ready to be a precious metals investor, rather than someone who intends to use gold as a hedge against uncertainty. Do you want to chase high returns, or are you a more conservative investor? Exactly what is your risk tolerance? This is something you need to answer before stepping into the water.

Do you want to take full advantage of this gold/silver bull market, and get the most out of it that you can? Or, do you want to limit your risk and focus on gold? For those of you who are leery of stepping out on the ledge, understand that risk can be managed, and I will be discussing this throughout the book. The key is not to be afraid of it. It's all about risk-reward. You have to expose yourself to all of the angles to get the best reward. In other words, a little bit of risk is not a bad thing (not in a bull market).

While silver is more risky than gold, Junior Gold Explorer companies are much more risky than investing in gold coins. However, gold coins are going to have a limited upside, whereas Junior Gold Explorers can have enormous upside potential. The gains can be truly stunning. Those gains will not be possible unless you go for it and try to understand what it means to be a precious metals investor.

I could have simply opened this chapter by explaining why gold is the best investment you can make today. But I wanted you to understand the true focus of this book. This gold bull market is a once in a lifetime investment opportunity that should be approached from all angles. This is why the majority of this book is focused on gold and silver mining stocks.

Risk Tolerance

Many of you probably aren't interested in exposing yourself to substantial risk. After all, isn't gold supposed to be a hedge against uncertainty? You're likely reading this because you want to own gold for safety. You want some exposure, but you are not interested in risky stocks. That's fine. I cover that, too. If you want safety, stay away from the miners. If you want big returns, follow me through the rest of the book. Let's see how deep this rabbit hole can go....

The Best Investment: Gold

I read a book in 1989 which convinced me that gold was the best investment one co I read a book in 1989 which convinced me that gold was the best investment one could make (I became a gold bug). At that time, I was still in college and didn't have any money. But as soon as I started working, every dime of my investments went into gold-related assets. During the 1990s gold prices languished and it was a heady time for making money in the stock market. Some people laughed at me when I told them where I put my money.

People no longer laugh at me for investing in gold, and more and more people recognize the value of gold. Those gold investments in the 1990s put me in the position where I can retire early. It was the smartest thing I have done in my life. While I may have been early, it is not too late to invest in this gold bull market. My motives for investing in gold back in the 1990s are still valid today. Let's list a few:

1. Gold has one purpose, and that is to hold value. Thus, gold is an asset that can be converted to money. In fact, gold has acted as money for 5,000 years and will act as money for the foreseeable future.

   Note: Only 12% of gold demand is industrial/fabrication demand, mostly from electronics and dentistry, 50% is jewelry demand, and 38% is investment demand.[16]

2. Gold has no counter-party risk. When you hold an ounce of gold in your hand, there is no claim against it. Its value is determined by only one thing, the going spot price on that day.

   Note: This is not entirely true. Governments can attempt to confiscate gold or manipulate the price through taxation. But gold is not like a stock or bond asset which relies on a third party for its value.

3. Gold is rare. Approximately 190,000 tons of gold exist, enough to fill two Olympic-sized swimming pools.[17] Only 3,000 tons or so are mined each year.
4. Gold retains its value. An ounce of gold a hundred years ago could essentially purchase the same thing as an ounce of gold today. For instance, one ounce will purchase a nice suit, and nearly always has.
5. The U.S Government is steadily devaluing the dollar through deficit spending. Eventually, these deficits (which increase the national debt and inflate the money supply) will lead to a significant increase in the value of gold.

The first four reasons are essentially facts. However, it is that last one that you need to convince yourself is true. Because if it is true, then gold is the logical investment. The following charts show the correlation between U.S. Government debt and the price of gold. The first chart shows the gold price from 1989 to 2019.[18] Notice that gold did not reach $500 until 2006. The second chart shows U.S. Government debt to 2016.[19]

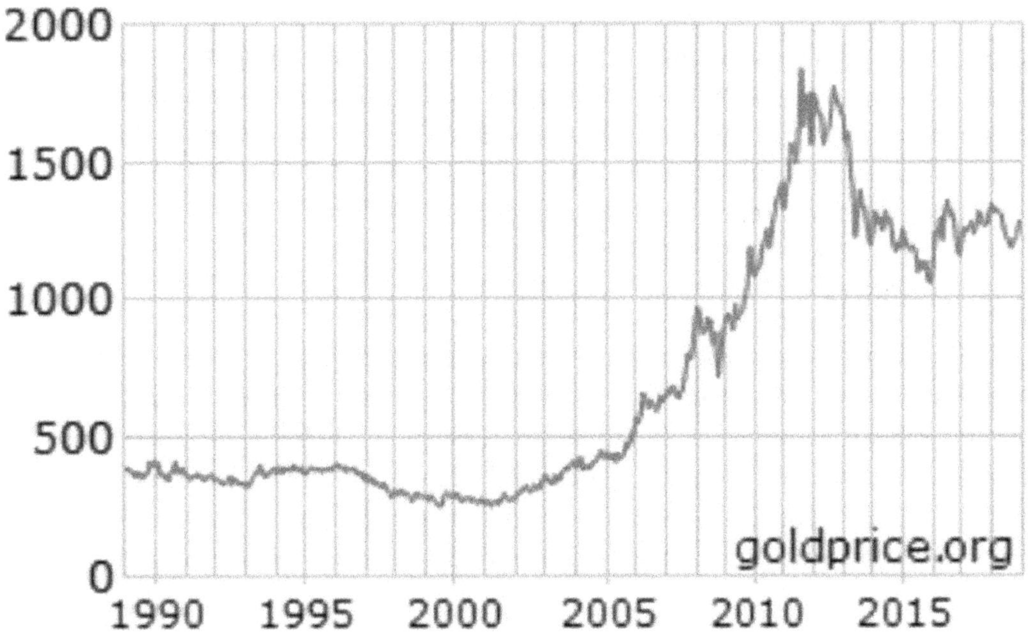

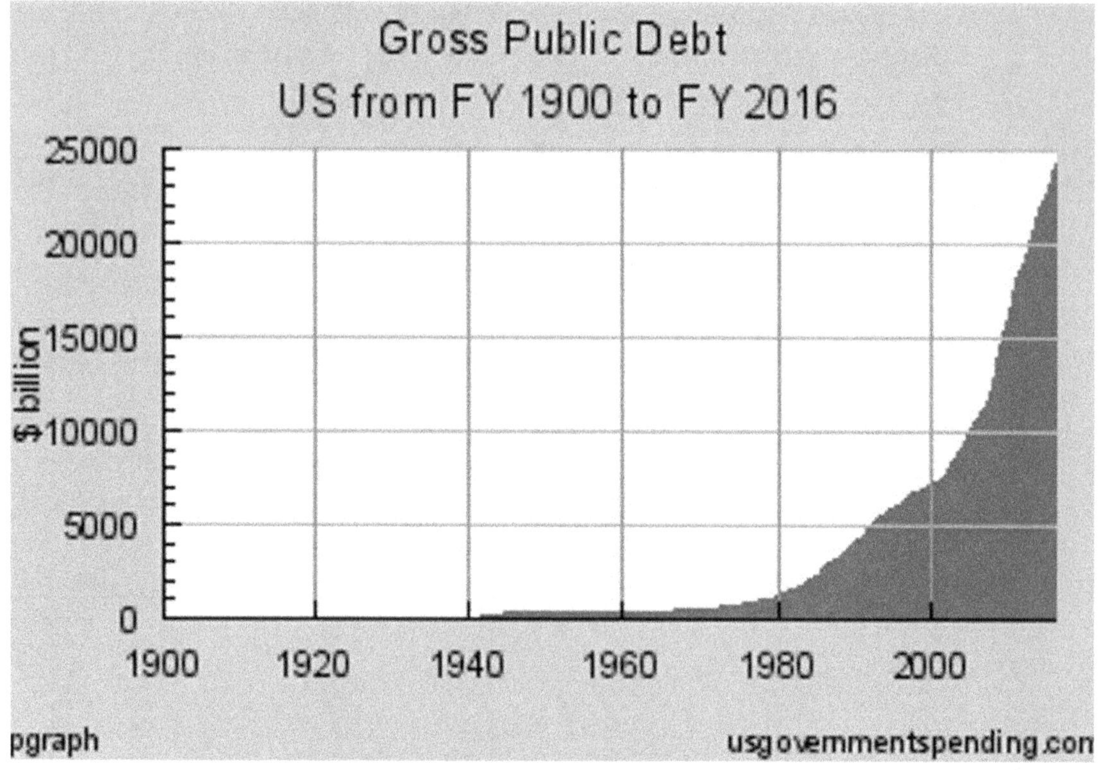

The correlation is quite clear: if debt continues to rise at its current rate, then the gold price will likely rise with it. Conversely, if the economy comes back to life and the rate of debt slows, then the gold price will likely fall. However, it is beginning to become obvious that substantially more U.S. debt is inevitable. It is estimated that the national debt will reach $30 trillion before 2030.

More Evidence

I believed in all five reasons when I started investing in gold. At that time, I knew it could take years for a gold bull market to manifest, but I was convinced of the outcome. Today, I am more convinced than ever. The U.S. Government has about $27 trillion in debt, and the annual interest expense is about $500 billion dollars.[20, 21] This interest payment could easily double if interest rates increase. Are you worried yet about whether we can manage this debt? Perhaps, worried enough to invest in gold? Me, too.

If you have your doubts about gold continuing its bull market price rise, and you are also optimistic that the U.S. economy is going to bounce back, then perhaps gold is not where you should invest. I think everyone should have at least 10% of their investments in gold and silver related assets. But if your heart is not in it, then don't buy gold.

Gold is for people who are nervous about the future of the U.S. economy and want to hedge against that uncertainty. It's not for people who believe that the dollar and the stock market can remain strong over the long term. Everyone should invest in what they believe in. You should trust your gut. Of course, if you have any doubts about the future, then hedging with some gold makes a lot of sense.

I like this quote by Bill Rogers, the investment billionaire:

> *I've owned gold for many years, I've never sold any gold, and I can't imagine I ever will sell gold in my life, because it is somewhat of an insurance policy ... I've never sold any gold and if gold comes down and I expect it to go down, doesn't mean it will, I'll buy more. I'm certainly not going to sell.*

I agree with Bill; gold is the ultimate asset (you don't sell it). I believe that gold is going to $2,500 and beyond. From an investment perspective, it is the one thing I believe without any doubt. Thus, my investment choices are heavily weighted in gold and silver related assets. Depending on your beliefs, your choices will be less weighted in gold and silver.

The Trend Is Our Friend

Some investors are not interested in the five reasons I gave for investing in gold. What they are interested in is the trend and the fact that gold is in a bull market. For those of you who are not versed in this technical jargon, all you need to do is look at the gold price chart since 2002.

The gold price has been in an upward trend since 2002 (refer to the gold chart on the previous pages). This upward trend is called a bull market. In bull markets, you make money if you buy and hold. There is a saying for riding out bull markets: sit tight and be right. The saying implies that there will be price swings, but hold on until the bull market is over.

Some investors think the bull market in gold ended in 2011. These last nine years have been quite challenging as the 45% correction (from $1,925 to $1,062) has been severe. However, from a technical perspective, the upward trend has not reversed. A correction of that size is not unusual during bull markets. The last gold bull market from 1970 to 1981 had an even larger correction (from 1974 to 1975, the gold market corrected 47%). For this bull market to be over, we would need to see the price stay under $1,000 for an extended period. I think that is unlikely based on the economic fundamentals we face. Instead, it is much more likely that gold will remain in an upward trend well north of $2,000. Moreover, this bull market should last for several more years.

Long-Term Fundamentals

The upward trend, as reflected in the gold price chart, is what is considered to be a technical chart. Once a trend is reflected in a price chart, investors gravitate to these technical trends. I don't invest long term on technical price charts, although I do in the short term for finding good entry prices. For the long term, I rely much more on the fundamentals, and this is where I think gold shines.

In my opinion, the world is in a mess economically. This is like manna from heaven for gold, because gold always rises in periods of crisis. The last time we had high inflation and slow growth was the 1970s, and gold promptly exploded from $35 to $850 per oz. (2,300%). Today that same degree of uncertainty exists, perhaps more because of the high amount of debt that exists.

The various central bank's infatuation with MMT (modern monetary theory) implies a bad outcome. This theory assumes that debt doesn't matter and can be managed by injecting liquidity. In other words, the only reason debt can be a problem is if the money supply is not large enough. I call it insanity economics, but as of today, it is all the rage. Printing a trillion digital dollars today is a minor event that doesn't even make the front page of the major newspapers.

We have never come close to experiencing the kind of economic turmoil that exists today. Nearly every western nation is on the brink of an economic crisis, which is only being averted by central bank manipulation. This economic mess is not going to rectify itself for several more years, and during that period, gold is likely to rise substantially.

When I wrote the paragraph above in 2010, it was still fairly early in the debt crisis. Today we are much further along, and it is becoming apparent that it is going to get worse before it gets better. Today a poll was released that revealed 67% of American's think we are on the wrong track, heading in the wrong direction.[22] I would bet the majority of those who think we are on the right track are concerned about the direction we are taking. Anyone who thinks we are going to get out of this debt crisis without any pain is deluding themselves. I would go as far as to say that our country's future is literally at risk if the economy does not turn around soon. But even if it does turn around, what happens to our debt when interest rates rise?

This economic turmoil is not going unnoticed. Already, China is importing about 30 to 100 tons of gold per month (see chart below),[23] and other countries, such as India, Russia, South Korea, and Vietnam are becoming steady buyers. Central banks have also become net buyers. This strong demand a telltale sign of things to come.

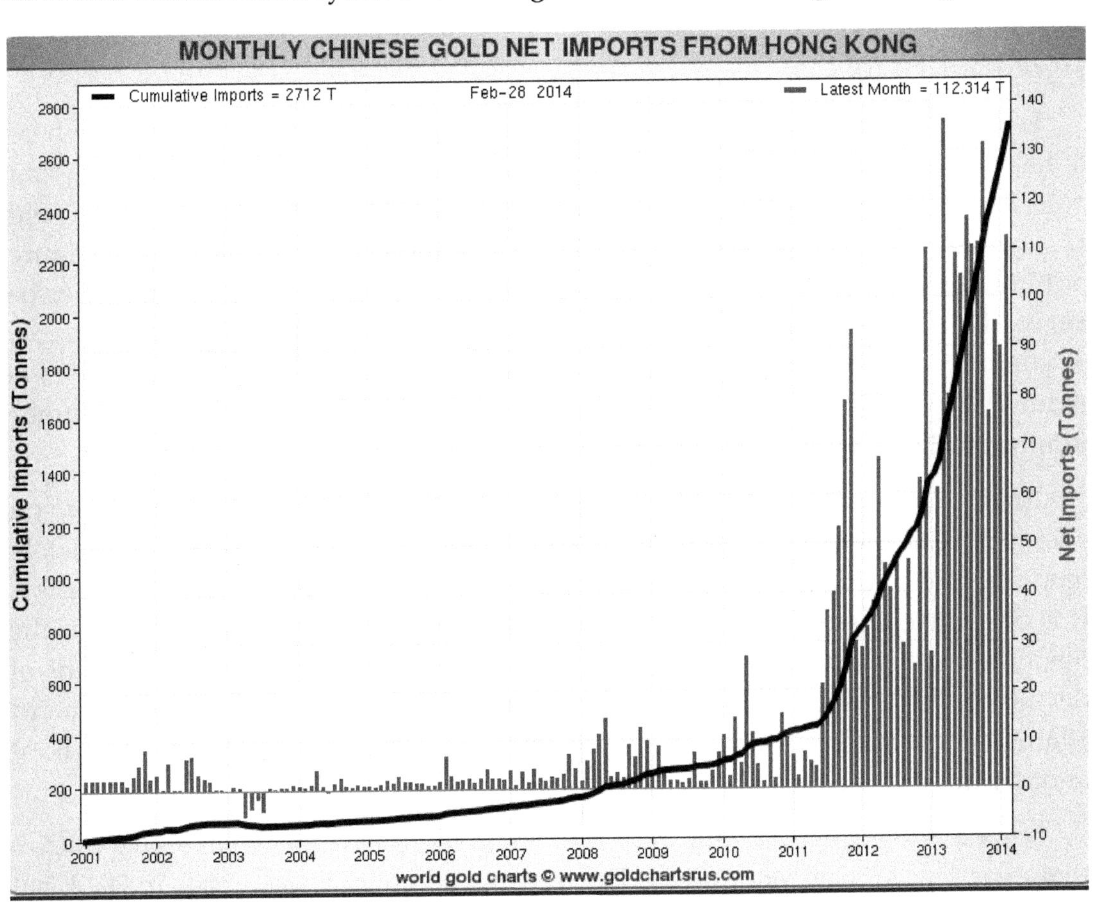

I invest in gold purely from a U.S. debt standpoint. I believe the U.S. Government cannot restrain from deficit spending, and thereby will be forced to increase its debt load. This ongoing deficit spending devalues the dollar and will inexorably lead to the rising price of gold. The global economic turmoil will also help the overall rising pressure on gold prices. But from my standpoint, this is just another factor that pushes up the price of gold. If the rest of the world is going to also implode economically, that is just a correlation to the problems the U.S. is having.

From a fundamental standpoint, the only thing that could stop gold prices from rising is if the U.S. economy begins a vibrant period of growth. If the U.S. begins growing at 3% to 4% annually, we will lift the European and Asian economies. If that happens for an extended period, gold will fall below $1,500 and stay there. However, over the next few years, I think that is highly unlikely because of the debt crisis in the U.S., Japan, and Europe, as well as constrained economic growth.

Gold as a Hedge

While gold makes sense today from an investment standpoint, perhaps where it makes even more sense is as a hedge against financial uncertainty. Knowing that gold is going to shine if things do not straighten out, it makes sense to utilize gold as a hedge. This logic seems like a no-brainer to me. Now you just have to figure out how much you want to hedge, and what strategies to use. You can either be aggressive or conservative. The most conservative would be to invest as little as 5% of your investments into some form of physical gold bullion. The most aggressive would be to utilize all of the various options of gold investing, including Junior mining stocks and perhaps even options.

If you are dubious about gold being the best hedge for today, then perhaps you should invest only a small portion of your money in gold. However, completely ignoring gold during this momentous period of history might not be a good decision. It is one of the few investments that can guard against impending inflation or the devaluation of the dollar. In fact, if a new U.S. currency is issued as a means of devaluing the currency, then your standard of living could drop overnight. To guard against an event of this magnitude, you should be hedged with gold, or perhaps another inflation hedge.

Since I wrote the first edition of this book, there have been several countries that experienced a currency crisis. The most well known was Cyprus in 2012, but citizens in Russia, Venezuela, and Argentina also experienced severe losses due to currency devaluation. The corollary is that those who held gold in these countries were protected. Gold is priced in dollars, which did not crash with these currencies. When will people begin to awaken to the hedging power of gold?

I read something recently by Richard Russell (a leading investment analyst),[24] where he said something to the effect that if you own 10,000 ounces of gold, you are rich. And that no matter what happens to the price of gold, you will remain rich. If gold goes to $500, you are still rich. And if it goes to $2,500, you are just richer. Do you get his point? If you own enough gold, you will likely always be rich. Gold is practically the only investment where you can make this argument. Thus, it is the ultimate hedge.

The Stigma of Gold Investing

Investment advisors like to make the argument that gold bullion does not generate income, and that, historically, it does not appreciate over the long term as well as stocks and bonds. While gold bullion may not generate income, gold mining companies do generate profits and return that to investors in the form of dividends and capital gains. I usually receive a dividend check annually for my gold mutual funds. (Refer to the Internet for historical dividend payouts for gold mining companies.)

Yes, gold languished from 1981 to 2001. During this twenty-year period, everyone focused on stocks and bonds and ignored gold. And from 2011 to 2015, gold dropped from $1,925 to $1062. But gold has risen 600% ($259 to $1,850) since 2001, which is more than the stock market during that period.

The investment community dislikes gold for a few other reasons. The first of which is that gold is a buy and hold investment. Generally, when someone buys gold, they never sell it. Thus, there is no turnover and no additional fees. Second, as an investment category, gold competes against stocks, bonds and other financial instruments that have higher fees. If a financial company sells a bond or an IPO stock, they get very large fees to do so. They get paid by the company who wants to sell the bonds, and by customers who purchase them. If investors are putting their money in gold, then that is less money for these other assets that investment banks like to sell to their customers.

Also, gold is an asset that most investment advisors do not understand. For instance, I have a friend who asked his financial advisor about gold investments, and he was told that they don't sell them. Can you imagine? Gold has risen 600% since 2001, and some financial advisors aren't even offering gold investments to their clients. There is a significant bias in the financial investment community against selling gold or even understanding gold. The average stock mutual fund in the U.S. has less than 1% of their assets in gold or silver related assets. I doubt if there is one 401K plan in America that includes a gold mutual fund in their list of available funds. I have asked several of my friends, and they have never seen one offered in their 401K plans.

Gold as Risk

There are a few risks for gold investors. The first one is government confiscation. This happened in 1933 when possessing gold was made illegal, and it could happen again. I don't think it will happen again because of the global nature of the economy. One way to anticipate such a move is to diversify your gold holdings internationally.

For instance, you can easily store gold in foreign countries using Internet-based companies such as BullionVault.com or GoldMoney.com. You can also travel to Canada and purchase gold bullion and store it in a Canadian safe deposit box. These are just two examples, but you can be flexible with your investments. I can't imagine the U.S. Government passing a law stating that American citizens cannot hold gold in a foreign country, but you never know. One benefit of holding gold internationally is that you can hold it in a foreign currency and protect yourself against a dollar devaluation. Who is to say that gold will always be valued in dollars?

Taxation is always a risk. There is a possibility that the government could decide to make it less appealing to own gold and impose extremely high capital gains taxes.

Another risk is what to do with your physical metal. Where can it be stored safely? How comfortable are you with a home safe? Are safe deposit boxes really safe? If you use an ETF, there is always the risk of some type of unforeseen event (such as trading being halted). And, of course, mining stocks always carry risk. In the subsequent chapters, I will be discussing all of these options and the risks associated with each one.

From my perspective, owning physical gold is essentially riskless if it is stored in a safe place, and especially if that location is insured. This, of course, depends on your entry price. For those lucky enough to have purchased gold below $1,000, I think physical gold is a riskless investment. The higher your entry price, the more risk you hold.

> Note: The riskless price level is likely to increase. By the time you read this book, it could be much higher than $1,000.

Blow-Off Phase

The biggest risk for gold investors is that the price of gold could drop at any moment, and drop considerably. During the last gold bull market (1971-1980), there was a final "blow-off" phase, where the price went from $300 to $850 and then back to $300 in only a few months (see chart below).[25] If you got in before 1978, you would have made a lot of money, even if you didn't time your exit. However, if you bought at the top, then you probably lost money. In that bull market, the floor turned out to be around $300. This was about 800% higher than where the bull market started. This current bull market started at $250, so I would expect the floor to be around $1,500. Although, it could be much lower, and it is impossible to know where the gold price will land after we get the final blow-off phase.

One other point I want to make. Bull markets in commodities that last for a decade or longer usually always have a blow-off phase. This is one of the reasons I think the gold price correction from 2011 to 2019 was not the end of this bull market. We clearly have not yet had a blow-off phase. If you look at the current gold price chart, it has not yet spiked straight up. The sign of a blow-off peak is a straight up rise, followed by a straight down fall. See the chart below that shows the 1980 gold peak and the 2000 NASDAQ peak. This is what we can expect to find when this bull market ends.

World Gold Holdings (2011)
(Source: United States Geological Survey)[1][23]

Location	Gold holdings (in tonnes)	Share of total world gold holdings
Total	171,300	100%
Jewellery	84,300	49.2%
Investment (bars, coins)	33,000	19.26%
Central banks	29,500	17.2%
Industrial	20,800	12.14%
Unaccounted	3,700	2.2%

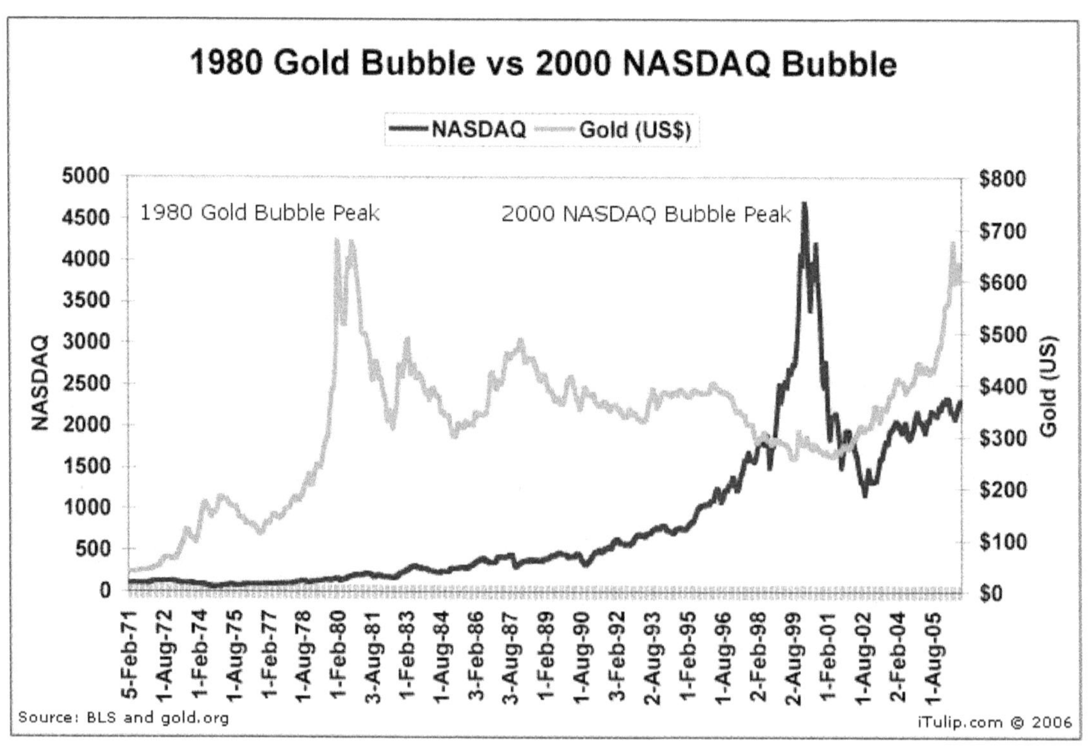

Exit Strategy

Due to the risk of this gold bull market eventually coming to an end, I think everyone should develop a plan for when they want to begin diversifying out of gold. For me, that price is around $2,000. At that time, I plan to begin selling some of my gold-related assets. As gold moves from $2,000 to $3,000, I will steadily diversify out of gold. My final exit point is when the DOW/Gold ratio reaches 2 to 1 or perhaps 3 to 1, which I think will signal the coming end to the gold bull market.

Currently, I am about 90% invested in gold and silver, but I am not going to maintain this level forever. I'm keenly aware that this gold bull market will eventually end. As I diversify out of gold/silver, I will keep a small portion of my investments in gold and silver related assets (perhaps 10%).

From my perspective, I think there is a high probability that gold will reach $3,000 over the next few years. However, the final rise could be part of a blow-off rally that will not last very long. I think it will be wise to be very careful once we get past $3,000 and to take some profits and run. Although, if you have bullion and coins, you might want to keep some in case we get hyperinflation (devaluation of the dollar).

With the economic turmoil that we are experiencing, I think there is a chance we could see $4,000 gold, and perhaps even $5,000 gold. So, whereas price is the biggest risk, it is also the biggest opportunity. I will likely cash out most of my remaining mining stock profits at $3,000 and thus miss out if gold rockets to $4,000 and beyond. But I can afford to since I got in early. You may want to let part of your portfolio ride once we hit that magical $3,000 level. I will talk more about exit strategies in Chapter 9.

If you own gold coins and bullion, then you will have a hard decision if prices explode. Do you sell some and book the profits? Or do you hold and continue to hedge against inflation? I think this is where a small percentage of your assets in gold is the way to go. If gold prices explode, it won't make a lot of sense holding a large percentage of your assets in gold.

Be smart by getting in early and out early, although don't sell everything too early. Remember, it's not inconceivable that we could see gold prices beyond $5,000. A 30% move on $3,000 is $1,000. Once gold prices take off, small percentage moves become big in dollar terms. Of course, this works in both directions. Gold can drop

$1,000 very quickly once we get to $3,000. Expect a lot of volatility, with large price swings on a daily basis.

Cash and Bonds

Nearly everyone today still thinks that cash is king and government bonds are safe. People would rather have cash in the bank or investments in government bonds than own gold. The current consensus is that gold is a risky asset, and that cash and U.S. Government bonds are essentially risk free. This belief is so pervasive that less than 3% of the population owns any physical gold. If this mindset reverses, the move into gold will be explosive, and gold prices will rise very quickly and quite dramatically.

The global bond market is a $100 trillion market. And when you add in the global multi-trillion money market and CD (certificates of deposit) markets, the dollar amounts make the gold market tiny by comparison. If a time comes when people want to convert their cash, money market funds, CDs, and bonds for physical gold, there won't be enough physical gold to purchase.

So, how much gold is available today to purchase? Let's do the math and make an estimate:

The World Gold Council in 2011 estimated that total inventory was 171,000 tons. It breaks down as follows. Jewelry at 49%, Investment at 19%, Central Banks at 17%, Industrial at 12%, and Lost at 2% of the total.[26] Since 2011, the total has increased to about 190,000 tons, but the distributions are about the same.

My estimate is that perhaps 5,000 tons are available for sale. That equates to 160 million ounces, or $235 billion (at $1,500 gold). This is just a rough estimate, but that is not very much money when you are comparing it to the trillions of dollars held in bonds, money market funds, and CDs.

Even if my estimate is off by a few thousand tons, the amount of gold that is available to purchase is substantially less than the amount of money available in these funds. If there is even a tiny move away from so-called safe investments of bonds, money markets, and CDs, the price of gold could rise very quickly.

Another thing that is very bullish for gold investors is that the amount of available gold continues to shrink as more and more investors purchase gold and take it off the market. Private investors of gold ETFs are gobbling it up at a very fast pace. The chart below shows how quickly ETFs are proliferating.[27] Notice that gold ETFs did not even exist at the beginning of 2004! Less than a decade later, they have taken 2,000 tons off the market. At this rate, soon all of the available gold will be sitting in warehouses.

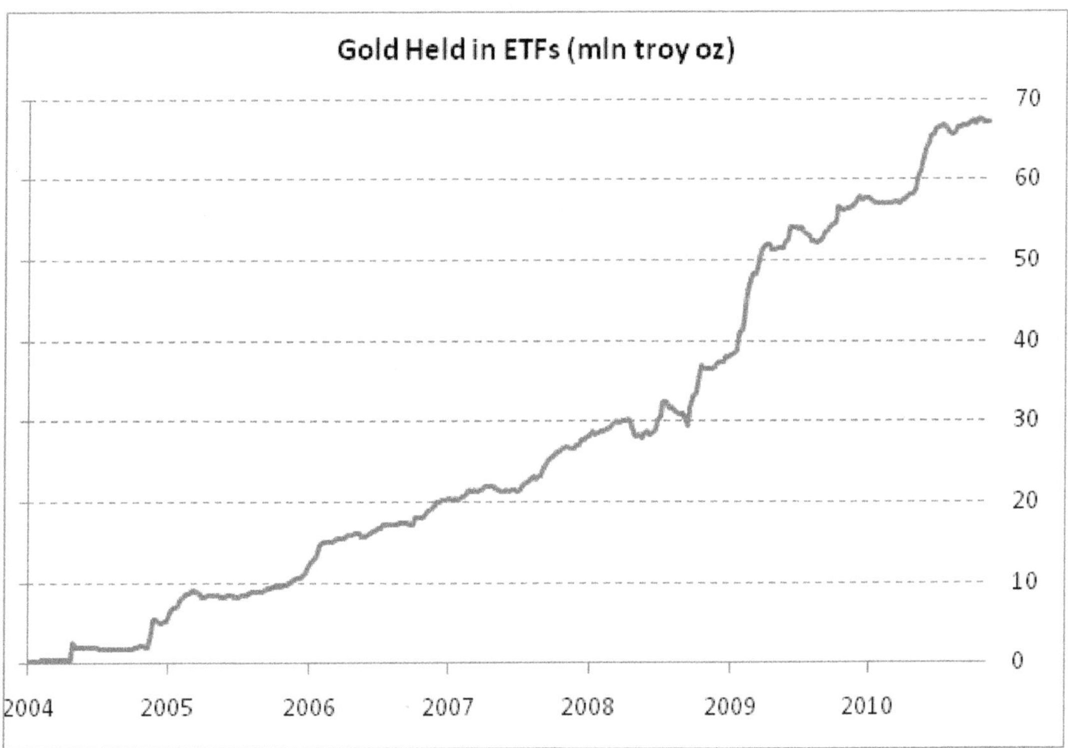

The Fear Trade

Until recently, I was concerned that the price of gold was vulnerable to a significant price drop if the stock markets crash. However, now that central banks and governments have become buyers of gold (fearing uncertainty), I think there is a floor under the gold price of at least $1,500. And even if we get a major correction below this floor price, I don't think the price will stay below $1,500 for very long. My opinion is that any price below $1,500 will bring in large buyers of physical gold until there is none available to buy.

Also, the psychology around gold as an investment is steadily improving as more people are losing confidence with the strategies of the Federal Reserve and other central banks. It is my opinion that we are literally on the precipice of a major move in gold and a surge to $2,000 and beyond. This surge is going to happen mainly from this change in psychology as the fear trade takes hold.

> Note: I wrote the previous paragraph several years ago, and clearly I was wrong that we were on a precipice. I did not anticipate a 7-year correction in the gold price. But I did anticipate further erosion in the financial system. That erosion is evident and points to the likelihood that gold prices will surge soon.

I think the reason gold is so under-owned in the West is because of psychology. To buy gold you have to lose confidence in our economic system and invest in something contrary to your normal behavior. Converting dollars into gold can be quite disconcerting the first time you do it. You quite literally have to question your beliefs about our economic system. And to do that you need an understanding of why our economic system is faltering. It becomes a very complex question and one that most people do not want to contemplate. It is far easier to simply have faith that our economic system is sound, and that gold is not needed.

Once this faith begins to break down and fear becomes pervasive, I think it is inevitable that the move towards gold will be powerful. People will follow the herd, and it is only a matter of time before enough leaders show them the way. At what point do insurance companies and pension funds begin to buy gold? Or perhaps 401K plans add gold mutual funds to their list of available funds?

Anyone who says that gold is in a bubble is wrong, although it will eventually become one as the herd begins to buy gold. The fact is that gold is only owned by a tiny portion of the populace. Less than 1% of Americans have a significant portion of their assets in gold. Moreover, the total value of gold and silver related assets as a percentage of total financial assets is tiny. For gold to form a bubble, it has a long way to go. Many are expecting gold to reach $10,000 per ounce, which is not as crazy as it seems. Once the fear trade kicks into gear anything is possible.

The fear trade will move gold to $2,000, but it will speculators who move it $2,500 and beyond. There is a saying, "why get rich slow when you can get rich fast." That is the motto of the speculator. The other saying is that "there is no fever like gold fever." In other words, speculators love a gold rally. So, the trend is our friend, but speculators are our godsend.

Paper Gold, Gold Leasing, and Gold Swaps

The purpose of this book is to help you to invest in gold and silver related assets and to share what I have learned. I added this section in the fourth edition because I think it is important to understand. It is somewhat technical, but is something you should be aware of as a gold investor.

Paper gold is when you own gold via an IOU (a paper contract). It is any form of gold ownership where you do not have physical possession. There are many different types of paper gold, but they all rely on the seller of the IOU to produce either physical gold or cash when the paper gold holder turns in their IOU.

Common types of paper gold are ETFs, gold certificates, futures contracts, leased gold, and gold swaps. Today, there is much more paper gold than physical gold. Some say there is 100x more paper gold versus physical gold. I think that number is ridiculously high. If paper gold ownership was 15x physical ownership, this equates to about 900,000 tons. At $1,500 per oz. gold, one ton equals $54 million. So, 900,000 tons is $48 trillion! That is a huge number. It is almost as much as the global GDP.

I did some research, and I could not find a single source that would give a total of paper gold ownership. My guess is the number is closer to $10 trillion, but that it is still a very big number.

While we don't know how much paper gold is outstanding, we do know that the amount of paper gold is huge. We also know that it is a potential problem. Why? Because paper gold owners are reliant on the seller of the IOU to pay them on demand. This is called third-party risk. Conversely, if you hold physical gold, there is no third party risk. If you want to convert your gold into cash, you simply take it to your local "We Buy Gold" shop, or sell it online using eBay or to one of the precious metals websites, such as APMEX.

Most of the paper gold is owned by banks and financial institutions, which they claim as assets. For instance, Central Banks have leased out approximately 10,000 tons. Central Banks lease their gold to bullion banks who in turn sell it as paper gold to investors. It is called leasing, but technically they loan their gold out for a specific period at the current gold lease rate. You can look up the lease rates at Kitco.com (below is the current chart).[28] In 2019, one-year lease rates were less than 1 percent, which was very cheap.

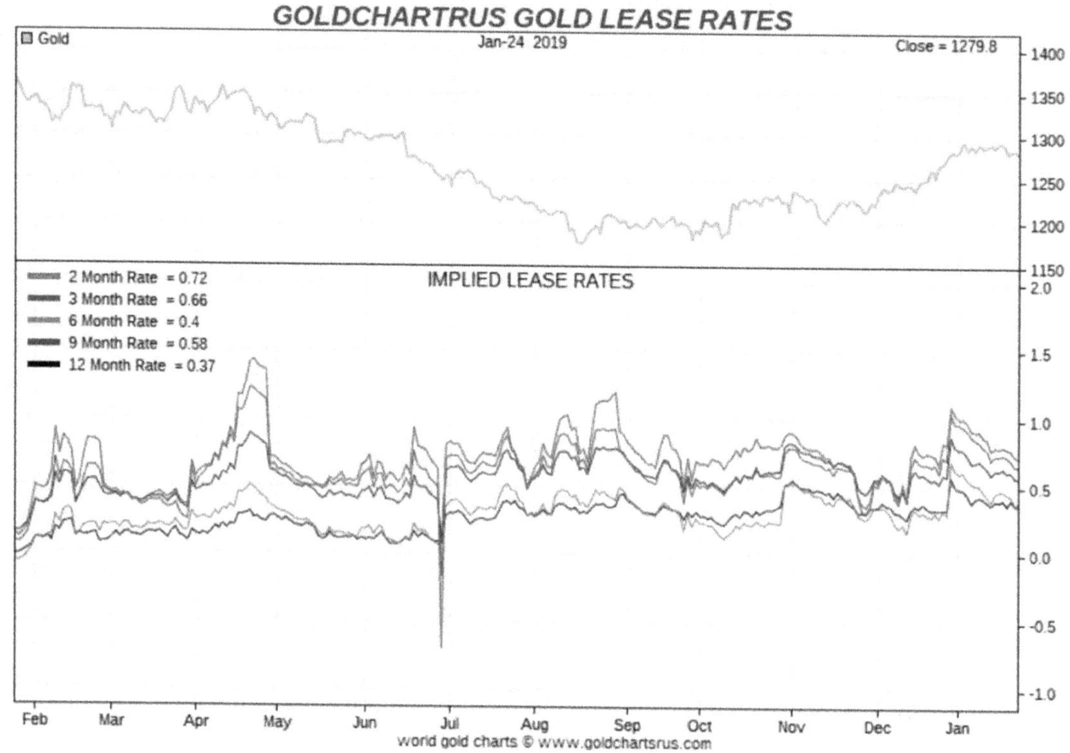

Once bullion banks receive the loaned gold, they sell it to multiple investors. This is legal. They can sell the same gold to multiple investors! The bullion banks use a fractional banking system in the same manner as normal banks, thereby keeping only a fraction of the gold they lease or purchase. Moreover, the same way a bank run on cash can happen, so to can a run on bullion banks that have a large paper gold exposure.

Bullion banks sell their gold to investors using allocated and unallocated accounts. These are paper gold IOUs and are also called gold certificates. An allocated paper gold IOU is supposed to be backed by physical gold and includes storage fees that are paid by the investor. However, many allocated accounts are pooled accounts. Thus, bullion banks normally only keep a limited amount of physical gold in inventory. This is their "pool" of gold. Unallocated accounts are also pooled accounts, but they do not include storage fees and are not contractually backed by physical gold.

Some bullion banks have been caught charging customers storage fees for allocated accounts, only to be found out to have no inventory when the IOU (gold certificate) was presented by an investor. It is not uncommon for bullion banks to sell their gold and keep very little in inventory. They do this because most investors never request physical delivery and because the bullion banks would rather invest in an asset that generates income rather than hold gold in inventory.

How much paper gold is in allocated and unallocated accounts globally? It is hard to say because it is not published. I would say about $2 trillion, but that is just a guess, and it is probably much more. Many of these allocated and unallocated accounts have the right to demand physical gold for their IOUs. This makes it a problem waiting to happen, because the amount of physical gold the bullion banks have in inventory is minuscule versus their IOU exposure.

To pay holders of paper gold IOUs who demand physical gold, bullion banks rely on both their inventory and the supply of physical gold in the global market. If they run out of gold inventory because investors turn in their paper gold IOUs for physical gold, then they must purchase more physical gold. This can easily become a problem if there is a gold shortage.

> Note: Some people argue that there can never be a shortage of gold because the price of gold can always rise to meet demand. However, if there is no physical gold available for sale at the current gold price, I would consider that a shortage.

If there is ever a mild stampede out of these paper gold IOUs and into physical gold, the gold price will take off. Why? Because the bullion banks would likely run out of gold inventory and be forced to purchase gold on the global market. This increased demand for physical gold would likely result in a physical gold shortage. And if a physical gold shortage appears, holders of paper gold will likely get nervous and turn in their IOUs for physical gold. This could create a negative feedback loop. If one bullion bank goes bankrupt, there could be a feeding frenzy for physical gold, thereby bankrupting many bullion banks.

One question you should be asking is how paper gold could impact the future price of gold? Let me show you a chart. Below is the Gold Forward Offered Rate chart from 2007 to 2014. This is the one month rate to swap physical gold for dollars.

In other words, you can use gold as collateral to get a loan at a very low-interest rate. They call it a swap because you have to hand over your gold to get the loan.

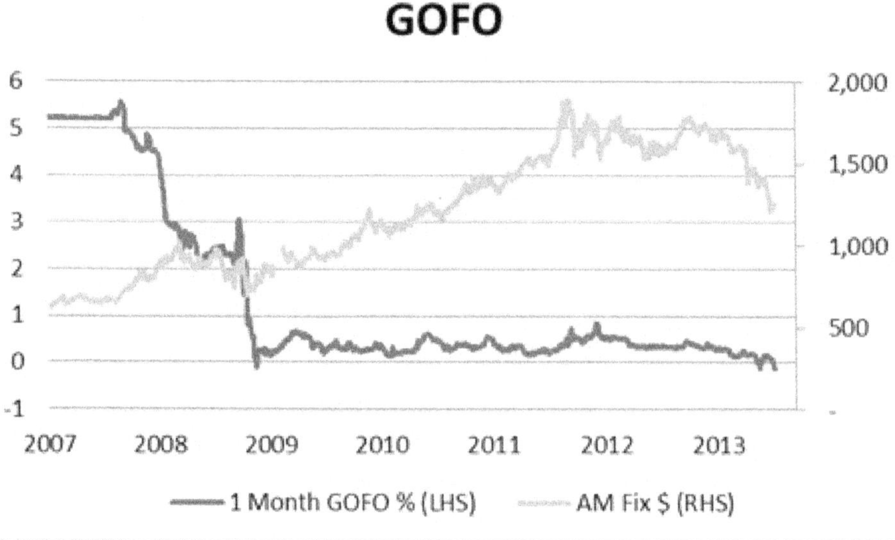

Notice that the rate crashed in 2008 and had not recovered. After it went negative, the LBMO (London Bullion Market Association) stopped publishing it. Why did it go negative? Because those who have gold no longer want to loan it out for dollars. I don't want your stinking dollars! When it is negative, it means that those who have physical gold no longer want to swap it for dollars unless they are paid a premium. In other words, you will be paid to borrow money if you use gold as collateral.

Why would the gold swap interest rate (GOFO) go negative? Because of third-party risk. Low GOFO rates exist today because investors fear they will not get their gold back after the swap. This is where it gets interesting. Remember all of those paper gold IOUs out there? Owners of paper gold become nervous when GOFO rates are negative. The reason why is because negative GOFO rates imply physical shortages are possible.

This chart is signaling a potential run on paper gold. It is also signaling that investors are beginning to stop swapping gold for dollars. This has the effect of restricting the gold supply. No wonder the LBMA stopped publishing the GOFO rate. They don't want web bloggers or television analysts shouting to the world that the rate is negative.

The entire paper gold market could easily blow up if there is even a small run on paper gold. This seems inevitable to me because of the size of the paper gold market and the potential for increased physical demand. For instance, if there is a run on a bullion bank and it goes bankrupt, many investors are going to begin converting their paper gold into physical gold. Once the selling of paper gold begins, it could easily push gold prices much higher. Bullion banks will be forced to buy physical gold to close out many of their IOUs that demand physical gold.

Here is a chart that shows how this could happen. It is called Exter's Pyramid.[29] It shows the inverted risk of financial assets. You will find derivatives at the top and gold at the bottom.

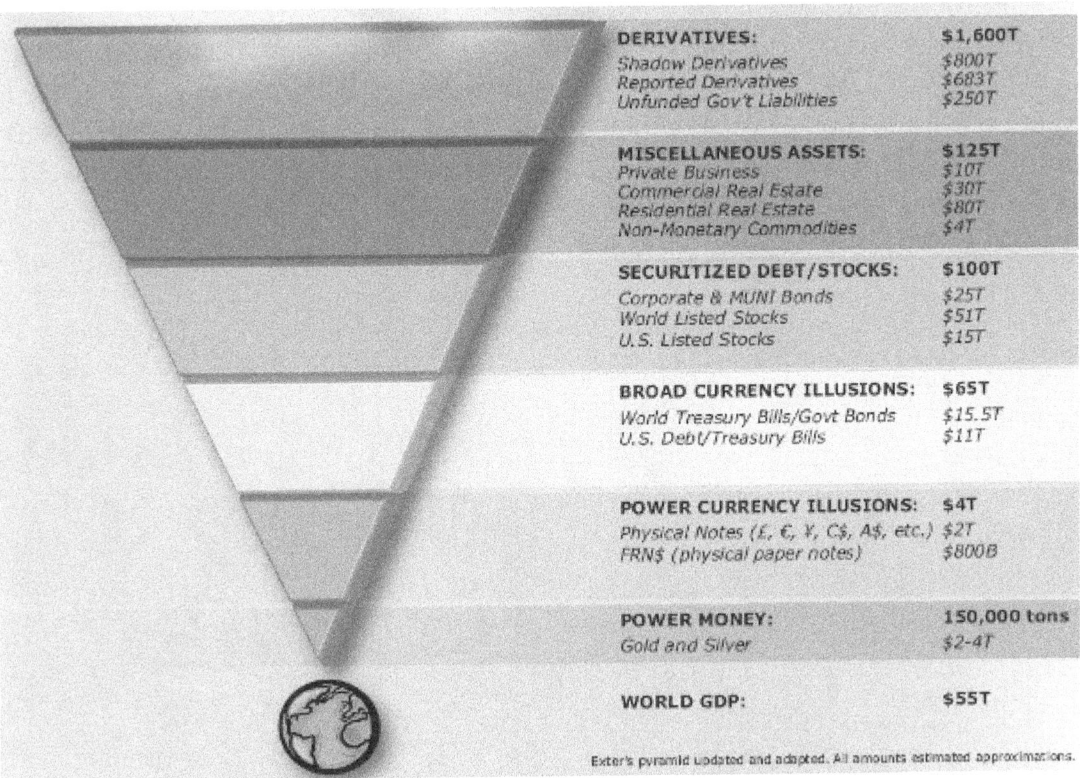

If the global financial system becomes unstable (isn't it already?), investors will move down the pyramid into safer assets. What is fascinating about this pyramid is the relationship of physical gold to paper gold. While physical gold is the safest asset, derivatives - IOUs - are the riskiest! Many people think their paper gold is just as safe as the real thing. This pyramid shows how foolish that assumption can be. As I have pointed out, without enough physical gold, those paper gold IOUs are at risk. .

* * * * *

Another large holder of paper gold is investment banks, which trade in the futures market. Today there are about 40 million ounces of gold held in futures contracts on the COMEX. [30] That is about 1,200 tons of gold. Holders of those contracts can demand delivery in physical gold. Currently, the COMEX only keeps about 3 million ounces in their inventory. That is a problem waiting to happen if investors begin to demand delivery.

Historically this has not been an issue because physical gold is rarely demanded to close out futures contracts. However, if we experience a tight supply of gold, investors could use the COMEX as a method of obtaining large quantities of physical gold. There is evidence this is already happening. Below is a chart[31] of the gold inventory at the COMEX, which has been shrinking quite dramatically. In 2019, it only had 700,000 ounces in registered gold. This is a fraction of what it had at the beginning of 2013. It appears perilously close to a default.

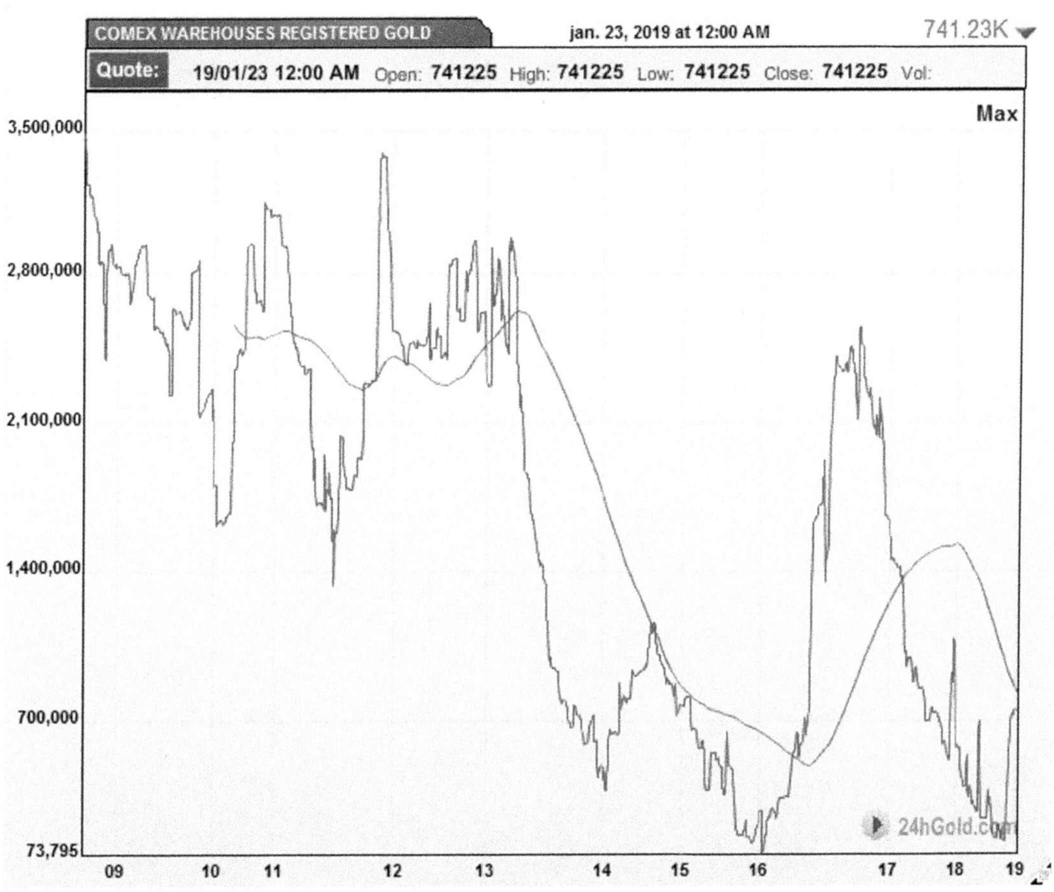
COMEX WAREHOUSES REGISTERED GOLD
jan. 23, 2019 at 12:00 AM
741.23K
Quote: 19/01/23 12:00 AM Open: 741225 High: 741225 Low: 741225 Close: 741225 Vol:
Max
3,500,000
2,800,000
2,100,000
1,400,000
700,000
73,795
09
10
11
12
13
14
15
16
17
18
19
24hGold.com

CHAPTER 3

PHYSICAL METAL: BULLION & COINS

The one thing I have heard over and over from gold/silver analysts is that the starting place for investing in precious metals is physical metal. So I will repeat that suggestion here. It is recommended to include some physical metal as part of your portfolio. This is the "riskless" portion of your investment that you "own." Ideally, you want to take possession of this metal and keep it close at hand. If an economic calamity ever occurs, you will always have access to it.

The Ultimate Insurance

If you have a few dozen gold coins, then you have considerable wealth in your possession. Those coins can go a long way in financing your day to day affairs. Thus, you will not be broke in a short period of time. Think of them as the best insurance you can buy. Stated another way, when dollars are worth much less than they are today, you are going to be glad you stocked up on some gold or silver metal.

Another benefit of owning physical metal is that it is not a stock. Whereas a mining stock can go to zero, bullion tends to hold its value. When you own physical, your only concern is the value of gold or silver.

You don't purchase physical metal to get rich. Silver has the potential to rise perhaps 5-10 times, which is considerable, but gold is likely only to double or triple. Yes, those are nice gains, but these metals are all about retaining their value. They represent inflation hedges and insurance for maintaining your wealth, rather than investments.

> Note: If you purchase a gold or silver bullion ETF, I would consider that a "paper" investment. But if you purchase physical metal and take

possession, I would consider that an inflation hedge and insurance against a financial crisis.

Real Money

Think of physical bullion and coins as "real" money, and that you are simply exchanging one form of money for another. Yes, you are foregoing other potential investments, but the time has come to create a "stash" of real money. If you don't do it, you face the possibility of the dollar being worth much less in value in the future, and your net worth getting shrunk. My suggestion is to exchange a portion of your paper dollars for gold and/or silver metal, and then find a place to store it. You will likely be glad you did.

What is the worst thing that could happen? Someone could steal it. However, that can be avoided with careful planning. What is the second worst thing that could happen? Gold and silver could drop dramatically in price, and you could lose some money. Trust me when I say that you want that to happen! That means that the world did not fall apart, and the economy came back to life. Let us pray that we are all crying because our gold investments went down in value.

Purchasing Coins

Okay, this is a practical guide, so let's get started. How do you purchase bullion or coins? And which do you choose?

It starts with how much money you have to work with. If you have less than $100,000 to invest, then the choice is easy: purchase gold and silver U.S. American Eagle coins (or the most popular coins in your country) and take possession. You could also purchase 10-ounce silver bars, or perhaps some pre-1965 U.S. silver coins (90% silver).

Bullion has a lower markup than coins and sells closer to the spot price. However, many investors prefer coins because of their popularity and ease of conversion into cash. If you have a 10-ounce gold bar, you have two potential problems. 1) The coin dealer may want to do an assay analysis (which you will pay for) to verify the metal is pure. 2) The coin dealer might not have that much cash on hand (although they will likely have enough cash for a few gold coins). When you own coins, neither of these problems arise.

Purchasing U.S. Mint American Eagle coins takes nearly all of the risk out of the equation. These are the most commonly traded coins, so people will always recognize them and want them. Your local coin shop (or Internet website) will pay you approximately the going market rate (called the spot price) for your Eagles. Yes, you will pay a premium above the spot price for coins, but they will likely also return a premium. I will discuss these premiums below.

As for storage, that is a topic all unto itself. There are many possibilities. I used to think that safe deposit boxes were secure, but now I have my doubts. Home safes are an option to consider, but they can be a target. There are lots of creative ways to hide it. You can make false floors, false walls, even bury it. I think storage is a personal choice. The one thing I would suggest is to use multiple locations to diversify your risk of theft.

For those of you with a small portfolio and who only want physical metal, you're done. Well, almost. You need to know where and how to buy them, how much you will pay, and some tax information.

Gold American Eagles

Where to Buy Gold/Silver

You have two choices when it comes to purchases, your local coin shop or the Internet (I mention my favorite precious metals websites on the next page). I prefer the Internet because they have lower prices. When you are going to spend a small amount of money, then paying a bit more at your local coin shop may make sense. However, the difference in price can be substantial the more you purchase.

Prices at local coin shops will vary widely because of their random markups. This is because coin shops generally price for the local market. Local coin shops know what the Internet prices are, and you can expect to pay more. For instance, today APMEX.com, one of the largest Internet coin sellers, is charging a 5% premium for 1 oz. Gold Eagles and a 23% premium for 1 oz. Silver Eagles. It is unlikely your local coin shop will match these prices, although they will be close.

Normally, Gold Eagles sell for about a 3.5% to 5% premium on the Internet. Silver Eagles can have a wide range depending on availability. The range can fluctuate from 20% to 30%. It's not unusual for the U.S. mint to halt Silver Eagle sales due to silver supply issues.

If you want to get a general idea of what your local coin shop is charging for these coins, go to APMEX and check the prices. Also, it's a good idea to calculate the current premium. This is very easy to do. You divide the markup by the spot price:

Internet Price: $1,371
Spot Price: $1,306

Markup: $65
$65 / $1,306 = 5%

If you buy a large quantity of coins (10 or more), you will get a discount. You can buy 500 Silver Eagles in what is called a Monster Box. These are sealed green plastic boxes that come from the U.S. Mint. The coins are brand new. Normally the premiums for a Monster Box is about 15%.

So, for Silver Eagles expect to pay somewhere between 15% to 30%, depending on how many coins you buy, and where you buy them. The best price you will find for Gold Eagles is about 3% above spot. However, this price is hard to find and will require purchasing multiple coins. More likely, you will pay about 3.5% to 5% above spot on the Internet. Gold Eagles also sell in denominations below 1 oz. These smaller denominations generally have higher premiums than 1 oz. coins, especially in coin shops.

Currently (on Internet websites) you can sell back your Gold Eagles for a few dollars above the spot price and your Silver Eagles for about 5% above the spot price. Your local coin shot is more likely to buy them back for lower premiums.

The Internet is your friend if you want the best prices. There are many sites you can use, although not all of them are reputable. I recommend checking the following sites for the best prices and availability: APMEX.com, JMBullion.com, SDBullion.com, and ProvidentMetals.com. These sites are all large distributors, and they have remained that way by providing value to their numerous customers. All of them provide free insurance and free shipping for orders over $99. Plus, all accept PayPal and Bitcoin as payment options, and soon all will accept eCheck ACH payments.

APMEX is perhaps the largest distributor, and they have competitive prices, although generally not the lowest. I use APMEX because they give me a high comfort level. I also use the other websites I listed when they have better prices than APMEX. Today APMEX and JMBullion are both charging a 5% premium for 1 oz. Gold Eagles. ProvidentMetals is charging 4%, and SDBullion is charging only a 3.5% premium. The obvious choice for me today for Gold Eagles would be SDBullion.

You may see a TV advertisement by Monex, GoldLine, or another precious metals seller. These companies can offer excellent prices, but buyer beware. They use salespeople who are paid to get your business. These are not customer service reps who are taking your order. They are salespeople who want to sell you products.

Here are some issues to consider when you are looking for a website online. Check if they offer free shipping and free insurance. Normally there is no sales tax, but they have begun taxing orders to some states, such as California. Just like at gas stations, they usually have two prices, one for personal checks or bank wires, and another for credit cards. Some websites require that you fund your account before you can buy or use a written check before using eCheck. Lastly, make sure they display their inventory for each product. You don't want to purchase coins or bullion and have to wait for an extended period for delivery. I've heard stories where people have had to wait months for delivery.

There are several different ways to pay on the Internet: Credit Card, Bank Wire, Cashier's Check, Money Order, Personal Check, eCheck (ACH), Paypal, or Bitcoin. If you use a credit card or Paypal, then you have to pay a 3% additional premium, and your purchase can be limited to $5,000 or $10,000 per month. If you use a bank wire, then you have to pay your bank a fee, which is usually around $25 for each wire transfer. Cashier's checks, money orders, and personal checks all have to arrive within five business days of the order, or else your order price will no longer be "locked." If your check is late, you might have to pay more if the price of gold/silver rises.

Generally, your order price will lock-in when you place your order. If you can't lock-in the price at the time of the order, then don't buy it. The minimum shipment date is 1 day for bank wires, 1 to 3 days for credit cards, eCheck, or Paypal, 1 to 5 days for cashier's checks or money orders (after mail arrival), and 5 to 10 days for personal checks (after mail arrival).

The best way to pay in my opinion is by eCheck, which I think is the most convenient. However, you usually can't use this payment method for your first purchase. After you have paid by a personal check, then you can use eCheck. It won't cost you anything to use a personal check other than a few extra days for the check to clear. Why make a trip to the bank to pay for a bank wire, when you can write a personal check? However, some websites require a bank wire for purchases over a certain amount.

If you use a bank wire, you could receive your order in perhaps as little as three days. If you use a personal check, then you will wait a minimum of two weeks. However, with tight supplies of physical metals, it is becoming common to wait two to four weeks for delivery. Also, when you are planning to keep this investment for the long term, why is it important to arrive as soon as possible? Waiting a couple of weeks is not that big of an issue. As long as you can monitor the status of the order and track shipping, you should be comfortable waiting.

Another website that sells gold and silver is eBay. Many people like to use eBay and play the bidding game for the lowest price. I would say that most of the highly rated sellers on eBay are reputable and that this is a legitimate way to purchase gold and silver coins and bullion. I think it is safer to utilize the large Internet websites, but if you like to bid and get deals, then go for it. Also, eBay is a good place to sell your precious metals to get the best price when you cash out.

Tax Rules

In most states, there are certain sales tax exemptions for precious metals. In California, if you spend more than $1,500, there is no sales tax. In many states, there are no sales taxes for bullion or coins. Check your tax laws. Also, you may be able to legally save taxes if you use the Internet for out of state purchases.

Here are the current state tax laws[32] for gold and silver purchases, although I would suggest to confirm this data for your home state:

No sales tax:

Arizona, Delaware, Georgia, Idaho, Illinois, Iowa, Michigan, Mississippi, Missouri, North Dakota, Oregon, Pennsylvania, Rhode Island, South Dakota, Utah, Washington, Wyoming.

Sales tax:

Arkansas, D.C., Indiana, Kansas, Kentucky, Maine, Minnesota, Nebraska, New Hampshire, New Jersey, New Mexico, North Carolina, Ohio, Oklahoma, Tennessee, Vermont, Virginia, West Virginia, Wisconsin.

Special Cases:

Alabama: The State charges 4% on everything. There are also County & City taxes, which can add another 4-5%.

Alaska: No state sales tax, though local governments may still tax.

California: Exemption on Coins and Bullion when over $1500.

Colorado: Sales Tax on Coins and Bullion varies by City. The State does not charge any sales tax.

Connecticut: No sales tax on Coins. Exemption on Bullion when over $1,000

Florida: No sales tax on U.S. Coins. Exemption on Bullion when over $500.

Idaho: No taxes on precious metals (buying or selling).

Hawaii: General Excise Tax is collected on Coins and Bullion.

Louisiana: Exemption on Coins and Bullion when over $1,000.

Maryland: Numismatic items and Bullion are exempt when over $1,000.

Massachusetts: Coins and Bullion are exempt when over $1,000.

Montana: No sales tax collected on Coins or Precious Metals by the State. There is a 3% Provisional tax in some communities.

Nevada: Sales tax is collected on anything that sells for over 50% of its "Face Value." Private Mint Bars and Rounds are exempt.

New York: Coins are Taxable. Bullion is Exempt when over $1,000.

Texas: Coins and Precious Metals are exempt over $1,000.

Wyoming: No taxes on precious metals (buying or selling).

The last thing you need to know involves the IRS (Federal Taxes) reporting laws for coins/bullion:

> **Purchases:** If your purchase is over $10,000, then the seller must report it to the IRS using a 1099B form. This is actually for a calendar year, per business. If you purchase from two coin shops, you can spend $9,999 in each and have no 1099B forms. Out of state Internet sales are currently not taxable.
>
> **Sales:** The current Obamacare law (still in effect in 2021) requires purchases made by businesses more than $600 to be reported to the IRS. Thus, if you sell bullion or coins to a business (local coin shop or website) for a value more than $600, then they need to fill out an IRS form.
>
> **Sales (previous law):** If you sell your gold coins to a dealer, they do not have to fill out an IRS form, unless the sale was for more than 24 gold coins. Gold bullion and silver appear to be exempt from sales reporting by dealers. But do your own due diligence.

Capital Gains: Gold and silver are subject to capital gains if they are sold at a profit. This must be reported on your annual tax statements as capital gains. Sadly, bullion and coins are considered collectibles and are taxed at 28% for federal taxes. State tax rules for capital gains will vary. Again, do your own due diligence.

Purchasing Bullion

Now we turn to large investors, those who plan to invest more than $100,000. The first option is to buy and store your own bullion. The second option is to have someone else store your bullion. The easiest way to own large quantities of physical bullion is to find a reputable Internet website that sells and stores your bullion.

For instance, at BullionVault.com there is practically no premium to purchase gold. You can buy gold at a sales fee of just .2% (not 2%, but .2%) above spot. Then you can store and insure it for only .12% annually. That is as cheap as you will find. Also, you can choose the location where your gold is stored: New York, London, Hong Kong, or Zurich. All of your bars will have serial numbers and will be audited annually. Because it is your gold, you have the option to sell it at any time in the currency of your choice. One problem with BullionVault is that if you ever want to take possession of your gold, the fees and taxes for withdrawal can be exorbitant.[33]

Go to the BullionVault.com web page and read the FAQs and customer comments. They are hard to beat. I rate them at the top of the list. GoldMoney.com is nearly an identical site and also has a good reputation. GoldMoney's gold storage fees are a bit higher and about the same for silver. There are others you can research, but these are the only two I would use.

Note: Currently at GoldMoney you can only withdraw (take possession of) a minimum of a 400 oz. gold bar or 30,000 ounces of silver.

If you have a lot of money to invest in gold, it might make sense to open accounts with both BullionVault.com and GoldMoney.com. Then store your gold in two different countries to diversify your risk. Again, these are websites for large investors. If you are a small investor, simply take possession of your gold or silver.

These are not the only options for buying and storing gold. The large investment banks on Wall St. all have bullion banks that they use. If you have a financial adviser or stockbroker, he can sell you gold bars in a bullion bank vault. The problem with this approach is that you can't trust the bullion banks, which are deeply embedded in the financial system. This was explained in the last chapter regarding paper gold. You may think you have allocated gold, but when you go to collect your physical gold, it possibly won't be there.

Silver Storage Issues

If you decide to purchase silver bullion, understand that storage fees are high (generally three or four times higher than gold storage). For this reason, I would suggest either taking possession of silver bars or using a silver bullion ETF. Storage fees for silver will eat you up over a long period. The bulk weight of silver also makes it much more costly for larger safe deposit boxes.

Silver bullion is an unwieldy investment to store since it is relatively inexpensive. If you want to purchase $100,000 worth of silver bullion (at $20 per oz.), that would weigh about 300 pounds. I don't think you want to store 300 pounds in several safe deposit boxes or pay for the storage fees at BullionVault.com (.48% annually). That leaves you with the option of a large home safe (these are quite affordable), or an ETF.

Because silver bullion becomes problematic to store, most large investors should stick with gold. However, if you do want some silver bars for your home safe, you can easily purchase .999% pure silver bars from the Internet websites that I mentioned above.

Standard Size Bars

When you purchase bullion, you want to get a good price (and markups vary widely). The standard size bar for silver is 10 ounces, although 100-ounce bars are popular. I prefer 10-ounce bars because a 100-ounce bar won't be as easy to sell once silver prices explode. Always purchase bars that are stamped with a known brand. These bars will be easy to sell and are much more difficult to counterfeit.

For gold bullion, my favorite bar is the PAMP Suisse Lady Fortuna. It is a well-known brand from Switzerland (where gold is refined into .999 pure bars). They have many sizes to choose from. There isn't a standard size bar for gold because it comes in so many sizes (ounces and grams). However, the 1-kilo bar is the size of choice in Asia.

You can also purchase 1-ounce silver rounds. Rounds are essentially blank .999% pure silver. Some of them come with stamps from the manufacturer. Some people like rounds because they sell at a lower premium over spot price but still hold their spot value. As long as they are .999% pure, they are good. You can even purchase these directly from mining companies at great prices. For instance, First Majestic Silver currently sells their own stamped silver coins on their web page.

If you do buy silver rounds and bars that do not have stamps, there is a chance you will have to pay to have them assayed when you go to sell them. This is the reason I prefer to purchase coins or bars with stamps. I think it is always a good idea to have your coins, rounds, or bars stamped in one form or another.

There are several handheld devices that can authenticate silver and gold bullion. However, these devices are still expensive and have not made their way to all of the local coin shops. At some point in the future, the possibility of counterfeiting bullion and coins will be a thing of the past.

Junk Silver

Some of you may want to have some "junk" silver coins in your safe. These are U.S. dimes, quarters, and fifty cent pieces made before 1965. They are 90% silver and are worth 90% of their weight. These could be very handy if people start using silver for payment or barter. You can buy these coins from your local coin shops, or on the Internet. Currently, there is still a large inventory, but I don't expect that to last.

In my opinion, junk silver is a very misleading term. I think these coins have the potential to be both an insurance plan and an investment. For example, what would you rather have in your safe today, $10,000 in twenty-dollar bills, or a canvas bag with 1,000 1964 Kennedy half dollars? Each of those half dollars is worth about $15 today. But in the future, they will likely be worth more than $50 each. And those twenty-dollar bills could be worth about half their current value. Junk? Not from my perspective.

If a website is selling junk silver, you will see something like "Silver 720 oz. $1,000 90% Junk Coins." This will be a bag of pre-1965 U.S. silver coins with a face value of $1,000. A face value of $1,000 will equate to approximately 720 ounces. This means that each $1 in face value is worth 72% of an ounce of silver. A $1 face value would be two half dollars, four quarters, or ten dimes. Multiply these quantities by

1,000, and you will know how many coins should be in the bag. For instance, if you bought dimes, then there will be 10,000.

The standard size bag is $1,000 face value (720 ounces), although you can also find $500, $250, and $100 face value bags. In addition to purchasing bags, you can also buy the coins individually. Currently, on APMEX, you can purchase any quantity you desire, from a single coin to several thousand.

Until recently, junk silver had low markups, often as low as a 2% premium over spot. This has changed. Now premiums can exceed 35%. Currently, APMEX is charging a 15% premium for a $100 face bag of 1964 Kennedy Half Dollars. I was surprised by this large increase in premiums, but then I realized why. They don't make these anymore.

I wrote the following back in 2010:

> *Junk silver is probably one of the best investments one can make. Why buy silver bullion bars and rounds, when all you will get for them is the spot price? Why not buy junk silver that you can sell in the future for large premiums? I would not be surprised if at some point you can no longer find junk silver coins for premiums under 50% the spot price.*

A Troy Ounce

I suppose I'd better clarify that an ounce isn't an ounce when it comes to precious metals. An ounce as we are used to it weighs 28.3 grams, but an ounce for precious metals is 31.1 grams. Thus, if you weigh your bars or coins, they will weigh a little bit more than you are expecting (unless you are on the metric system). Odd, isn't it! This system dates back to the original gold coins from Rome. Thus, precious metals are weighed in troy ounces.

Gold is often listed as tons. But there are three different types of tons, so you need to know which one is being used. U.S. short tons (2,000 lbs.) is 29,166 troy ounces. British long tons (2,240 lbs.) is 32,665 troy ounces, and a metric ton (1,000 kilos) is 32,150 troy ounces. A common mistake is to expect 32,000 ounces of gold in a U.S. short ton.

Silver Bars

For those of you who want a lot of silver bullion, they do sell silver bars that weigh 1,000 ounces. Oddly, they rarely weigh exactly 1,000 ounces, but instead weigh somewhere between 980 ounces and 1,100 ounces. Thus, the price will vary based on the actual weight.

These are the bars that manufacturers purchase for fabrication, and they are pretty hefty, at 65 pounds or so. Currently, you can purchase these from large Internet websites. Northwest Territorial Mint (nwtmint.com) specializes in these bars and is good places to locate large quantities and get good prices.

COMEX Trick

One trick to purchasing large quantities of silver bars is to take delivery from the COMEX (New York Commodity Exchange). However, they are starting to have supply issues and have threatened to stop this practice. As it stands today, you can purchase a call option contract on the COMEX for a set price. After you purchase the contract, you can immediately demand delivery at the contract price. A full contract is 5,000 ounces (5 bars). A mini contract is 1,000 ounces (1 bar). I know of one guy in New York who purchases contracts and then drives to New Jersey and picks up the bars at a COMEX warehouse. You pay the contract price per ounce, which is the best price you can get, so this unorthodox method makes sense.

To purchase contracts through the COMEX, you need a futures account with a stockbroker. Also, make sure your stockbroker is comfortable taking delivery. When you demand delivery, the stockbroker will then receive a depository receipt, which includes the serial numbers and location of your silver bars. Have your stockbroker send you the receipt. You now can either leave it at its current location (an insured warehouse), and pay storage fees, or you can move it.

The only reason to move it is to take delivery. To take delivery, you must sign the back of the receipt and write a letter explaining who is going to pick up the silver and when. It is a good idea to contact the location on the receipt and ask them if there are any other details required to take delivery.

I found all of this information on an obscure web page.[34] What is amazing is that whoever wrote this article (there was no name) knew his stuff. I smiled when

I read the quote below by the author since our opinions matched. This was solid confirmation that BullionVault and GoldMoney are the best places to store gold.

> *I still think that BullionVault (BullionVault.com) and GoldMoney (goldmoney.com) are superior to any form of paper gold, including ETFs, futures, Perth mint certificates, etc. They are relatively cheap, liquid, and have lower transaction costs. However, there is something to be said for owning real metal directly.*[35]

A note for the millionaires out there: You can use this same method for taking delivery of gold bars from COMEX. (Note: COMEX settles gold delivery in 100-ounce bars.) But I don't see a reason for that since there is no shortage of gold. You can always buy gold bars direct from an Internet website, or the London Bullion Market Association (LBMA) if you can afford 400-ounce bars.

London OTC (Over the Counter) Market

Most of the world's physical gold is bought and sold in London at the LBMA. This is considered the OTC market for gold, where you can purchase physical gold bars. These are the ubiquitous large gold bars that you have likely seen before. However, you have not likely held one in your hand. They weigh 400 ounces (28.4 lbs.). At $1,500 per ounce, one bar costs about $600,000 dollars. Buy two bars and you are a millionaire.

Understanding Coins

Gold and silver coins have been a part of the American monetary system dating back to the foundation of this country. It is only in modern times that we stopped using gold and silver coins as currency. The first paper money was not printed until the Civil War in the 1860s. The first U.S. Silver Dollar was minted in 1794, and we used silver coins from that early period until 1965.

Gold coins have also had a long history in the U.S. Until 1933, when gold was confiscated by the Federal Government, the American public held gold coins in abundance. Until that time, it was quite common for families to own gold coins. The original Gold Eagle coins date from the late 18th century (1795). See the image below for the first minted U.S. Gold Eagle.[36]

American Eagles

In my opinion, all you need to know about gold and silver coins starts and stops with modern American Eagles. The U.S. Mint began issuing the modern version of these in 1986, and they are, by far, the most popular coins. Since 2010, an average of about 40 million American Eagles were minted. Of this total, less than 1 million Gold Eagles are minted annually.

From 1933 until 1986, Gold Eagles were not minted. This was the "dead period" of gold coins. The U.S. Treasury tried to make gold coins go away, but they failed. If you want to own a U.S. Gold Eagle, your choices are from 1849 until 1933, or a modern version (1986 until the present).

While Gold Eagles are a resumption of minting practices from the past, Silver Eagles are a modern invention that replaces the U.S. Silver Dollar. The first silver dollar was minted in 1794 and was 90% silver.[37] Since 1794, there have been several versions, including the widely used Morgan Silver Dollar (originally minted from 1878 to 1921). Most of the older versions are approximately 90% silver, along with other base metals, such as copper, to make them harder to bend. The U.S. Treasury began minting Silver Eagle coins in 1986, and they are .999% pure. They are stunningly beautiful and will hold their value better than any other non-numismatic silver coin.

A note about Morgan Silver Dollars, which are quite popular. They only weigh 26.7 grams and have .77 ounces of silver. These odd measurements can be confusing for valuing the coins versus the spot price. Here is a method you can use:

Spot Price: $20
Morgan Price: $25
Morgan silver
content spot price = ... $20 x .77 = $15.40
Silver Markup: .... $25 - $15.40 = $9.60
Silver Premium: ....$9.60 / $15.40 = 62%

As you can see, if you are not careful you can pay a very large premium on the actual silver content. The reason you are paying for this large premium is the numismatic value, which I am going to discuss later in this chapter.

Non-Standard Eagles

Modern "standard version" Eagles are not yet classified as a collectible (numismatic). This will inevitably change in the future, once they are no longer minted. That is basically what a numismatic coin is, one that is no longer minted. Thus, by buying modern Eagles, you are likely buying a future collectible. This will never be true of a bullion bar.

The U.S. Mint sells different versions of Eagles to make more income. What they do is issue collectible versions. For instance, for Silver Eagles, in addition to the standard version, they also issue proof versions and uncirculated versions. These last two are considered collectibles and cost more than standard Eagles. It's just a game of trying to invent rarity so that the U.S. Mint can make more money for essentially the same coin.

The only thing different from these non-standard collectible coins and the standard coins is that they have an additional letter on them designating the mint they came from (such as P for Philadelphia or W for West Point or S for San Francisco). These letters are used to signify their rarity since the standard versions do not have letters. Everyone knows that these coins will all eventually become numismatic coins, so the collectible market is already forming.

My suggestion is to stick with the standard Silver Eagles (the ones without letters), but I would try to keep them blemish free by using plastic covers or airtight cases. However, even if they are scratched and blemished, they will not lose their spot value. If you do have an Eagle with a minted letter, know that it is worth a few dollars more.

If you happen to have a 1995W, it is worth more than $1,000. This is the only rare Silver Eagle, because only 30,000 were made. If you want a list of the quantities of all the Silver Eagles ever minted, refer to this web page: *http://en.wikipedia.org/wiki/American_Silver_Eagle*.

Eagles Denominations

Silver Eagles only come in one size: 1 ounce. Modern Gold Eagles come in four sizes: 1 ounce, ½ ounce, ¼ ounce, and 1/10 ounce. These have face values of $50, $25, $10, and $5. The face values are only for show, as they are priced by weight.

Modern Gold Eagles weigh more than their denomination size. Let me explain why. While Silver Eagles are .999% pure, Gold Eagles are 22 karats, or 92% pure. The reason for this is that gold is a soft metal and will bend easily at 24 karats (.999%). The additional metals used in modern Gold Eagles are 3% silver and 5% copper. Each 1 ounce Gold Eagle contains 31.1 grams of gold (a troy oz.) and weighs 33.9 grams (the remainder is silver and copper).

Eagles Designs

The design of the Modern Gold and Silver Eagles are similar, with Lady Liberty on the front and an eagle on the back. Both are quite beautiful. The front of the Gold Eagle is nearly identical to the Double Eagle designed by Augustus Saint-Gaudens in 1905. It's not quite as stunning as the Saint-Gaudens, but still beautiful in its elegance. The Modern Gold Eagle coin is considered the official gold bullion coin of the United States.

Just like Modern Silver Eagles, Modern Gold Eagle collectibles are minted with letters, such as W for West Point Mint. These coins are worth more than standard gold bullion Eagles because of their rarity. They are minted with the same terminology (proofs and uncirculated). Proofs are minted when the dies are being cleaned or tested. Uncirculated versions are rarer than proofs and are made specifically for collectors.

Other Modern Coins

While I like Modern American Eagle coins (minted from 1986 forward), they aren't the only game in town. Several countries mint gold and silver coins that are comparable to the American Eagles. The ones I like the most are the gold and silver Maple Leafs from the Canadian Mint. The markups for these foreign coins can be considerably less in the U.S. than that of Eagles, due to supply/demand dynamics. Also, when Eagles are hard to find, these coins tend to be available.

In addition to American Eagles and Canadian Maple Leafs, there are three other sovereign coins that have an extensive inventory and are very popular: South African Krugerrands, Great Britain Britannia, and Austrian Philharmonics.

Gold Maple Leafs, Britannia, and Philharmonics are pure gold. South African Krugerrands are the same as Modern Gold Eagles: 22 karat, or 92% gold. All five of these coins contain a troy ounce (31.1 grams of gold), with the American and South African coins weighing about 34 grams for the additional metals used for hardening. You may want to buy Canadian Maple Leafs for this reason. Why not buy a pure gold coin when it costs less than an American Eagle? One reason is that in the future, Americans may not accept a Canadian coin for payment. If we ever begin using gold coins in the U.S. for payments, the Modern Gold Eagle might be the only accepted coin in some situations.

The remaining popular coins: Chinese Pandas, Australian Kangaroos, American Buffalos, etc. are not as extensively owned. These are okay for collectors, but I wouldn't purchase these to be the bulk of your investment portfolio. Stick with coins that dealers are going to want.

I should mention that silver Chinese Pandas have had the highest appreciation in value over the past few years. If you Google the value of Chinese Pandas from the year 2000 onward, you will be a bit surprised. The other coins that collectors prefer are silver African Elephants. These two coins appear to not only hold their value but increase in value.

> Note: Gold American Buffalos are pure gold and older versions have numismatic value. These are quite popular because they are currently the only pure gold U.S. minted coin (no copper or silver used for hardening).
>
> Note: Silver Maple Leafs are the only pure silver sovereign coin at .9999%. That's four 9s. You can use these coins for creating colloidal silver simply by soaking them in water.

Numismatic Double Eagles

The last category is numismatic coins. This is a category that most of you will avoid, but the late Bob Chapman (The International Forecaster), whose opinion I respect, said that Double Eagle gold coins (1849 to 1933) would explode in value when gold prices rise because of their rarity. He thought you would get double the return versus standard gold Eagles. Thus, if you purchase a few of these rare coins as an investment, you could make a nice return. See the image below of a $20 Double Eagle coin from 1849.

Old silver coins are also excellent collector items, such as the Morgan Silver Dollars from the late 1800s. These, along with the old gold coins, are the ultimate collector pieces. I envision these coins escalating in value as the price of gold and silver rises.

The old Double Eagle coins are expensive, so it takes a bit of nerve to purchase them. They were minted with two different designs. The design above was from 1849 to 1907. The Saint-Gaudens (see below) was from 1907 to 1933.[38]

Nearly all of the 1933 coins were melted down. A 1933 Double Eagle was sold for $6.6 million dollars at an auction in 2002. In 2011, a family in Pennsylvania found ten 1933 Double Eagles worth more than $50 million dollars, and the U.S. Government confiscated them. The Langbord family sued to get them back and lost.[39] Today, you can purchase a Double Eagle for anywhere between the spot price and $6,000 dollars.

For those of you with a lot of money and who like to collect things, it might be a good investment to stock up on these rare gold Double Eagles. While your local coin dealer will not likely have these in inventory, he or she might be able to get them for you, and you can use the dealer's expertise to confirm their current value. You want to make sure you do not pay too high a premium, but something close to their current value.

Also, make sure you have somewhere to sell them. These coins could increase in value to more than $10,000 each. Will your local coin dealer want to buy them? Worst case, you may have to drive to another town. I wouldn't be too concerned about finding a buyer. These are Double Eagles, after all, the most prized gold coin ever made.

Numismatic Valuations

Numismatic coins are valued based on two factors. The first factor is the grading, which is completely based on quality (the lack of blemishes). The grading of a coin is quite complicated. I will include an extensive explanation of how coins are graded at the end of this chapter.

The second factor that determines the value of a coin is its rarity. Every coin that has ever been minted is part of an inventory for that year's minting. The coin community knows how many pieces of your coin were minted. Thus, what is rare is very well understood. The combination of rarity and grading can make a Double Eagle coin worth thousands of dollars.

Currently, a blemished Double Eagle will sell for about the price of gold. A pristine Double Eagle can sell for about three times the price of gold. We should see blemished Double Eagles selling for about double the price of gold when the mania phase begins, and everyone wants to own gold.

In my opinion, Double Eagles are the ultimate collector's item. If you own a few of these coins, you can consider that a significant savings account of real assets.

Buying Double Eagles

If I were going to buy Double Eagles, I would work with my local coin dealer. This is something they like to do. They love to go shopping for their clients and find these valuable old coins. Then they get their commission.

I personally don't feel comfortable buying numismatic coins on the Internet. Of course, it's easy to do, and some Internet sites have a large inventory. Check out AmericanGoldExchange.com (see screen shot below). eBay is always an option, too.

1909-s Gold $20 **Saint Gaudens Double Eagle** Choice Bu
Better Date $20 Gold **Saint Gaudens Double Eagle** from 1909-S. Desirable MS63/64 Coin. Excellent addition to your Collection or Perfect Gift. ....
Add to Shopping List
$1,925.00 ne
eBay

1909-s Gold $20 **Saint Gaudens Double Eagle** Bu+
Better Date $20 Gold **Saint Gaudens Double Eagle** from 1910-S. Desirable Coin. Excellent addition to your Collection or Perfect Gift. ....
Add to Shopping List
$1,775.00 ne
eBay

Beauty 1909-s Gold $20 **Saint Gaudens Double Eagle** (189
Better Date $20 Gold **Saint Gaudens Double Eagle** from 1909-S. Desirable Coin. Excellent addition to your Collection or Perfect Gift. ....
Add to Shopping List
$1,675.00 ne
eBay

If you are going to invest in numismatic coins, I would suggesst purchasing only MS (mint state) graded coins. These are the coins that are most likely to hold their value, as well as increase the most in price. And they are also beautiful to behold because of their high quality. Below is an explanation of how coins are graded and a description of each grading.

Grading Coins[40]

The first thing to understand about grading coins is that for accuracy you need to have your coins graded by a professional grading company. The most popular grading company is Professional Coin Grading Service (*www.pcsg.com*). They charge approximately $30 per coin, plus shipping. Coin shops can guess the grade, but the service companies will give you a certificate, which you can use when you sell the coin. These service companies use a scale from 0 to 70, with 70 being the best (zero blemishes). Along with this 0 to 70 number scale, they use an abbreviation to identify the grading level that the number represents. However, not all of the 70 grading numbers are used, and not all grading levels get numbers or abbreviations. Confused yet? It's actually pretty simply, once you read the grading levels.

There are nine grading levels that the service companies use. The first one we have all heard of before: mint condition, or mint state.

Mint State (MS)

An MS-70 graded coin is as good as it gets. This is perfection. Under a magnifying glass, there are no blemishes and it is shiny new. MS coins are graded from 60 to 70, and the bottom level for mint condition is MS-60. To the naked eye, this would look like a brand new coin, with no discernable blemishes.

Almost Uncirculated (AU)

These are graded as AU-58, AU-55 and AU-50. These coins have only a trace of visible wear on the highest points. The differences for some of these coins are so minor that the grading is not precise. One person might give it a 55 and another person a 58. Some of the rules that graders use are strange. For this reason, an AU-58 nearly always looks better to the layman than an MS-60. Also, often the XF graded coins can look better than the AU graded coins.

Extremely Fine (XF)

These are graded as XF-45 and XF-40. They have very light wear on only the highest points. The differences between XF and AU are not always discernable to the layman.

Very Fine (VF)

These are graded as VF-35, VF-30, VF-25, and VF-20. These coins show medium wear, but are still in good condition.

Fine (F)

These are graded as F-12. These coins have moderate wear, but you can still see most of the design.

Very Good (VG)

These are graded as VG-8. These coins have moderate to heavy wear, but the design is almost in full detail.

Good (G)

These coins are heavily worn, but the design is visible.

Almost Good (AG)

The design is barely perceptible, but you can make it out.

Fair

You can identify the coin, but that's it.

Note: The last three grades do not get number ratings, and this last grade does not have an abbreviation.

CHAPTER 4

ETFs (Exchange Traded Funds)

ETFs (Exchange Traded Funds) have become popular investment funds for investors. These funds trade on the major stock exchanges, using a stock symbol no different than that of a corporation. For instance, the symbol GLD is traded on the New York Stock Exchange (NYSE) as if it were just another company. However, the symbol GLD is actually a trading vehicle that is managed by a major investment bank (Mellon Bank of New York).

Today there are more than a thousand ETFs that trade on the NYSE or the American Stock Exchange (AMEX). You can purchase ETFs for everything from commodities (DBA for food, PHO for water), stock market indexes (SPY for the S&P 500 Index, DIA for the DOW Jones Index), currencies (ERO for the Euro/Dollar exchange rate), to bonds (IEF for 10 Year Bonds). You can invest in nearly any commodity, stock index, currency, or bond using an ETF. With the Internet, it is easy to find these ETFs. All you have to do is search Google. Enter a search request such as ETF Gold, ETF Energy, or ETF Agriculture. You will easily find a list of available ETFs.

ETFs vs. Mutual Funds

The difference between a mutual fund and an ETF is often imperceptible. However, there are several significant distinctions. The main difference is that a mutual fund is generally actively managed by a fund manager and, an ETF is passively managed. For this reason, ETFs tend to have lower annual fees and lower premiums to purchase shares. Another big difference is the way they are taxed, with ETFs tending to have lower annual capital gains.

I use gold mutual funds for income because they payout annual capital gains and larger dividends than ETFs. I use ETFs for long-term capital gains. The only time I would consider buying a gold mutual fund is if I were looking for annual income. Otherwise, I would be focusing on ETFs.

There are two types of gold/silver ETFs. The first type tracks the price of gold or the price of silver. Note that these ETFs use different methods for tracking the price, which I will mention below. The second type purchases shares of mining companies, and acts a lot like a gold mutual fund, but with lower fees and lower premiums.

Bullion ETFs have become very popular. These are ETFs that track the price of gold or silver by purchasing physical bullion and placing it in a warehouse. Thus, the value of the ETF coincides with the price of gold or silver. In theory, the ETF share price is supposed to match the price of gold or silver. However, in practice, there is always some type of premium which can vary based on supply and demand of the ETF.

No Guarantees

Most ETFs do a good job of tracking their underlying assets (commodities, stock indexes, currencies, or bonds). However, nearly every ETF prospectus will claim that certain factors can impede this close tracking. In other words, they do not guarantee a close correlation, and sometimes the correlations are way off.

For instance, in 2009 an ETF that tracks the price of natural gas (symbol UNG), did not perform as advertised. The price of natural gas went down to $2.50 in early September 2009, and then it jumped to $6.00 in December. However, investors in UNG did not double their money. The price for UNG only moved from $9 to $10.85 (see chart below).[41] Investors were not happy. What happened is that because this fund is so large ($4 billion market cap), UNG lost control of tracking the price. This fund relies on futures contracts, and once prices rise, they cannot go back in time and buy cheap futures contracts. Thus, they missed the bottom of the market.

Google.com

What happened to UNG can happen to any commodity ETF that relies on futures contracts. So, buyer beware. To avoid this situation, GLD (SPDR Gold Shares) and SLV (iShares Silver Trust) were created. These gold and silver bullion ETFs are not backed by futures contracts, but by physical metal. Thus, in theory, they should always closely correlate to the price of silver or gold. And since they were introduced, this has been true.

SLV

When you purchase a share of SLV, you essentially purchase one ounce of silver. If you notice the chart below from 2013, you will see that there were 344 million shares outstanding, and 331 million ounces of silver in the trust (not an exact match, but close).[42] According to BlackRock Asset Management, the fund manager, these ounces of silver are located in a warehouse in London.

Profile as of 11/27/2013	
Description	Value
Total Net Assets	$6,619,621,795
Shares Outstanding	344,050,000
Sponsor's Fee	0.50%
Inception Date	4/21/2006
Ounces of Silver in Trust	331,442,709.900

The iShares Silver Trust's silver and other assets are valued on the basis of each day's announced London Silver Fix, the price for an ounce of silver set by three market making members of the London Bullion Market Association, minus all accrued fees, expenses and liabilities.[43]

Ease of Investing

There are many benefits for using an ETF to purchase gold or silver. The first one is ease of investing. Instead of having to worry where to purchase your gold or where to store it, all you have to do is purchase a stock. How simple is that? Moreover, you get all of the benefits of a stock. You can hold it for as long as you want and do not have to pay capital gains until you sell it.

Not only is it simple, but it is very cheap to purchase and sell. On TD Ameritrade, you can purchase an unlimited amount of an ETF for free, without a fee. And you can sell it for that same zero fee. Because ETFs are so inexpensive to buy and sell, many people like to trade them and use them for short-term investments. With gold and silver being highly volatile, this can be a very profitable trading strategy.

Brokerage Firms

Since I mentioned TD Ameritrade, I wanted to share my experience with several brokerage firms that I have used. TD Ameritrade is currently the best in my opinion if you want to purchase junior mining stocks. They are the only large online brokerage firm that has a flat rate for all trades. Other large brokerage firms, such as Fidelity or any bank, all charge extra fees to purchase stocks under $1 per share. E-Trade also charges extra fees for junior stocks under $1. If it wasn't for these extra fees, the differences between E-Trade, Fidelity, and TD Ameritrade is minimal.

I have used Wells Fargo, E-Trade, Scottrade, TD Ameritrade, and Interactive Brokers. From my experience, I can say that TD Ameritrade is the only one that I have been satisfied with. I like their 24-hour phone support and I buy a lot of stocks that trade under $1, so TD Ameritrade is the only one that saves me money on trades. I'm sure that there are other online brokerages that also have flat rates for all trades, but I have not done the research to find these firms.

Interactive Brokers (IB) has been useful for buying stocks on foreign exchanges. I use it for some stocks that do not trade in the U.S. or have very low volume on the OTC market. I have found that IB is very useful for this purpose and the fees are not outrageous, although not low either. One nice feature when using IB, is that you can let your stocks ride in a foreign currency. After you sell the stock, you can convert it back into your native currency on their website for small fee. Currently, they charge $2.50 to do currency conversions.

Fees and Premiums

A benefit of ETFs is their low management fees. The management fees associated with ETFs are generally much lower than mutual funds because ETFs have lower costs. Whereas ETFs generally have annual fees of less than .5%, it is quite normal for traditional mutual funds to charge 2% or more.

Annual management fees are built into the premiums that you pay to purchase a fund. Premiums are the percentage difference between the purchase price and the sale price. Premiums can vary anywhere from 1% to 15%. If you purchase a fund with a 10% premium, then it has to increase 10% in value for you to breakeven.

From my experience, because ETF fees are low, the premiums tend to be low. Conversely, the opposite is true for mutual funds. This is just a generalization because there are thousands of funds. Moreover, while most ETF premiums tend to be low, and most mutual fund premiums tend to be high, this is not always true.

The only fees associated with SLV are the .5% annual fee that BlackRock Asset Management charges for managing the fund and storing/insuring the silver. These fees are translated into the premium that you have to pay to purchase SLV. I have found that the premium for SLV is barely noticeable. For instance, today you can purchase SLV for $23.78 (the ask price), and you can sell your shares for $23. (the bid price). The difference is only 1 cent. Basically, there is no premium other than your brokerage fee. The reason for this is the size of the ETF and the low annual fee.

These low premiums are not always the case for all ETFs. The premiums for PSLV and CEF (both bullion ETFs) tend to be higher. These are both based in Canada and have very good reputations for safety. Their premiums tend to vary based on the demand of these ETFs. Both have historically volatile premiums. Many savvy investors recognize when an ETF has a historically volatile premium and waits for a good entry point with a lower premium.

Real-Time Pricing

Another benefit with ETFs is that they track their underlying asset in real time. For instance, the price of SLV follows the price of silver during trading hours. As silver goes up, so does the price of SLV.

This can make an ETF advantageous versus a mining stock. If silver or gold spike in price, you will get that return immediately in SLV or GLD. However, if you own a mining stock, it might take months for that stock to incorporate the new price of the metal into the value of the shares. If silver or gold prices spike really high, the mining shares may not ever match the price spike. The reason for this is that investors may not believe that the spike will last. This happens all the time when investors anticipate the price of gold/silver coming back down. Mining companies are constantly complaining that their share price does not reflect the current price of gold or silver.

SLV Concerns

I bought SLV at $13 and thought I made a good investment. I was confident silver would reach $75, and I would get my five bagger (500% return). At the time, I was still a rookie and didn't think it was a risky investment. Now I have concerns. If you do some research on the Internet regarding SLV, you will find that there is a large number of investors and analysts who do not trust this ETF. Most of these skeptics do not believe that SLV has all of the silver they claim to have. However,

SLV claims to do audit inspections,[44] and you can view a copy of the audit report at the URL on this footnote.[45]

A silver analyst that I follow told his readers to stay clear of SLV. Then I read the same thing from many other investment analysts that I respect. They all said the same thing: You can't trust it. Ironically, it is called the iShares Silver Trust. For many SLV detractors, trust is not something they associate with this ETF. Note that many analysts have said the same thing about GLD, the largest gold ETF.

I think the audit is valid and they have their silver. But if word ever gets out that they have significantly less silver than what they claim to have, the share price could fall dramatically and very quickly.

That is one risk. There are a few more. The next one is if BlackRock has financial trouble. What would happen to the SLV fund under this scenario? Would it get audited? Would it be liquidated? Also, what happens if the fund stops trading due to a financial crisis? That is a long shot, but still a risk.

And lastly, perhaps the worst risk of all, what happens if the U.S. Government decides to appropriate all of the silver in SLV due to a physical shortage? They would likely pay the going market price, which could drop dramatically in only a few hours after the announcement. A simple rumor of this event could lead to a cascade out of the fund, depressing the price. This is actually not so farfetched. If silver prices increase to $75 due to silver shortages, then corporations are going to be lobbying governments for this type of appropriation. I will not be surprised at all if lobbyists begin calling silver a strategic metal with a critically low inventory.

All in all, you can see why owning physical gold is truly the only riskless investment. The next best is not an ETF, but having gold stored somewhere, such as BullionVault.com or GoldMoney.com, which is directly owned by you. While using storage does take some risk out of the equation, it also costs you money for storage fees.

Storage or ETFs always include third-party risk. My favorite example of third-party risk is from the movie Blow when Johnny Depp goes to his bank in Panama and expects to withdraw money. They tell him his account has been closed. Thus, you can never be certain that a third party will keep their promise to pay.

Most Popular Gold and Silver ETFs

ETF	Exchange	Symbol
iShares Silver Trust	NYSEMKT	SLV
Spider Gold Shares	NYSEARCA	GLD
Aberdeen Physical Silver Shares	NYSEMKT	SIVR
Global X Silver Miners	NYSEMKT	SIL
VanEck Gold Miners	NYSEARCA	GDX
VanEck Junior Gold Miners	NYSEARCA	GDXJ
Direxion 3x Bull Junior Gold Miner	NYSEARCA	JNUG
Direxion 3x Bear Junior Gold Miner	NYSEARCA	JDST
Direxion 3x Bull Gold Miner	NYSEARCA	NUGT
Direxion 3x Bear Gold Miner	NYSEARCA	DUST
Velocity Shares Silver 3x Long	NASDAQ	USLV
Proshares Ultra Silver	NYSEMKT	AGZ
iShares Global Silver Miners	NYSEMKT	SLVP
Prime Junior Silver Miners	NYSEMKT	SILV
Sprott Physical Gold & Silver Trust	NYSEARCA	CEF
Sprott Physical Silver Trust	NYSEARCA	PSLV
Sprott Physical Gold Trust	NYSEARCA	PHYS
Sprott Gold Miners	NYSEARCA	SGDM
Sprott Junior Gold Miners	NYSEARCA	SGDJ

More Gold and Silver ETFs

ETF	Symbol
Global X Gold Explorer	GOEX
Powershares Global Gold Miners	PSAU
US Global Go Gold Precious Metals	GOAU
Microsector Gold Miner 3x Long	GDXU
Microsector Gold Miner 3x Short	GDXD
Physical Gold 2x Long	UGL
Physical Gold 2x Short	GLL
Physical Silver 2x Long	AGQ
Physical Silver 2x Short	ZSL

Other Silver ETFs

I no longer consider SLV as the preferred silver bullion ETF, because there are two other silver ETFs that seem safer. Today I prefer PSLV and SIVR.[46] I think both of these ETFs are safe and good options for investing in silver bullion.

PSLV was started in 2010 by Sprott Asset Management out of Canada. This silver ETF is highly respected for safety and currently has a premium of only 2%. You can buy it for $8.85 and sell for $8.84. When it first started trading, the premium was as high as 30%, which shows the demand for safety. I think it is a buy with a premium under 5%.

SIVR was started in 2009 by ETF Securities Ltd, which is based in London. They are one of the largest ETF management companies in the world and specialize in commodities. SIVR is nearly identical to SLV, except it is audited twice a year and their expenses are lower. SIVR has included annual auditing and lower expenses to attract customers. It looks pretty safe to me. You could compare the premiums between PSLV and SIVR and see which is cheaper.

There are two other silver ETFs, but they are not backed by physical silver. E-TRACS Silver is managed by UBS (trading symbol USV). It tries to track the price of silver by using silver futures contracts. I don't see the value in this type of fund, when SIVR and PSLV are around, which are much more adept at tracking the price. The PowerShares DB Silver (trading symbol DBS) is essentially the same thing as USV.

Many of the professional analysts that I follow recommend staying clear of ETFs, and to either take physical possession or use a storage facility such as BullionVault.com. However, if you want to invest in a large quantity of silver, storage fees can be significant (generally .5% per year). An investment of $100,000 at .5% is $500 annually. That is not cheap. Note that gold is much cheaper to store, at around .15% annually, and makes much more sense for storage in large amounts.

Gold ETFs

Using gold ETFs for long-term investing is not worth the risk when BullionVault.com and GoldMoney.com are around (with their low storage fees). If you are a large investor, then it makes much more sense to pay the fees and sleep well at night. Gold in these warehouses is yours, and it is insured.

However, there is one excellent ETF called the Central Fund of Canada, which trades on AMEX with the symbol of CEF. This ETF is managed in Canada and holds half gold bullion and half silver bullion (currently 53% gold, 46% silver, 1% cash). Their gold and silver are stored in Canada. It is essentially the same thing as SLV and GLD, except that CEF has its assets split between gold and silver.

There are a couple of other significant benefits for CEF. First, the physical metal is audited annually. Second, CEF is taxed at standard capital gains rates, whereas GLD and SLV are taxed at 28% as collectibles.

From a pure bullion play, CEF is an excellent investment. Perhaps not as safe as physical ownership or a storage vault, but pretty close. There is one negative: you generally have to pay a high premium to purchase the stock. However, today it is trading at a 1% premium. You can buy it at $22.45 and sell it at $22.35. After this gold price correction turns, I would expect this premium to rise.

If you are a long-term investor, then the safety of this ETF, along with the tax benefits, are enticing. Plus, if the gold/silver ratio tightens, silver should go up more than gold, making this a good way to get silver exposure. You won't get rich in a gold and silver bullion ETF, but you will increase your wealth in this gold bull market continues. Moreover, if capital preservation is your goal, then CEF is a good holding.

The other gold ETF that I like is PHYS, which is managed by Sprott Asset Management in Canada. I consider Sprott to be the safest company in the investment business, because of Eric Sprott, the CEO. He is a billionaire and made his money investing in the mining business. He is very shareholder focused. Currently, PHYS has a very low premium. You can buy it at $14.65 and sell it at $14.52.

Gold and Silver Mining ETFs

There are also gold and silver mining stock ETFs that are essentially stock mutual funds with very low fees and premiums. GDX is an ETF that includes most of the gold and silver Majors. GDXJ and GLDX include mostly gold Mid-Tier stocks. SIL includes nearly all of the silver producers. SLVP includes silver Mid-Tier stocks and riskier silver Juniors. I will mention these ETFs in subsequent chapters and consider them excellent investment choices.

Leveraged ETFs

In addition to tracking the price of gold and silver with ETFs such as GLD and PSLV, there are other ETFs which provide leverage. The Proshares Ultra Silver and Ultra Gold ETFs track double the bullion price (2X) going either up or down. The Velocity Shares ETFs are triple the bullion price (3X). The Direxion ETFs (DUST and NUGT) allow you to leverage against a gold miners index.

Here is the list:

Proshares Ultra 2X Silver .... AGQ
Proshares Ultra 2X Silver .... Short ZSL
Proshares Ultra 2X Gold .... GLL
Proshares Ultra 2X Gold .... Short UGL
Velocity Shares 3X Long Silver .... USLV
Velocity Shares 3X Short Silver .... DSLV
Velocity Shares 3X Long Gold .... UGLD
Velocity Shares 3X Short Gold .... DGLD
Direxion Shares 3X Short Miners .... DUST
Direxion Shares 3X Long Miners .... NGUT

These leveraged ETFs are useful for trading or hedging. You can also purchase options for these ETFs to create substantial leverage. With the high volatility in the price of gold and silver, using these leveraged ETFs is popular. It is a highly risky investment strategy, but the potential exists for large returns in very short time periods.

While I don't normally like leveraged ETFs due to their risky nature, this bull market will provide opportunities. If you can anticipate a price spike, they can be lucrative. For instance, in 2010, the price of silver rose 80%, and then in early 2011, it rose an additional 50%. Both of these situations provided an opportunity for large returns if leverage was utilized. If you want to bet on this occurring again, you can purchase an option (more on this in the next chapter) or a leveraged ETF once the trend materializes.

Another thing ETFs are good for is short-term trading. Because it is so cheap to buy these ETFs, you can easily afford to make multiple trades for short periods. We are likely to see a lot of volatility that will be conducive to trading in the near future. In Chapter 9, I will talk about the fluctuating price of precious metals and how to analyze the short-term technicals and fundamentals. There is one excellent system of selling into strength and buying into weakness. This is the same thing as buying low and selling high, although you do it as the price fluctuates. This is not day trading, but more like month trading. You buy the dips and then sell the spikes. You can use an ETF for this type of trading system. In a bull market, you can make money trading the volatility, as long as the trend is up.

Problems with Leveraged ETFs

There are 2X and 3X leveraged ETFs as mentioned above. These ETFs attempt to emulate twice or triple the daily movement in the underlying asset. You can purchase a 2X and 3X ETF that tracks the price lower, also called a short fund. Or you can purchase a 2X and 3X ETF that tracks the price higher, also called a long fund. I do not use leveraged ETFs for long-term investing, although using them for hedging can be okay (more on this later). They were created specifically for short-term traders.

The problem with 2X and 3X ETFs is that they do not track the underlying price accurately, and over time the correlation becomes highly skewed. There was a major lawsuit against a 2X Real Estate ETF with the symbol SRS because investors tried to use it for long-term investing, and it did not track the price of its underlying asset. They lost their lawsuit because the prospectus spells this out.

While researching leveraged ETFs, I found this example on the Security and Exchange Commission's web page warning about leveraged ETFs.[47]

> *Between December 1, 2008, and April 30, 2009, a particular index gained 2%. However, a leveraged ETF seeking to deliver twice that index's daily return fell by 6%, and an inverse ETF seeking to deliver twice the inverse of the index's daily return fell by 25%.*

This is an excellent example of why you should not use leveraged ETFs for long-term investment purposes.

Hedging

Hedging is a method of insuring against losses by betting on the other side of an investment. Many investors, especially professionals, like to hedge against significant price drops to protect their investments.

Hedging costs money, so you are potentially reducing your returns by betting both sides of an investment. One special benefit of ETFs is that they offer the ability to hedge the entire gold/silver market or hedge against a stock market crash.

I normally don't hedge because I am so bullish on the price of gold. However, I have hedged on occasion (explained below). I experienced both the 2008 and 2011-2015 corrections when gold and silver stocks got obliterated. From this experience,

I am inclined to analyze hedge options for potential stock crashes. The next time gold reaches a new high, I might consider a hedge.

The hedge I chose was an option on a leveraged 3X short ETF for the financial sector (FAZ). What I like about FAZ is that it is an ideal hedge against a stock market crash. If the stock market crashes, the financial sector is likely to get hit hard. FAZ is already a leveraged ETF, and when you combine that with an option, the leverage is extreme. It could return 1,000% or higher if the stock market crashes.

Another 3X short ETF that is popular for shorting the market is TZA. This is a small cap short ETF that has a lot of liquidity and generally good prices. Moreover, the small caps tend to be very volatile and are perfect for hedging a potential crash.

You don't have to buy options to hedge. I could have just bought FAZ shares and held them. Other ETFs that protect against a drop in gold/silver prices are DUST (3X miners short), ZSL (2X silver short), or DSLV (3x silver short). However, by using options, you can more than double the possible returns.

With hedging, you can use risky options because you don't care if you're wrong and it does not pay off. You want to be wrong. If the hedge pays off, that means your portfolio took a big hit.

Some of you may want to purchase options in DUST, ZSL, DSLV, or UGL to insure against the price of silver or gold dropping. This will hedge your investments in precious metals, especially if you own a lot of bullion and want to maintain your net worth. You can purchase options called leaps that are good for up to two years.

I have not used DUST options as a hedge, but I wish I would have in 2011 when gold reached an ATH. DUST is a good way to protect a portfolio that is heavily weighted with gold/silver mining stocks. It is a 3X short fund that attempts to emulate the Arca gold miners index. This is the same index that GDX is based on. GDX is an ETF of the largest gold and silver mining stocks. I will be mentioning it in the chapter on Majors.

DUST and NUGT can also be used during volatile periods as trading vehicles. Because these are 3X leveraged ETFs, if you time a move either up or down, you can make significant returns in a very short period. Gold and silver are likely to be highly volatile in the years ahead. If you spot a trend either up or down, you can use these ETFs to make a quick return.

While DUST is used to hedge against a mining index, and FAZ is a hedge against the stock market, you can also hedge against a bullion price crash. When silver runs up past $50 (or gold to $2,500), you might want to get an option to guard against a price crash. Then if the price crashes over the next year or two, you are insured to a certain extent. An option on one of the bullion 3X leveraged ETFs can create extreme leverage. This method of hedging is becoming more common by professionals. They don't want their clients exposed to what happened in 2008 when silver dropped nearly 60% in a very short period.

While you may never hedge or speculate on a price spike by purchasing an option, you should try to understand how they work. I will be explaining options in the next chapter. When silver dropped from $21 to $9 in 2008, and from $49 to $14 in 2011-2015, I wish I had purchased an option. That would have been handy. To receive a windfall right when stocks are cheap is a good way to rebuild your portfolio and recoup some of your losses.

As I mentioned before, I have experimented with leveraged ETFs using options. What I learned was that the risk is unbelievably high. The odds of an option becoming worthless is quite high. The reason why is because you normally purchase these options out of the money. Thus, they start out being worthless. They only pay out if your expectation comes to fruition.

Because of this high-risk level, I have lost my taste for them. When gold and silver reach a new ATH, I probably won't hedge with an option on a leveraged ETF. However, at least you will know that this opportunity will exist, and you can do some further research. Perhaps refer back to this chapter and the following chapter when that event occurs.

CHAPTER 5

OPTIONS

Most of you will never purchase an option. In fact, I recommend skipping this chapter if you find the material too technical. However, if you have an interest in understanding options, stick around.

I think options are important to understand for two reasons. 1) Options provide opportunities to make significant returns in short time periods. 2) Options provide an easy way to hedge investments.

Understanding how to invest with options is not that difficult. All you need is some basic information about how it works. Options are generally associated with professional investors, but anyone can purchase them. Professionals use options because they provide leverage and the potential for big returns. For instance, instead of making 10% in one year, you can make that much in a single day. Of course, you can't have those kinds of returns without immense risk.

While all investing is basically a gamble on predicting the future, options are truly gambling instruments. Most options expire worthless, meaning you lost what you paid for your option.

Puts and Calls

There are various types of options, but I am going to focus on "puts" and "calls." These are options that have limited liability. This means that the most you can lose is the amount you pay for the options.

There are other types of options, such as writing options. These options require a margin account and can have *unlimited* liability. I consider unlimited liability options for professional traders only, and urge against their use by amateurs. If you want to understand how to write options, you can research them on the Internet or purchase a book on options trading.

The main difference between puts and calls and writing options is that puts and calls have limited liability - the amount you pay for the option. Conversely, writing options can have potentially unlimited liability.

Another difference is that unlimited liability options require margin accounts, and limited liability options do not. Moreover, many professional options traders who write options do so with borrowed money for extra leverage. A trader can open a margin account with several thousand dollars in borrowed money and begin writing options - betting on the price direction of stocks, commodities, currencies, etc. Professionals call this putting "on" a trade, or "taking" a position. For example, instead of buying a stock or ETF, they can write an unlimited liability option and bet on the inverse direction of the option - either long or short.

The precarious thing about this kind of trading - writing unlimited liability options - is that you can lose more than the amount you paid for your options - potentially an unlimited exposure! One trader - Nick Leeson - bankrupted Barings Bank by losing $1.4 billion while trading options.[48] The movie *Rogue Trader* is a fascinating account of Nick Leeson's debacle.

> Note: Even though professionals who write options are exposing themselves to potentially unlimited liability, they can still use stops and closeout positions whenever they want. The higher risk they assume is when they are losing money on an option and they continue to add margin, instead of closing out the option with a loss.

Options Explained

Put options (limited liability) are used to predict that a commodity or stock will go down, while call options (also limited liability) are used for the opposite, predicting that the price will rise.

The main benefit with put and call options is that you have a fixed liability and a non-fixed upside potential - due to the leverage involved. Of course, you have to be very smart - or lucky - to predict that upside within a specific time frame.

Options came into existence because, essentially, you can price risk. One party - the buyer - agrees to purchase the risk, and the other party - the options seller - agrees to assume the risk at that price. The seller is essentially a bookie. They know that most options will end up worthless, so they are willing to assume the risk. They know how to price it so that, in the long run, they make a profit.

Put and call options are always purchased with an expiration date. The start date is the date that you buy them. And the expiration date can be as short as one week or as long as two years. These longer dated options are called leaps.

Option Price Quotes

The way that puts and calls work is that you purchase an option contract with a specific duration. These contracts have vacillating prices that are quoted on the Internet and you can easily view them online. For instance, I copied the following chart from *www.finance.yahoo.com.* These are put options for SLV (iShares Silver Trust) that expire on January 16*th*, 2015.

Put Options				Expire at close Friday, January 16, 2015			
Strike	Symbol	Last	Chg	Bid	Ask	Vol	Open Int
15.00	SLV150117P00015000	**0.58**	0.00	0.53	0.66	5	416
16.00	SLV150117P00016000	**0.68**	0.00	0.63	0.80	70	2,498
17.00	SLV150117P00017000	**0.83**	0.00	0.81	0.93	2	34
18.00	SLV150117P00018000	**1.02**	↓0.03	0.99	1.10	2	129
19.00	SLV150117P00019000	**1.20**	0.00	1.18	1.29	1	40
20.00	SLV150117P00020000	**1.40**	0.00	1.40	1.51	50	228
21.00	SLV150117P00021000	**1.67**	0.00	1.65	1.75	10	66
22.00	SLV150117P00022000	**1.90**	0.00	1.92	2.05	5	10,342
23.00	SLV150117P00023000	**2.17**	0.00	2.23	2.35	20	149
24.00	SLV150117P00024000	**2.59**	0.00	2.53	2.69	51	124
25.00	SLV150117P00025000	**3.00**	↑0.10	2.88	3.00	4	647

www.finance.yahoo.com

Before I explain the details of this chart, let me describe a sample trade. Since this is a put option, you want the price to fall. Thus, you have to decide how far you think the price of SLV might drop before January 16, 2015. Currently, SLV is trading at $29, about the same as silver bullion. You want to look at the ask price (how much you will pay for the option) and the strike price (how much the stock *must* drop for you to make any money), and then decide which option to choose.

You want to pick a strike price that is substantially higher than you think silver could drop. As of today, I think silver could fall to $17 if there is a major crash. With this projected potential bottom, I now select a strike price substantially higher. I think $25 is a good choice, because it is substantially higher than $17 and a few dollars below the current silver price. Today, I can pay $3 (the ask price) for the option to purchase a share with a strike price of $25.

Basically, you purchase as many options as you want at the ask price, and then:

1. If SLV never drops below the strike price, you will lose potentially the entire amount of the contract, as your option will expire worthless. However, when you initially purchase the option, it will have some extrinsic value (time value). This extrinsic value will decrease as you get closer to expiration.

   Note: You can sell an option for its extrinsic value at any time.

2. If SLV drops below the strike price, you will be "in the money." You can then sell your option before the expiration date for both the intrinsic and extrinsic value.

3. If SLV drops substantially below the strike price, then you will make much more money. That is what leverage does.

Option Terminology[49]

Strike: The strike price. This is also called the exercise price. In our put option example, it is the price that SLV must drop below before the expiration date. If it drops below, it is said to be "in the money."

Symbol: This is the trading symbol associated with SLV at a particular strike price and expiration date. Every option contract has its own trading symbol and can be quoted just like any stock symbol.

Bid: The bid price. This is the amount an option buyer is willing to pay for an option. It is a combination of the intrinsic value and the time value (both defined below).

Ask: The ask price. This is the amount you have to pay for an option contract. Generally, this is the bid price, plus the commissions you have to pay. Note that each contract represents 100 shares of the stock, so you have to multiply the ask price by 100.

Last: This is the last bid price at which the contract traded. Normally, this is very close to the bid price. However, option prices can be volatile due to the changing price of the underlying stock or commodity, as well as other risk factors, such as time, interest rates, and stock dividends.

Chg: This is the change in price from the current bid price and yesterday's closing bid price.

Vol: Daily Trading Volume, or the number of option contracts traded today.

Open Int: Open Interest, or the total number of option contracts open.

Additional Definitions

Intrinsic Value: This is the strike price minus the current price. In the case of a put option, it cannot be negative, or else it has no intrinsic value. Note that if an option has an intrinsic value, it is "in the money," and can be sold for both the intrinsic and extrinsic value.

Intrinsic Value = Strike Price - Current Price

Extrinsic Value (Time Value): This is the ask price beyond the intrinsic value. It is based on the time remaining before the option expires. Note that the time value is always shrinking and reaches zero on the expiration date. If there is no intrinsic value, then the ask price is all time value.

Extrinsic value = Ask Price - Intrinsic Value

Premium: The total cost of the option contract (ask price plus commissions). On TD Ameritrade, the commission is $7.99, plus .75 per contract.

Expiration Date: This is last day that you can sell or exercise an option. Thus, for the option above, the last day you can potentially sell it is anytime on January 16*th*, 2015 (before trading closes for the day).

Exercise: When an option is "in the money," you have the right to purchase (puts) or sell (calls) the underlying stock at the strike price. This is done approximately 12% of the time. Most investors never exercise their options; instead, they sell them for cash.

Exercising a Put Option

If you want to exercise (and not sell) a put option, it is messy, and generally doesn't make a lot of sense for a typical investor. Professionals occasionally do it, but I wouldn't recommend it.

Let me give a put option example using the chart above. You purchase a put contract with a strike price of $25 per share. The ask price is $3, so you have to pay $300 for each contract (100 shares). Let's project that the silver price will drop to $17, giving you an intrinsic value of $8.

The approximate profit per share (excluding commissions) is easy to calculate in this example.

$25 strike price

$17 current price

$3 cost of option

===============

$5 profit per share

Paid $300 (1 contract for 100 shares at $3)

Plus $17.48 in commissions ($7.99 + .75 x 2)

Profit $500 (100 shares x $5)

Return 150% (($300 + $500 - $317.48) / 317.48))

This estimated profit of $5 per share excludes any extrinsic value (additional time value). If the option does not expire for a few months, it will have a higher profit. The bid price should be close to the intrinsic price ($8), but it could be significantly higher if there is a lot of extrinsic value (time until expiration).

You have a few choices, now that the option is in the money. The first choice is to sell the option and receive cash (bid price x 100 = approximately $800) into your account. The next choice is to wait and hope that the option becomes more valuable (the stock continues to drop in price) before it expires. The last choice is to exercise it.

If you exercise it, and you happen to own the underlying shares (which is unlikely), then you can sell them at the strike price. However, if you do not own the shares, then you will enter into a short position (with unlimited risk). Unless you know what a short position is, you don't want to do this (and unless you have a margin account, you won't be allowed).

Exercising a Call Option

Exercising a call option is easier to understand. You simply purchase the underlying shares at the strike price. (Note that you will need to have enough funds in your account to accomplish this.) Also note that by purchasing the shares, you are letting your profit "ride." If the stock keeps going up, you will have additional unrealized profit. But if it drops, you will have given up your profits.

There are really only a few reasons to ever exercise a call option:

1. You own an "in the money" call option and a dividend payout is coming up that is worth more than the extrinsic value. Just make sure you exercise the option prior to the ex-dividend date, otherwise you won't get paid the dividend.
2. You own a call option in the money, and the bids do not match the stock price. Thus, it can be more profitable to acquire the stock and then immediately sell it. This does happen from time to time.
3. You already have a short position with unlimited risk, which you want to offset and close.

Selling an Option

The reasons to sell an option instead of exercising it are fairly clear:

1. It is simple.
2. There is less risk.
3. The remaining extrinsic value is not lost.
4. Commissions are generally lower.

Put Options							Expire at close Friday, January 16, 2015
Strike	Symbol	Last	Chg	Bid	Ask	Vol	Open Int
15.00	SLV150117P00015000	**0.58**	0.00	0.53	0.66	5	416
16.00	SLV150117P00016000	**0.68**	0.00	0.63	0.80	70	2,498
17.00	SLV150117P00017000	**0.83**	0.00	0.81	0.93	2	34
18.00	SLV150117P00018000	**1.02**	↓0.03	0.99	1.10	2	129
19.00	SLV150117P00019000	**1.20**	0.00	1.18	1.29	1	40
20.00	SLV150117P00020000	**1.40**	0.00	1.40	1.51	50	228
21.00	SLV150117P00021000	**1.67**	0.00	1.65	1.75	10	66
22.00	SLV150117P00022000	**1.90**	0.00	1.92	2.05	5	10,342
23.00	SLV150117P00023000	**2.17**	0.00	2.23	2.35	20	149
24.00	SLV150117P00024000	**2.59**	0.00	2.53	2.69	51	124
25.00	SLV150117P00025000	**3.00**	↑0.10	2.88	3.00	4	647

www.finance.yahoo.com

Intrinsic & Extrinsic Value

Let's continue with our example. Let's assume that we purchased a put option with a strike price of $25, but today's price is $28. Since the current price is higher than our target strike price, our option is not in the money.

Intrinsic Value = Strike Price - Current Price

Extrinsic value = Ask Price - Intrinsic Value

On the chart above, the strike price is lower than the current price. Thus it does not have any intrinsic value. When this is the case, the entire ask price (minus commissions) is the extrinsic value (the time value). Got that? That is important to understand. The value of an option is the combination of the intrinsic value plus the extrinsic value. Unless you grasp that, you will be confused regarding options.

Because the extrinsic value decreases over time, it often makes sense to sell an option immediately after it reaches your investment goal. However, this is not always the case, and you can limit your returns dramatically by selling early. For instance, in the put example above, if the price drops to $17, then the return of this option will be approximately 150%. However, since this is a two year option, if it reaches $17 early, there will be significant extrinsic value. Moreover, the closer you get to expiration, the less extrinsic value will remain. Eventually, the extrinsic value will go to zero.

How Options Work

For this put example, we are assuming that once the option gets "in the money," below the $25 strike price, we are going to let it ride until it reaches $17. We could have sold it just below the strike price, but that is merely the break-even point for the intrinsic value. You must go beyond the strike price to make a profit. And to really make big returns, you have to go significantly past the strike price. In fact, the returns are limited unless you get big moves in price.

Here is another example, using the same chart above. Let's say you pay 58 cents for a contract with a strike price of $15. You won't make very much money unless the price goes below $10. What are the chances of that? Thus, that 58-cent contract might seem cheap, but it is a fool's bet.

Hedging with Put Options

The chance of silver dropping 25% or more is always possible. For that reason, you could invest, perhaps, 3% of your investment into put options. Let's say your portfolio has a value of $100,000. You could invest $3,000 in options. For example, ten contracts with a $3 ask price and a $25 strike price. Then if the option price hits $17, your profit will be approximately ($25 - $17 - 3 = $5 per share) $5,000. That gives you a degree of insurance for a market crash.

If you are like me, you will look at this example and come to the conclusion that the risk/reward is not very good by hedging with SLV. If you invest $3,000 and only get back $5,000, that is only a 150% return. This is why I suggest using leveraged ETFs, such as FAZ (2X financial short) or ZSL (2X silver short), when hedging with options. Although, once silver rises substantially, SLV might make sense. As an example, when silver rises to $60, you could hedge with a strike price of $55. If silver drops to $35, you will have an intrinsic value of $20, and your profit will likely be $55 - $35 - 2 = $18 per share. The return would be approximately 800% if you pay $200 per contract.[50] If you invested $3,000, you would get back approximately 1,500 shares x $18 = $27,000. Not bad, although options for the 2X or 3X leveraged ETFs will do better.

Profiting with Call Options

Call options are perhaps more enticing during a bull market than puts, although these are used as an investment instead of a hedge. Many people are expecting a blow-off rally before this market is done, and a call option is perfect if we get one. If you happen to own a call option during that period, you will do very well. Let's look at an example for SLV.

Today, SLV trades at $29 and you can purchase a January 2015 call option with a strike price of $50 for $1.87 per contract. Thus, if silver spikes to $65, your approximate profit would be $65 - $50 - $1.87 = $13.13 per share, or a 550% return. If it spikes early in the year, you would have additional extrinsic value. Moreover, if it spikes higher, your leverage will add to your profits.

If you are bullish on silver over the next two years, a call option can leverage you a nice return. If silver rises substantially, then you likely will be in the money by the end of 2014. Your break-even point for a $50 strike price will be around $52. If silver cannot break through $52, then you will lose most or all of your investment.

Options Clearing Corporation

Everything was fairly clear to me when I learned about put and call options except one thing: What happens when my contract is in the money and I want to sell it at a profit? Who takes the loss? How is it matched up with the individual who originally sold me the contract? From my perspective, I am going to sell it into the open market at the bid price.

Well, it turns out there is something called the Options Clearing Corporation. Somehow, they know how to match up the buyers and sellers. Basically, the sellers are a "group of people" who are randomly selected to close out the options. A random person writes the option that you purchase, and then another random person closes it out when you sell it. Investors never know who was on the other side of their transaction. The trading system is not even noticeable, and it all works seamlessly.

Options in the Money

With options that are "in the money," you will have a profit. However, to collect that profit, you have to either sell them (or exercise them) prior to the end of trading on the expiration date. If you happen to forget, you are out of luck. It will have expired.

Once an option is in the money, it can increase in value or decrease, and potentially fall out of the money. For instance, if you have a put option with a strike price of $25, and the underlying stock or ETF is at $24, it will be "in the money" and have an intrinsic value of $1. However, tomorrow the price of the underlying stock or ETF can do anything. It can drop to $23 or rise to $26.

Thus, you can see how volatile options can be. You are never guaranteed a profit until you sell them (or exercise them) when they are in the money. For this reason, sometimes it can be difficult to know when to sell an option. The more conservative you are, the more difficult it will be for you to be patient and let the option rise in value.

One of the factors that adds value to an option is called the time value of money, which is the extrinsic value. If the stock in the previous put option example still has several months before it expires, it will have significant extrinsic value. Those extra months will add value to the option, because investors will expect the stock price to drop further. However, that extrinsic value is not guaranteed. In fact, as you get closer to the expiration date, the time value will steadily wither away until all you have left is the intrinsic value (the strike price minus the current stock price).

So, if you purchase an option with a strike price of $25, and the price quickly drops from $32 to $26, you will have significant extrinsic value. However, the option will not be in the money, and you cannot cash in on any intrinsic value until it drops under $25. You can sell the option for the extrinsic value, but it is better to wait and see if it drops below the strike price. As time goes by and the underlying stock or ETF does not drop below $25, the extrinsic value will steadily wither away as the expiration date approaches.

As should be clear by now, the value of an option is a combination of the strike price, the expiration date (time value of money), and the current value of the underlying stock or ETF.

Options Review

Are you clear on puts and calls? They are not that complicated. Basically, you are betting on the direction a stock or ETF will go. Moreover, you are locking in a period of time and how much you think the stock will increase or decrease. These are high-risk investments, so consider the entire amount of the investment to be at risk of loss.

There are two ways to use options. The first way is as a hedge in order to protect your portfolio against a major drop. Most gold and silver investors do not hedge because they are bullish that the price of gold/silver is going to continue rising. Another reason hedging is not popular is because options reduce your returns when they do not fall in the money.

The second way is to use call options to predict large increases in stock prices or ETF prices. This is more commonly used because gold and silver are so volatile. Options are ideal for turning big price moves into big profits.

You now know all about both puts and calls. If you are interested in options, you should read this chapter again.

Purchasing an Option on TD Ameritrade

Below is the options trading screen from TD Ameritrade. At first glance, it looks complicated. However, for puts and calls, it is simple. Let me explain it for you:

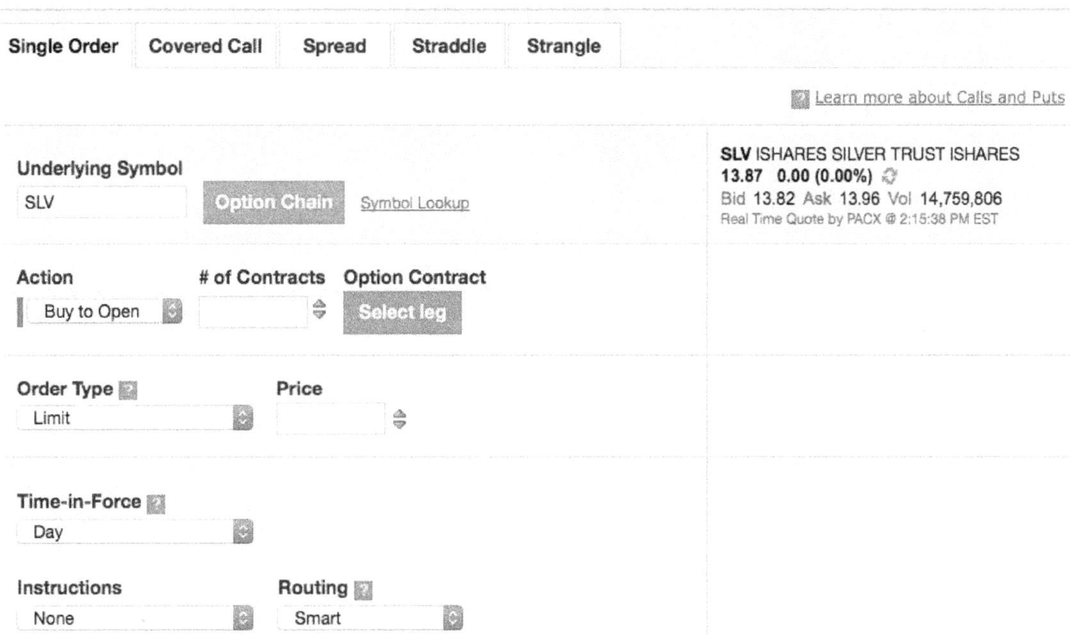

1. **The Underlying Symbol**. This is the stock or ETF symbol that underlies the options. For example, SLV.

2. **Action.** This is the order type. Normally you will use either "Buy to Open" or "Sell to Close." Rarely, if ever, will you select "Exercise." The "Sell to Open" and "Buy to Close" choices are for writing options with a margin account. These are for professionals who take the other side of an option and expose themselves to potential unlimited liability.

   Buy to Open is when you purchase either a put or call option contract. This is how you buy options.

   Sell to Close is when you sell your put option contract. This is basically the same as creating an open order to sell a stock. If the order gets executed, then your brokerage account will get debited with the value of the option.

3. **# of Contracts.** Enter how many contracts you want to purchase (1 = 100 shares, 2 =200 shares, etc.). Each contract usually costs 75 cents.
4. **Option Contract**. This is the same option symbol you use to get a price quote.
5. **The Order Type.** This is usually a limit order or a market order. A limit order allows you to choose how much you are willing to pay (entered in the **Price** box). If the ask price is less than your limit price, it will execute. A market order will trade immediately at the current ask price.
6. **Price.** This is used for limit orders to set a minimum price that you want to pay for an option.
7. **Time in Force.** This is usually Day or GTC (Good 'Til Cancelled). This is when the option order expires. These are only used for limit orders, since market orders execute immediately (if the market is trading).
8. **Special Instructions** are usually None or AON. AON means all or none. If you keep it at the default of None, sometimes you will get different prices for some of your options, although they will be very close. Also, if you use None for a limit order, sometimes only part of it will trade before the ask price rises above the limit. Thus, AON ensures that your entire trade is completed, but you may have to wait longer since it has to trade as one order, and there is the rare chance it won't trade if you buy/sell a lot of shares.
9. **Routing**. Leave it on auto at TD Ameritrade. They use proprietary technology.

Online brokerages charge you for both the transaction and for each option contract. At TD Ameritrade it is $7.99 for the transaction, plus 75 cents for each contract. This is close to industry average pricing. There are a few online brokerages who charge less.

Option Color Coding

Once you purchase your option, it will appear in your online portfolio just like a stock, and will show the current market price. It will be colored white when it is out of the money, and shaded when it is in the money. This same color coding is used when you receive option quotes. Below are the quotes for SLV call options that expire in January 2015. Notice that the options below $28 are in the money, as indicated by the darker shade.

View By Expiration: Dec 12 | Jan 13 | Feb 13 | Mar 13 | Apr 13 | Jul 13 | Oct 13 | Jan 14 | **Jan 15**

Call Options							Expire at close Friday, January 16, 2015
Strike	Symbol	Last	Chg	Bid	Ask	Vol	Open Int
15.00	SLV150117C00015000	**14.75**	↑0.05	14.50	14.75	17	53
16.00	SLV150117C00016000	**16.09**	0.00	13.65	13.90	4	4
20.00	SLV150117C00020000	**10.60**	↓0.10	10.40	10.65	2	270
21.00	SLV150117C00021000	**12.85**	0.00	9.65	9.90	1	1
22.00	SLV150117C00022000	**11.95**	0.00	8.95	9.20	20	20
24.00	SLV150117C00024000	**7.85**	0.00	7.60	7.85	5	121
25.00	SLV150117C00025000	**7.15**	0.00	7.00	7.25	6	49
26.00	SLV150117C00026000	**6.70**	↑0.01	6.45	6.65	8	2,096
27.00	SLV150117C00027000	**5.90**	0.00	5.90	6.10	44	57
28.00	SLV150117C00028000	**5.50**	0.00	5.40	5.60	20	27
29.00	SLV150117C00029000	**5.15**	↑0.05	4.90	5.15	13	179
30.00	SLV150117C00030000	**4.65**	0.00	4.50	4.70	21	3,134
31.00	SLV150117C00031000	**4.35**	0.00	4.10	4.30	4	831
32.00	SLV150117C00032000	**4.05**	0.00	3.75	3.95	22	1,334
33.00	SLV150117C00033000	**3.59**	0.00	3.35	3.60	30	2,672
34.00	SLV150117C00034000	**3.05**	0.00	3.10	3.30	76	5,701
35.00	SLV150117C00035000	**3.00**	0.00	2.79	2.98	60	4,008
36.00	SLV150117C00036000	**2.75**	0.00	2.55	2.74	20	1,252
37.00	SLV150117C00037000	**2.50**	↑0.12	2.33	2.49	2	526
38.00	SLV150117C00038000	**2.27**	↓0.05	2.14	2.29	236	34,760
40.00	SLV150117C00040000	**1.87**	0.00	1.76	1.91	34	1,042
45.00	SLV150117C00045000	**1.14**	↓0.02	1.14	1.28	4	1,139
50.00	SLV150117C00050000	**0.85**	↑0.05	0.75	0.90	6	13,294
53.00	SLV150117C00053000	**0.68**	0.00	0.58	0.74	11	11
55.00	SLV150117C00055000	**0.55**	0.00	0.55	0.67	50	50
56.00	SLV150117C00056000	**0.56**	0.00	0.47	0.69	12	12

www.finance.yahoo.com

Note: TD Ameritrade does not give you the right to purchase options until you request them. However, this is just a formality. They just ask a few questions (on the screen) to make sure that you know what you are doing. Also, I don't suggest opening a margin account and going short/long. As I mentioned previously, that is for professionals only.

CHAPTER 6

MINING COMPANIES: MAJORS

The asset class of major gold mining companies (Majors) is where I started investing in precious metals. Most gold and silver analysts say to begin with physical metal, and I agree with them that bullion or coins is a good foundation. When you think in terms of managing risk, it is always good to have either bullion or coins in your possession. After you have accumulated some bullion or coins, then you can consider owning a few Majors.

Pyramid of Risk

Below is a pyramid of risk that I have created, and you will see that Majors are just above the bottom foundation. Because mining is a high-risk industry, even the largest companies need to be considered a risky stock. All it takes is for them to have problems at one mine and it can impact their share price significantly.

I think it is a good idea to use all gold and silver investment opportunities available to you (except perhaps options and leveraged ETFs), but you need a strong foundation. Once the foundation is created, then you can build a portfolio with a diversity of miners. If you use my pyramid approach, you will have less risk exposure, while at the same time giving yourself an opportunity for significant returns.

There are many different investment strategies that you can use. For instance, you can focus on physical bullion and coins, which is the most conservative way to limit risk. However, this strategy will also limit your potential returns. Conversely, you could focus entirely on Junior mining stocks. This strategy will have the most risk, but the returns could be phenomenal.

My preferred strategy is to have a balanced portfolio of gold and silver investments that diversifies risk by investing in each group. Think of it as a pyramid of risk (see below), with each tier being more risky than the previous one. Your foundation should be bullion and perhaps ETFs. The next level of the pyramid is Majors and

Mid-Tier Producers. After that are the Junior mining stocks. Finally, at the top, are options and leveraged ETFs, which should be used sparingly (if at all).

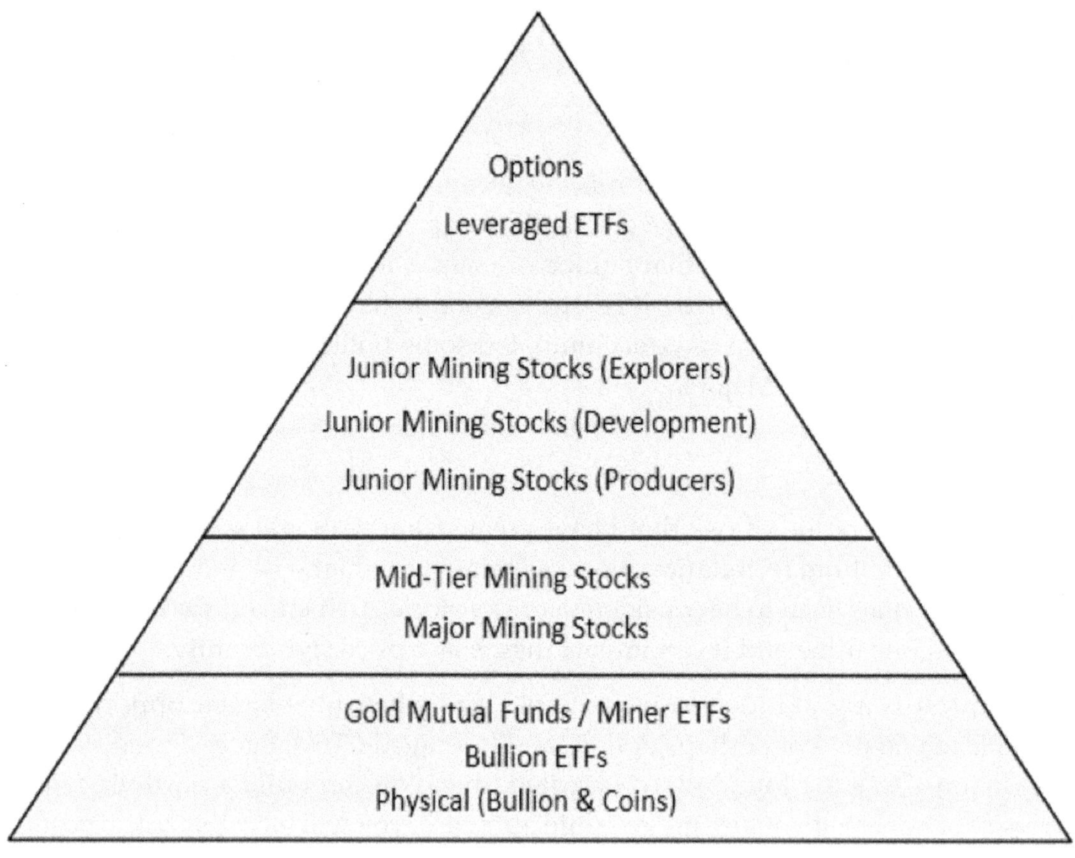

I have followed this pyramid to balance my risk. The list below is close to my current portfolio distribution. This is the cost basis from my overall portfolio, which includes more than these asset classes.

5% Physical Bullion

20% ETFs (Silver Bullion, Gold and Silver Producers)

20% Gold Mutual Funds (Gold and Silver Producers)

20% Mid-Tier Producers

25% Juniors (Producers, Development, Exploration)

My focus has always been on large returns (goal of 500%), so I have a larger percentage of Juniors that you may be comfortable. If you are more risk averse, then you should limit your Juniors to about 10%. Also, I have a lot of gold mutual funds. I like these for annual income from dividends and capital gains payouts. Mutual funds payout capital gains on an annual basis.

If your focus is on large returns, you will be tempted to bypass the bottom tier of the pyramid and instead focus on Mid-Tier producers and Juniors. That is your decision to make, but I don't suggest it. I have learned that having a foundation of less risky assets is advantageous during periods of volatility. Junior mining stocks can go down 90% or more during big corrections, but bullion and ETFs will not go down nearly as much.

Having a balanced approach makes it much easier to endure downtrends, because high-risk portfolios of only Junior mining stocks will get slammed. Moreover, there are few investors who can have a portfolio that is down 70% and continue buying. However, during big corrections is when you make your biggest gains. This is the time to buy. As Warren Buffett says, "You want to be greedy when everyone else is fearful."

Kinross Gold

One of the best major gold mining stocks today is probably Kinross Gold. If you invest in it today (this was written in 2019, when it was trading at $3.34), you will most likely triple your money as gold goes higher. It is a relatively safe investment, and a 200% return in these dismal economic times is fantastic. However, it is not a guaranteed investment. Here are my comments from my database at *www.goldstockdata.com*:

> *Kinross Gold is a Major with 2.5 million oz. of gold equivalent production. Their all-in costs for 2018 are projected to be around $1100 (gold equivalent cash cost per oz. around $750). Their net profit in 2017 was about $450 million, which they plan to achieve in 2018 if gold prices remain at $1300. They are a growth company with plans to expand production to 3.5 million oz. of gold equivalent.*
>
> *Their share price dropped from $17.50 a share in 2011 to $1.49 in January 2016. Someone got an excellent entry price. Now it has popped back to $3.84, on its way back to $17. It is an attractive income stock. While the dividend today is only*

about 1.5%, this stock could triple in value and triple the dividend return on your investment.

There are two red flags for this stock. The first is the location of their mines, which include Russia and West Africa (combined 40% of production). I don't think this is a significant risk, but the political risk does exist. The other red flag is their balance sheet. They have $1.7 billion in debt and $470 million in cash. Also, they are a growth company. Thus, they are not going to slow down development budgets to pay down their debt. I prefer cash focused companies with good balance sheets. That said, I would like to have this stock in my gold mutual funds.

Mining is a risky business, and a lot of things can go wrong. Even for a company as large as Kinross Gold, there are several significant risks. They have no control over the gold price, which can drop below their costs. Energy prices can increase and drive up their costs. Politics (regulations, taxes, civil war, etc.) are always hard to predict.

Mining Returns vs. Physical Metal

What is the difference between owning mining stocks versus owning physical gold? The obvious difference is risk. The other big difference is leverage. An increase in the price of gold/silver generally increases the value of mining company stocks substantially. This is because most of the price increase in gold or silver goes directly to profit. And these higher profit margins can make stock prices spike. This is the reason why mining stocks generally have higher returns than physical metal.

For instance, if you invest in Majors, your return as the gold price rises to $2,500 should be approximately 200% (gold prices today are $1,850). That is much higher than bullion will return. For this reason, you should consider creating an investment position in Majors.

One caveat is the price of energy, which could hamper their profits. However, I am bullish that their profits are going to be exploding when we reach the $2,500 level. I can't imagine these stocks being ignored by investors after gold reaches $2,500. And if investors stay away from mining stocks, then the Majors will just increase their dividends until they get everyone's attention.

Diversifying

I prefer to diversify when I invest in Majors. I do this by using mutual funds and ETFs. If you let a mutual fund manager pick a portfolio of stocks, they can make the adjustments faster than you can. Normally, the Majors are all going to track the price of gold. However, there are always unexpected events that can impact companies.

For instance, the risk factors that can severely impact a mining company are quite numerous: a political issue, a tax increase, a strike, a war, an energy shortage, a flood, a local dispute, an environmental issue, etc. These unique events can slam the stock price. Thus, if you try to pick three to five major gold/silver mining stocks, you have to watch them and manage them yourself. Also, if you do not react quickly to these events, share prices can drop significantly in a short period of time.

While picking a few Majors is doable, it's not the easiest strategy. Stick with either gold mutual funds or GDX. Also, GDXJ, which was originally a Mid-Tier ETF, has become mostly a large-cap fund.

For gold mutual funds, you have the option to either reinvest your dividends and capital gains, or receive an annual check. With one of my mutual funds, the annual checks have exceeded my initial cost. Something similar will likely happen to you. As time goes by, the annual returns (either shares or checks) will reduce your initial cost. I expect annual dividends to reach 4% or 5% of the share price for many Majors, so it won't take very many years to have a substantial reduction to your cost basis.

Mutual Funds / ETFs

There are not that many Majors, so the easiest way to play this sector is to purchase either a mutual fund or an ETF. The returns for mutual funds are slightly decreased by the management fees (about .5% to 1.5% per year) that you have to pay annually. But as long as gold hits $2,500, you won't notice. And from my perspective, these managers earn their fees. That fee is like insurance since they make sure that any blight in the portfolio is purged. They are also professionals with lots of experience, and they know which companies to add.

Below were the top performing gold funds in 2009-10.[51] I own the Franklin Gold fund (FKRCX) and the Van Eck Gold fund (INIVX). Both of these funds are well suited for investment income.

Symbol	Fund Name	2 Year Return (%)
TGLDX	Tocqueville Gold	169.4
OPGSX	Oppenheimer Gold A	153.7
UNWPX	US Global World Pr Mns	137.9
INIVX	Van Eck Intl Inv GoldA	135.2
PMPIX	Profund Prec Mtls Ultr	132.4
FKRCX	Franklin Gold & PrMt A	131.7
OCMGX	OCM Gold	125.9
MIDSX	Midas Fund	123.9
VGPMX	Vanguard Prec Metals	123.2

Note: The chart above is old, from 2009 and 2010, when mining stocks did very well. They have not performed nearly as well from 2011 to 2015. However, I think we will see this kind of performance again once gold prices rise.

Mutual Fund Research

When you investigate one of these funds, there are a few things to look for. First, go to a website like Yahoo Finance (here is the link for the Franklin Fund Gold A fund: *http://finance.yahoo.com/q/pr?s=FKRCX*). Then review the fees to purchase it (also called the sales load), the last dividend percentage, and the annual expense ratio (management fee):

FUND OPERATIONS	
Last Dividend (1-Dec-09):	2.21
Last Cap Gain (1-Dec-09):	0.59
Annual Holdings Turnover	17.17%
Average for Category:	75.46%

FEES & EXPENSES		
Expense	FKRCX	Category Avg
Total Expense Ratio:	%	1.47%
Max 12b1 Fee:	%	N/A
Max Front End Sales Load:	5.75%	5.36%

www.finance.yahoo.com

This fund has a nice dividend, and expenses are near the 1.50% industry average. The only downside is that they charge a 5.75% premium to purchase it. But that is normal for these funds, and not really that bad. Since you are going to hold it long term, the entry price premium will be paid for by your annual dividends and captial gains.

After you research a gold mutual fund on an Internet finance website (Google Finance, Yahoo Finance, etc.), go to the fund's web page. Check the dividend history and the current portfolio. You also want to understand the portfolio's focus and investment strategy. Some funds focus on investment income (dividends), others are more aggressive and include Juniors and Mid-Tiers for growth, while others diversify into silver and platinum. Make sure you are comfortable with the strategy of the fund.

Van Eck Gold Miners ETF (GDX)

In addition to the mutual funds I prefer, there is an ETF that I also like. Its trading symbol is GDX. If I were just starting out, this would be a fund that I might buy.

The beauty of this ETF is that the annual fees are low, and the premium to purchase them is also low. For instance, you can buy it for less than a 1% premium. That is an unbelievably low premium. If the stock goes up 2%, you make a profit.

The other thing I like about GDX is that it is basically a reflection of the entire gold Major market, because its holdings include nearly all of the gold Majors. In fact, its valuation closely follows the HUI, which is a popular gold mining index. You can pretty much follow the HUI and know how this ETF is doing.

Here are the top 10 companies in GDX (from January 2019), which make up 55% of its holdings:[52]

Holding Name	Ticker	Shares	Market Value (US$)	% of Net Assets
Barrick Gold Corp	GOLD US	90,612,554	1,182,493,830	11.20
Newmont Mining Corp	NEM US	25,869,990	872,077,363	8.26
Franco-Nevada Corp	FNV US	9,051,184	690,876,875	6.54
Newcrest Mining Ltd	NCM AU	37,312,324	656,278,114	6.22
Agnico Eagle Mines Ltd	AEM US	12,223,708	524,274,836	4.97
Goldcorp Inc	GG US	46,701,421	513,715,631	4.87
Wheaton Precious Metals Corp	WPM US	25,041,020	511,838,449	4.85
Kirkland Lake Gold Ltd	KL CN	14,122,205	440,001,736	4.17
Anglogold Ashanti Ltd	AU US	27,757,716	383,889,212	3.64
Royal Gold Inc	RGLD US	4,408,508	378,029,561	3.58

vaneck.com

These companies are all Majors, except for Franco Nevada and Wheaton Precious Metals, which are royalty stocks. This ETF's holdings include both gold and a few silver mining stocks, along with a few royalty stocks. There are no bullion or cash holdings. By purchasing this ETF, you have basically purchased all of the Majors. In 2019, this ETF held 46 stocks: five of them are silver stocks, four are royalty stocks, and the rest are gold mining stocks.

The advantage of GDX is that you get a mutual fund without the high annual fees and extra costs to purchase it. The other thing I like about it is that they only focus on the best stocks. If they see a stock stumbling, they quickly swap it out. Thus, the management team is very proactive in rotating underperforming stocks out of the portfolio. I think this is very bullish for GDX in the long term.

From my perspective, if you are going to invest any money in this gold bull market, then a gold mutual fund or gold/silver stock ETF makes sense. It is relatively safe for the long term and will return more than bullion. Again, if you only want to maintain your wealth, then bullion is the place to be invested.

If you want to at least double your money, then using Majors (or mutual funds and ETFs) is a good way to go. I consider this a good core position for investing in gold and silver miners. Once you have your core position, then you can move on to the more risky investment areas: Mid-Tier and Junior mining stocks.

Why There are Few Silver Miners

The reason there are so few silver Majors is that silver is normally mined with other metals, such as gold, copper, lead, and zinc. Thus, silver is primarily mined as a byproduct. In fact, there are currently only about 15 silver miners with more than 1 million oz. of production, who call themselves silver miners. And this list has been shrinking in the past few years from mergers. Also, there has also been a trend for silver miners to diversify into gold mining. Soon the list of silver miners with production above 1 million oz. is going to be less than 10.

Wheaton Precious Metals has the biggest market cap in the silver sector, and they don't even own a mine. They get all of their silver from long-term contracts with base metal and gold producers. Wheaton Precious Metals guarantees to purchase a designated amount of silver production at a fixed price for the life of the mine. This allows base metal and gold producers to hedge their silver production to a contracted buyer. As long as base metal production does not stop, this makes Wheaton Precious Metals incredibly profitable.

Best Silver Majors

Currently, there are only two silver Majors: Fresnillo and Pan American Silver. There is one Emerging Major: Hecla Ming. None of these companies would be considered a pure silver miner, because all of them produce a significant amount of gold.

Owning a few large silver producers is not only a good way to diversify risk, but also a way to expose yourself to upside potential. These are companies that have huge reserves and solid production numbers. They will likely do very well if silver prices rise. In my opinion, they are practically sure things in the long term. Why? Because they are the only big players in silver. Once silver reaches $50, investors are going to jump on the trend. (Don't they always?) And investors will have no choice but to buy them, for lack of any other choices.

> Note: I do not see much difference in risk between these large silver producers and some of the large Mid-Tier producers. These companies will be discussed in the next chapter.

Wheaton Precious Metals (technically not a Major since they do not operate any mines) also appears good, since they have enough contracts to make them the most profitable silver company for quite some time. However, their contracts make me nervous, which are amazingly one-sided because they use fixed prices. Many of Silver Wheaton's contracts allow them to buy silver at $4 for the life of the mine. Thus, they will be able to turn around and sell it for $50, $75, $100, or as high as silver goes. I can't imagine those contracts holding, but I could be wrong.

Also, I see a possible global economic slowdown coming, and that means less demand for base metals. Thus, I see Silver Wheaton as a risky stock. But that doesn't mean this stock won't explode in value. It might be one of the most profitable silver stocks over the next few years.

Pan American Silver is also going to do well. This is another solid stock with a lot of upside potential. I see this stock going up at least three times from where it is today. They have a lot of reserves and significant production growth.

An Ideal Low-Risk Portfolio

An ideal $100,000 low-risk portfolio would look something like this:

$25,000	Gold Coins	1 oz. Gold Eagles or Maple Leafs
$25,000	Silver Bullion	SIVR (ETF) or PSLV (ETF)
$20,000	Gold Majors	GDX (ETF) or Mutual Fund
$15,000	Silver Mid-Tiers	SIL (ETF)
$15,000	Gold Mid-Tiers	GDXJ (ETF)

I prefer using bullion and lower risk gold mutual funds and mining ETFs as a foundation for a diversified portfolio. If you are not comfortable with mining stocks, then you can exclude them and focus on bullion and coins. While I called this a low-risk portfolio, it is dependent on your entry point and if the gold bull market continues. It is my opinion that gold prices are heading to $2,500 and perhaps even higher. And if that happens, then these are the lowest risk assets for that scenario.

I excluded silver coins and physical silver from this portfolio, but if you want some physical silver in your possession, I think that is smart. Silver Eagles or a few junk bags of silver pre-1965 coins will come in handy. Also, a few 10 oz. silver bars make a lot of sense. Having an assortment of various forms of physical silver will add to the number of ounces in your possession.

Which Majors to Pick?

I can give you some pointers on finding the best gold Majors, but in this bull market it is easy to pick the gold Majors. You simply buy GDX, which gets you exposed to most of the gold Majors, and it gives you a return that reflects the mining industry as the gold price rises. If you prefer to own a gold mutual fund instead of GDX, so that you get perhaps a better dividend, I can't argue with that strategy. Also, GDXJ has become very similar to GDX after the fund was rebalanced with larger cap stocks.

After you have chosen your gold Majors, then you purchase two or three of the largest silver producers to capture silver's upside. This will give you a solid core position at the lowest rung of risk for mining companies. Moreover, the more you invest in the silver producers, the better your return will likely be. If silver increases from today's value of $25 to $150, the returns for the silver producers could be stunning.

Okay, for you stock pickers out there who want to pick your own Majors, let's look at the factors that are used for picking stocks.

Producing Properties

The most important factor for any company is the quality of their properties. You have to go to their web page and research their properties. You need to check the following:

1. Size

   How many ounces is the property producing? How many ounces are in the ground (resources and reserves) and what is the grade? What is the projected mine life? How many more years will it produce? For a Major, you want to see several properties that are producing significant quantities and have significant quantities in the ground (for a long mine life).

   An ideal gold property would be producing more than 150,000 ounces per year, with more than 2 million ounces in reserve. Also, you don't want to see a mine life with less than five years remaining (ideally 10 years or more). The stock market will punish that stock if production is going to drop in the near future.

   How many acres or hectares are there for each property? I prefer large properties with a lot of exploration potential. If a property has less than 500 acres, then the upside for exploration is limited. When it comes to property size, bigger is generally better.

2. Location

Safety

Safest: Canada, Australia, New Zealand, United States.

Moderately Safe: Brazil, Guyana, Nicaragua, Fiji, Ireland, Finland, Sweden, Norway.

Moderate Risk: Mexico, Argentina, Peru, Chile, Panama, Colombia, Mongolia.

High Risk: East Africa, West Africa, Russia, China, Russian Satellites (e.g., Kazakhstan), Ecuador, Turkey, Eastern Europe, Indonesia, Philippines, Middle East, Spain, Bolivia, Papua New Guinea.

Extreme Risk: Venezuela, South Africa, Central Africa.

Location safety is primarily related to threats from political issues, such as higher taxation, anti-mining groups, and nationalization. You don't want a Major that has several strategic properties in high risk locations. For instance, if a Major has all of their mines in Africa, you might want to avoid it. I don't avoid all African mining stocks, but I am aware of the added risk from this continent. To reduce my risk, I focus on West African miners, which tend to have the lowest risk on that continent.

Investors have been giving low valuations to properties in high-risk locations. All of the countries that I listed in the risky categories have been impacted. Moreover, there is a current bias against investing in African properties, and it is likely to last for some time. It doesn't seem to matter if the property is in South Africa, West Africa, Central Africa, or East Africa. It will be interesting to see how stocks in these regions perform in the future. They could do incredibly well, or investors could continue to stay away.

Infrastructure

Ideally, you want the location of the property to be next to an existing operating mine. This is one of the biggest factors if a mine will get built. For instance, if there are several existing operating mines in the vicinity, the odds are very good that this mine will get built (as long as it is economic).

A red flag for infrastructure is if the property is miles away from any roads or power sources. This will make it expensive and time-consuming to build the mine. Small mining companies generally cannot finance these types of projects. If you do invest in a company with a project without any nearby infrastructure, make sure you understand the additional risk you are taking.

Even if a project has infrastructure issues and is what I call infrastructure challenged, this does not always stop me from investing. In other words, this is not always a showstopper. If the economics are good, the management team is good, and they have a good shot at financing, then infrastructures issues can be overcome. There have been many mines built in the middle of nowhere, and this will continue. Just recognize that these types of mines are rarely built by small companies with small management teams.

Mining Friendly

The best places to invest are in mining friendly locations. These are places where mining is common, permitting is easy, regulations and taxes are low, and the national and local governments are not resistant to mining. For instance, in most locations in Canada, you can permit a mine in less than three years. Whereas, in the U.S., it can take five years or more to get all of the required permits.

While the U.S. can be a safe place to mine because of the rule of law, it is not necessarily a mining friendly country. The most mining friendly state is probably Nevada, because of the preponderance of active mines. This does mean that mining companies in Nevada do not have a lot of red tape. Conversely, many countries in South America can be considered mining friendly, because of the ease of permitting and reduced regulations, but they are not necessarily safe places to do business.

3. Local Issues

   Sometimes there are external issues that can impact properties. For instance, environmental issues, native cultural issues, anti-mining groups, labor strikes, lawsuits, etc. Read the past news releases on the company websites and search out recent impacting issues.

   Two of the biggest impediments can be native issues and anti-mining groups. Often the native ethnic issues are represented by groups that have significant political power, sometimes enough to shut down mines. These native issues are common in Canada, the Philippines, and South America, where there are a lot of native ethnic groups.

   Anti-mining groups are becoming more common, and this is primarily from ecological resistance. However, some communities are resisting open pit mining near their homes simply because they don't want the eyesore. Other communities are resisting because of potential harm to the local water supply.

4. Cash Cost Per Oz. / All-in Cost Per Oz.

   You always need to be aware of the current and expected cash cost per ounce. Is it a low cost or a high-cost mine? Note that costs are always in the local currency, and Third World countries have lower labor costs. For this reason, investing in companies that mine in Central America, South America, and West Africa can provide a cost advantage. The key thing to look for is whether it is a high-cost mine. Those high costs will hurt profitability and hurt the stock price.

   Some companies report their cash cost per ounce and all-in cost per ounce in their company presentation (found on their website). If they do not, then I use their most recent financial report (I'll explain where to find those later in the book). Their operating costs can be used to calculate their cash costs.

   It's easy to calculate cash costs. You take the revenue for the quarter and divide it by the cost of production. Then, you take the cost of production percentage and multiply it by the average spot price of gold. Here is an example.

Here is an example:

Revenue: $50 million

Cost of Production: $30 million

Cost of Production Percentage: $30 million / $50 million = 60%

Avg Spot Price Last Qtr = $1,300

Cash Cost Per Oz. = $1,300 x 60% = $780

Note: This calculation should make sense, but I'll explain. Because the cost of production was 60% of revenue, this means that the cost of production was 60% of the price of gold (the average spot price).

You want the cash cost per ounce to be significantly under the spot price of gold. Ideally, you want it to be 1/3 the spot price or less. At 1/3 the spot price, this would be considered a low-cost mine. If it is 2/3 the spot price or higher, then you have a high-cost mine. If the gold price is $1250, then any mine with cash costs over $800 is problematic for making a profit.

While cash costs are important, they are not as important as the all-in cost per ounce. The reason why is because the all-in costs determine solvency and profitability. Ironically, while the mining industry does a pretty good job of reporting the correct cash costs, it does a terrible job reporting the all-in costs. The fact is, they generally do not report their all-in costs. Instead, they report something called all-in sustaining costs (AISC). In theory, this is supposed to be their breakeven cost, but it generally is not.

Here are the costs not included in AISC:

1. Depreciation, amortization.
2. Taxes and royalties.
3. Finance and interest charges.
4. Working capital.

5. Impairments.

6. Reclamation, remediation (not related to current operations).

7. Exploration, development, permitting (not related to current operations).

As you can imagine, those costs can be significant. This is why the AISC number they report generally understates their breakeven point substantially. For this reason, I always ignore the reported all-in cost. Instead, I pad the all-in cost by at least 15% and sometimes as much as 50%.

For a typical gold producer with cash costs of $800 per oz., the company will report all-in costs around $1,000 per oz. I will generally pad that by 20% to $1,200 per oz. My padding varies based on their profit for the last quarter and if I can determine their expected free cash flow for the next quarter.

I wish there was an easy answer to tell you how to do the padding, but it is different for each company. Generally, what I do is check the net profit in their last financial statement and use that to calculate their all-in costs. However, net profit isn't always a reliable number to calculate free cash flow, because some companies spend their free cash flow on exploration and development. This spending should not be included in their all-in cost per ounce. For this reason, net profit is not always the best number to use for their all-in costs. However, if you use the net profit number, it is usually a conservative all-in cost per ounce.

If I do use net profit to calculate all-in costs, I will attempt to identify how much a company is spending on exploration and development (these are costs that are optional and could be curtailed). Then, I will pad the net profit by that amount. That way, when I calculate the all-in cost percentage, I will have a more accurate number. Here is an example:

Revenue: $50 million

Net Profit: $4 Million

Estimated Exploration/Development costs: $1 million

All-In Cost Percentage: 100% - ($5 million / $50 million) = 90%

Avg Spot Price = $1,300

All-In Cost Per Oz. = $1,300 x 90% = $1,170

I have found that it can be difficult estimating an accurate all-in cost per ounce that reflects free cash flow (break-even cost per ounce). There are often many intermittent costs, such as exploration costs, that generally should not be counted. When I see that a company's net profit is not in alignment with its free cash flow, then I will adjust the padding.

I have a tool to calculate a company's all-in cost per ounce. What I do is start with their cash cost per ounce, and then I pad it to get my all-in cost per ounce. Then I identify their expected free cash flow using their last financial statement (using the method above). Finally, I check to see if it matches their expected free cash flow (or is close). If it isn't, then I adjust the padding and try again. Usually, it takes me less than three tries.

You are probably wondering how I identify their free cash flow. Well, I hate to say this, but it takes experience reading financial statements. I start with their net profit and then look for items that could understate free cash flow. Then I pad the net profit using my judgment, as explained in the method above.

I analyze a lot of stocks. I find it amazing how often companies list their all-in cost per ounce below the spot price of gold/silver, yet lost money the previous quarter. Moreover, many of these companies are not building mines (development costs) and are not spending a lot of money on exploration. In essence, their all-in costs are misleading. This is why you have to pad them.

5. Recovery Rate

This is the percentage of gold/silver that is recovered versus the number of ounces that are mined. An average ton of mined ore today has only 1 gram of gold, but you never recover all of it. Ideally, you want to recover at least 90%, and anything lower than 80% is a red flag. If a company has a 2-million ounce gold property, but the recovery rate is only 75%, then it is really a 1.5-million ounce property. Companies will do metallurgy studies to determine their recovery rate and report them in their news releases or their website. The recovery rate can make a big impact on profitability and stock valuations. Stocks can get slammed if the recovery rate is low. Conversely, a recovery rate above 90% can help a stock and the economics of a mine.

If a company reports an expected recovery rate of 90% and then delivers a recovery rate below this target, the stock can get sold off. It is important that companies hit their target numbers, or else shareholders can be impacted. A lower recovery rate means lower production, which means less revenue.

Metallurgy is the science of determining the recovery rate of a metal from mineralized ore. This is performed by a third party company and is usually done when the 43-101 resource estimate is produced. Recovery rates are generally around 90%. This will vary depending on the geology, ore type, grade, and mining method. High-grade underground ore usually has very high recovery rates, often over 95%. Lower grades tend to have lower recovery rates. Surface ore recovery rates can vary significantly depending on the geology, mining methods, and ore grades.

6. Grade

This is the number of grams per ton that are found in the mined ore. Like the recovery rate, the ore grade can significantly impact the value of a stock. Some investors and analysts consider grade to be the most important factor in valuing a stock. The reason for this is that the grade can play a very important factor in the cash cost per ounce and the economics of a mine. High-grade deposits (which are becoming rarer) tend to have lower costs and high recovery rates.

Surface mines are steadily becoming mostly low-grade deposits. Anything two grams per ton or higher is becoming rare. I am happy with anything over one gram per ton, but I will still buy stocks as low as .5 grams per ton if there are offset metals to make the mine economic.

The grade is not as important to me as the all-in cost per ounce and the economics of the mine. I'm more concerned with potential cash flow at higher gold prices and production growth. I'll be talking more about this in the last two chapters.

I'm also more concerned with the recovery rate than grade because I feel that higher gold prices will make most deposits economic. For this reason, I'm more concerned with the number of gold ounces in the ground, and how many I can recover. I want to buy gold in the ground cheap and then mine it economically. From my perspective, grade is only one factor.

One key thing to understand about grade is that it can impact the stock price in a negative manner if guidance targets are missed. For instance, it won't be a good outcome if a company provides guidance to mine 1.5 grams per ton, and then the grade drops significantly during production. This will have two negative consequences. First, the cash cost per ounce will increase, thereby reducing profit. Second, the number of ounces mined will decrease, because generally each mine is built to mine a set number of tons per day. It's a lose-lose situation (more cost and less production), and the stock price will be impacted negatively.

7. Ownership

Ideally, you want the company to own 100% of their properties. However, often their properties are joint ventures, and they only own a percentage. In the mining business, there are five kinds of companies:

1. Exploration (project generators, also sometimes called prospect generators).
2. Development and Exploration (producers and potential producers).
3. Royalty (contractual owners of mining output).
4. Toll Milling (owners of a mining mill, also called a mining plant).
5. Investment Groups (debt holders and shareholders).

Because there are so many gold and silver exploration companies (about 1,000 globally), and so few producers (about 150 publicly traded), many exploration properties end up as joint ventures when these projects are developed into mines. An important thing to understand is that even though an exploration company might currently own 100% of a property, they tend to option their properties into JV deals. I will be discussing this in more detail in Chapter 8.

I prefer companies that own 100% of their properties, but this does not stop me from investing in companies that do not. Again, it comes down to economics and cash flow. The cut-off line for me is about 80%. As long a company owns 80%, and it is a large, profitable mine, then I could be interested. However, if it is a small project, then I likely would want 100% ownership.

Development and Early Exploration Properties

The same issues you researched above for Producing Properties, you need to analyze for development and early exploration properties. The purpose of this analysis is to look for value. For instance, if a company has a late-stage development project that is going to begin production in the next 24 to 36 months, this will significantly impact the future valuation of the stock. And if they have two or three mines under development, these future mines will make the future stock valuation that much better. All of this new, upcoming production will boost the price of the stock in the future.

New mines are one of the most important factors for boosting the price of a stock. It is often the most critical factor, other than the price of gold/silver, and the economics of the mine. Moreover, it is important to understand that the stock market will not completely price a new mine into the stock price until production begins. Often the stock market will wait until it is proven that the mine can produce what was promised in the feasibility study or company guidance before giving it a full valuation. Investors want to see if they are going to hit their various targets (production ounces, grade, recovery rate, cost per ounce, etc.). This delayed price reaction is where investors seize opportunities.

Because the stock price does not completely reflect development properties, you want to analyze these carefully. This is where you can find value and potentially large returns. When a company finds a large deposit, the odds are good that it will eventually be mined. Getting in early and buying before the stock price reflects this future production, is the key to making large profits. As an investor, you need to determine if these undeveloped deposits will get mined, and how much value that could add to the stock price.

For Majors, you want to invest in a company that is forecasting production growth, stable or lower all-in costs, with several development properties in their pipeline. You want to make sure they have new mines that are scheduled to come online. You also want to make sure they will not be losing any of their big mines due to declining reserves in the near future. In other words, production appears to be stable and is poised for growth. Or, better yet, production is forecasted to grow substantially over the next decade.

I am always looking for large returns. For this reason, the project pipeline (mines not yet in production) is where I focus. For these projects, I look for a number of factors: How long until production? Anything more than five years is too long to wait. How much is the capex? This is the cost to build the mine, also called the initial capital expenditure. Anything over $200 million can be difficult to finance. I prefer the capex to be between $25 million and $200 million, but I will go higher for projects I like.

What is the IRR (internal rate of return)? This is a fancy acronym for return on investment. I want it to be at least 20% after-tax at the current gold price. Anything above 30% is very good. What is the projected cash cost per ounce? I want it to be about 40% of the current gold price. I will go as high as 60% if I like the company. Remember, the gold price can rise, making projects very economic.

Management

In the mining business, management is crucial. It is much more important than in other industries. The reason for this is that operating mines, building mines, and exploration is very difficult. Finding a good management team that has a reputation for good stewardship should be one of your prerequisites before purchasing a stock. When you find a good management team, along with a good set of properties, you are likely looking at a good stock.

Management for Majors is usually driven by the CEO. Find out how long he/she has been in charge and their track record. Find out by visiting the company's web page and searching stock forums. Also, use Google to search their name. Before you invest in a company, make sure you are comfortable with the CEO, and perhaps the Board of Directors (BOD).

Some management teams are more focused on shareholders than others. This is not difficult to uncover and will be known by other investors. If a management team wants to continuously increase the size of the company by buying other companies, then they are going to take on debt or dilute their shares. This can be detrimental to shareholders, as profits are constantly pushed out into the future. Try to find management teams that are shareholder friendly, which will be reflected in their stock price history or corporate announcements. News releases are very useful for identifying shareholder focused companies. How often do they dilute? How often do they add debt? A good indicator is how much debt and cash they maintain, as well as how much dilution they increase annually.

I have found that good management teams who are shareholder friendly tend to keep their share structures tightly held (explained a few pages below in Share Structure) and a good balance sheet. When you see a company with very high share dilution, this is generally not a good sign that management is looking out for shareholder interest. This is not true for all companies, but some companies print shares like they are a central bank. Conversely, it is a good sign when management owns a substantial amount of stock. This is a good sign that management has "skin" in the game and wants the stock price to rise.

I like companies that have share structures with less than 150 million shares, and the fewer the number of shares the better. And I like it when management owns at least 10% of the company. Plus, I like it when management takes pride in announcing that they are focused on raising the share price and are trying to prevent share dilution.

Another good sign of a shareholder-friendly company is when they buy back shares. I would much rather a company buy back shares than issue dividends. In fact, I don't think it is shareholder friendly when companies issue dividends with a market cap under $1 billion. Why? Because I want them to use their cash to grow.

Another area of concern is hedging. This is the practice of selling future production at fixed prices. There will be many management teams tempted to lock-in profits or to use future production to borrow money, but this is not always shareholder friendly, as profit growth can be severely limited. If you see any significant hedging going on, identify that as a potential red flag that could impact the share price.

Hedging can sometimes be unavoidable for some Juniors to get financing. If you do see hedging used for borrowing money, then hopefully it is a small percentage of annual production and has little impact on profitability. Mid-Tier Producers and Majors should not be hedging significant amounts of production in my opinion. If large-producing companies are hedging significantly, then it is more in management's interest than that of stockholders. A little bit of hedging is okay, but after a certain point, it impacts potential profitability.

Execution is how you identify a good management team. The bad news is that it usually takes a few years to get an idea of how well a management team executes. This means that you might have to wait a long time before buying a stock. I often put pricey stocks with low upside potential on my watch list. Then I wait for them to come down in value. While I am waiting, I get the opportunity to watch how they execute. I have bought a lot of gold and silver mining stocks using this method of waiting and analyzing. I might look at a company several times over several years before buying it, waiting for the right entry price and the right execution from management teams.

How companies execute is crucial for the performance of their stock. This includes keeping their websites up to date and informing investors of their future plans. If companies take marketing lightly and ignore potential shareholders (which in the mining business means sharing information on their website), then they are not generally good management teams.

Execution means different things depending on the company type. A producing company has to "hit" their numbers. These are the numbers that investors are expecting, such as the forecasted cash cost per ounce, the amount of gold produced, expected recovery rate and grade, and profitability. Unfortunately, like most businesses, they have to perform quarterly, and all it takes is for one bad quarter to hurt the stock. This is another reason why management teams are so important.

For exploration companies, they have to return good drill results and advance their projects. Good steady news releases will drive these stocks higher. Conversely, bad news releases, or no news, will hurt the stock. And once they run out of cash, financing to raise cash will create share dilution and hurt the stock price.

Companies developing and building mines have to plan, finance, and permit projects. This can take several years, and often investors lose interest until production arrives. This is why there is usually a drop in the stock price between when the project is discovered and validated as economic, and when production begins. It takes a talented management team to keep investors interested during this development period. And it is usually a sign of a good management team if they can continue a steady stream of information all the way to production.

Stock Price History

Always check a company's stock chart. If the stock has done well over the last few years, that is a reflection of good management. You want to look back at least five years and compare the stock price to the price of gold/silver. If they have consistently outperformed the metal, that is a good sign. Next, compare their stock price to that of their peers. The good companies will stand out when you compare peers.

You don't want to see a lot of volatility in a stock price chart, although 2008 and 2011 to 2015 had severe market corrections in mining stocks. If a company has had an upward price trajectory, it is a good sign that investors know the story of this stock, and they are in it for the long haul. You want to find stocks that other investors like, and the stock price chart should reflect this fact. If a company has a good story, the word always gets out.

I also look at the chart to see if it is a good entry point. You don't want to buy stocks that have already had a major breakout, or if it has recently had a breakout. In those situations, you are generally late to the party and have missed your opportunity. For those situations, it is better to wait for the stock price to correct. When I look at a chart, and I don't see a breakout, or if it has had a breakout and came back down, then I am more comfortable buying the stock.

One thing that is crucial for making large returns and that is a good entry point. And you can't find a good entry point without looking at the chart. There is an expression in investing called buying the dip, and for getting a good entry point in mining stocks, you generally have to wait for the dip. From my experience, it usually always comes after you buy the stock.

In Chapters 9 and 10, I will be revisiting many of these concepts when I discuss how to make money and how to value a mining company.

Reserves/Resources Defined

Inferred Resources: These are resource estimates based on drilling results and geology. The better the geology is understood, the more likely the estimate will be accurate. These are generally unreliable without further drilling. Normally these are provided by third-party companies who prepare a resource estimate (often a 43-101 report) using drilling results and geology.

Measured and Indicated Resources (M&I): These are the gold/silver resources that were determined by drilling and a resource estimate by a third party. They are considered to be reliable. Generally, not all M&I resources are mined. A good rule of thumb is to expect about 80% of the M&I to be mined over the long term.

Proven and Probable Reserves (P&P): These are Measured and Indicated Resources that have been validated to be economic through a mine plan, usually called a Preliminary Feasibility Study. Thus, the only difference between M&I and P&P is a mine plan. There is a second difference, and that is you can reasonably expect 100% of P&P to be mined.

One of the most confusing things about mining stocks is the difference between resources and reserves. Until a legal mining plan exists in the form of a Preliminary Feasibility Study, all ounces in the ground are considered resources. Once a mining plan is generated, it can turn M&I resources into P&P reserves.

However, it is not that simple. From an investor's viewpoint, most of the M&I resources and some of the Inferred resources will eventually become reserves. For this reason, I usually include all of the M&I resources and some Inferred as part of my future valuation of a company. I add up all of the resources that I think they will eventually mine and count that as future reserves.

Because Majors have the funds to plan their projects meticulously, they tend to focus on P&P. When you hear analysts talk about Majors, they only seem to be concerned with reserves. For Mid-Tier and Junior stocks, they focus more on M&I. The reason for this is that smaller companies will save money by only funding a preliminary feasibility study for a project that is close to development. They might have several mine properties with M&I resources, but only one with P&P reserves. This does not mean that those M&I resources are not valuable and likely to be mined in the future.

For Juniors, inferred resources can also be very important. The reason for this is that drilling costs a lot of money, which is required to turn inferred ounces into M&I resources. Do not underestimate the value of inferred resources in a small company that has not had the time or money to turn those inferred resources into M&I.

Stock Valuation

I keep stock valuation fairly simple. I look at only a few factors: production ounces, future reserve ounces, cash, debt, cost per ounce, share structure, market cap, capex, IRR, NPV, future market cap, and future cash flow. Because the price of precious metals and the reserves in the ground play such a huge role in valuation, fancy financial models are not needed. At least, that's my opinion.

I recently heard an interview with the manager of a major gold mutual fund, and he mentioned the top five things he uses to value a company: 1) Management. 2) Production Growth. 3) Reserve and Resource Growth. 4) Cost per Ounce. 5) Projected price of gold.

I agree with him - keep it simple when it comes to valuing mining stocks. The most important thing is whether a company is growing (production and resources). Find future growth, and you are going to find an undervalued stock. Why? Because those new ounces are likely going to be revalued higher. That said, we can still use valuation methods to find undervalued stocks.

The company's balance sheet (cash and debt) is always important. You want a company that has low debt, cash in the bank, and if it is a producer, significant cash flow going to the bottom line. The more debt that a company has to finance, the less profit they can make and the less cash they will have to expand their business. Thus, debt is a bad thing, so always check it.

Do you remember Microsoft in the 1990s, or Apple in the 2000s? They had no debt, billions in cash, and were growing at a fast rate. As a consequence, Microsoft and Apple's stock made many of their shareholders millionaires. That is what you want.

Debt Coverage

Note: Valuation Formulas can be found in Appendix B.

A good way to measure debt is by calculating the debt coverage, which is a simple calculation of debt to cash flow. This is a no-frills method, but it captures numbers that are readily available.

Cash Flow = Production Revenue minus All-in Costs

(Production oz. x Current Spot Price) - (Production oz. x Cost Per oz.)

Debt = Debt - Cash
(Always subtract cash, since it could be used to pay off debt.)

Debt Coverage = Cash Flow / Debt

Note: Production ounces are often converted to equivalent gold or silver ounces, because production nearly always comes from multiple ore types. If a company lists their resources and costs using equivalent ounces, then I will too. This is more common with silver miners than gold miners.

Let's use an example:

Production = 100,000 equivalent ounces of gold

Cost Per Ounce = $800

Gold Price = $1,300

Cash Flow = (100,000 x 1,300) - (100,000 x 800) = $50,000,000

Debt = $125,000,000 (debt) - $5,000,000 (cash) = $120,000,000

$50 million Cash Flow, divided by

---------------- = 40% Debt Coverage

$120 million Debt

Thus, cash flow is 40% of debt. That is manageable and not a problem. They will likely pay off their debt soon with that much cash flow. However, if the ratio is less than 25%, then it is a red flag. And if it is close to 10%, it is a very serious problem. They may have to raise cash by issuing more stock, which would dilute the stock and thereby reduce its value. Or, worst case, they could default on their debt - bankruptcy.

Debt is one of the first things I look at. When I think of debt, I think of net debt, which is debt minus cash. Thus, when you look at debt, also look at cash. If they have no debt, but no cash, that is not good. You want a company with cash to fund operations and growth. Hopefully, they have enough cash to offset their debt, thereby increasing their debt coverage. You don't want a company with a lot of debt and very little cash. All of their cash flow is going to be used to pay off debt.

Another number to be aware of is the debt ratio, which simply cash divided by debt. I am much more concerned about the ability to afford debt payments, but the debt ratio is an indicator of a cash-focused company. Ideally, you always want a company to have more cash than debt, but this is not generally possible for juniors financing their first mine. But for producers, I look for balance sheets with more cash than debt. Ideally, you want a pristine balance sheet with zero debt and lots of cash.

One final comment regarding debt. Don't be fooled into thinking a company has a good balance sheet if they have a lot of cash, yet are currently building or expanding a mine. Their cash balance will shrink quickly once construction begins. Until cash flow begins, you are not going to know what their balance sheet will look like. However, if they have a solid debt coverage ratio, the balance sheet will clean up quickly.

> Note: I rarely calculate the debt coverage and debt ratio, although I always do it in my head by looking at the debt, cash, monthly burn rate, and cash flow. After you get some experience, you will look at these four numbers and know immediately if they have a debt problem. The calculations are the "math" that tells you if there is a problem, but generally you don't need to do the math.

Cost Per Ounce (Cost Structure)

The next thing to look at is the cost per ounce (cost structure). Cost has a direct correlation to profitability. For instance, if a mining company has a low-cost structure and the price of gold/silver rises, the stock price will likely rise, reflecting that low-cost structure. This is the leverage of mining companies that I mentioned earlier. This low-cost structure allows an increase in the gold/silver price to go directly to the bottom line - increased profit. This is also true for high-cost structures, but the low-cost structure stocks will be more rewarded by the market because they will have the highest profits.

Use the stock market's knowledge to your advantage. The stock market will reward companies that are profitable. If you know a company has a low-cost structure (such as Silvercorp Metals), then it has a big advantage over the competition. Compare each Major and see who has a high, medium, or low-cost structure.

You will often find that companies focused in Mexico, South America, or other Third World countries will have low price structures. But beware of energy costs. As oil prices rise, this will affect the bottom line - profit. Thus, do not assume that a low price structure can be maintained for the medium or long term.

When you look at the cost structure, you have to look at the cash cost per ounce and the all-in cost per ounce. The starting point is the cash costs. An easy way to determine if a company has low cash costs is to compare 1/3 of the spot price of gold/silver. If the cost per ounce is approximately 1/3 of the spot price, then the company has low costs. Conversely, if a company has a cost per ounce more than 2/3 of the spot price, it is high.

I try to find companies that have cash costs 1/2 of the spot price or less. However, this is not an ironclad rule, because I also like to invest in Canadian miners. Because of high labor costs, it is unusual to find Canadian miners with cash costs this low. However, there are many with moderate costs. I don't mind moderate costs in Canada, because I believe that these stocks will get a premium in the future because of their safe location.

After you analyze the cash cost per ounce, move on to the all-in cost per ounce. Here you are looking for free cash flow. Anything below 80% of the spot price is good, and below 70% is excellent. If a company is getting 30% (or more) free cash flow per ounce of production, that will be a very profitable company.

Currently, the gold price is about $1,800 per ounce. At that price, you want the all-in cost to be below $1,400. Anything above $1,500 can be problematic for a variety of reasons. First, the free cash flow is going to be limited. This will limit their ability to grow organically using cash that is generated through operations. Instead, they are likely to dilute shares to raise cash, or possibly add debt.

Without sufficient free cash flow, it puts a lot of pressure on the company and the share price. Ideally, with the price at $1,800, you want to all-in costs to be at $1,200 or lower. Note that 80% of $1,800 is $1,440. Anything below $1,4400 would be good, and anything below $1,200 would be excellent.

As metals prices rise, I expect many gold miners to have all-in costs less than 40% the spot price, and many silver miners to have all-in costs less than 30% the spot price. Silver miners have the potential to be huge performers. I don't think it will be a shock to see some silver miners with all-in costs at $25 per ounce and silver prices at $100. The margins could be huge.

* * * * *

Majors are relatively easy to value because you know:

1. Market Cap
2. Production Ounces
3. Resource Ounces
4. Share Structure
5. Cost Structure
6. Debt
7. Cash

I would also add another number to this list, which would be forecasted future reserves. I find this is fairly easy to estimate based on their current resources.

We have already looked at debt, cash, and costs. Let's look now at these other factors. I like to focus on resources (I generally exclude most or all of the inferred resources) and see how the market has valued them.

Here are four simple valuation methods:

Market Cap Valuation Per Resource Ounce

This is the valuation of the resources in the ground (excluding most inferred) on a per ounce basis. **<u>This is the most important valuation for identifying cheap stocks</u>.** Often you can buy Juniors at incredibly cheap valuations versus their resources.

Let's use Pan American Silver as an example (this is from 2019):

$2.3 billion	Market Cap, divided by
----------------	= $2.55 Market Cap Value Per Ounce
900 million	Resource Ounces (excluding inferred)

Each ounce in the ground is being valued at $2.55. Anything below $1 is very cheap. At $2.55, I would consider it undervalued, but not cheap.

Pan American Silver has 900 million ounces of silver in the ground (excluding inferred resources). When you divide that by their $2.3 billion market cap, you are paying $2.55 per ounce. Buying silver at $2.55 per ounce in the ground is about as cheap as you will find for a quality producer silver producer, let alone a Major. You should compare all of the Majors and Emerging Majors and see what it costs to buy these stocks on a per ounce basis.

Share Price Valuation by Resources in the Ground

This could also be called "Ounces Per Share," as this is the number of ounces in the ground that each share represents. Higher is better. This valuation is important because it shows the explosive potential of a tightly held stock. (I'll have more to say about this further down.)

Again, using Pan American Silver (from 2019):

900 million	Resource Ounces, divided by
----------------	= 5.8 oz. per share
154 million	Shares Outstanding

Each share represents 5.8 ounces of resources.

Each share is currently worth $92 worth of silver in the ground (5.8 x $16).

Thus, when you buy a share of Pan American Silver, it has an underlying value of 5.8 ounces of resources. That is not super cheap, but this a Major. Finding a company worth 20 ounces (or more) per share would be a very cheap valuation.

Note that this share valuation ignores the market cap or share price of the stock. It is strictly used to value the resources on a per share basis. As stated above, high valuations are positive because they reveal explosive potential in the stock price.

Resource Valuation as a Percentage of Market Cap

This is the valuation of the resources at current precious metal prices as a percentage of the market cap. This is a very useful valuation to see whether a company is undervalued. The general rule of thumb is that resources from a producing mine should be priced at 10%, or higher. You will find some companies priced at 20%.

Step 1: Value of Resources:

900 million (Resource Ounces) x $16 (Silver Price) = $14.4 billion

Step 2: Percent of Market Cap

$2.3 billion Market Cap, divided by

---------------- = 16%

$14.4 billion Value of Resources

The resource ounces in the ground are currently valued at 16% of the price of silver. This valuation is about right, but what happens when the price of silver doubles? The company becomes undervalued by 100%. In fact, if silver doubles, the company should more than double. This will be explained in a later chapter.

Quick and Dirty Market Cap Valuation

It is easy to do a quick and dirty valuation using resources and the current price of precious metals. This is just a guesstimate of its current market cap value, but it is considered a conservative estimate.

Step 1: Value of Resources:

900 million (Resource Ounces) x $16 (Silver Price) = $14.4 billion

Step 2: Value of Resources at 15%

$14.4 billion x 15% = $2.2 billion

Actual market cap: $2.3 billion

The current valuation of the resources is fairly valued.

Note: Resource ounces should include Proven or Probable, Measured and Indicated, and generally exclude Inferred.

Share Structure

Share structure is important to understand. I know one analyst who ranks it in the top three things he looks at to select a stock. Let's begin by defining the terminology:

Shares Outstanding: This is the number of shares that have been issued to shareholders, excluding Options and Warrants. These are the common stock shares that trade on stock exchanges.

Options: These are stock options given to employees, contractors, or others who are affiliated with the company. Each option has a specific price threshold (strike price), along with vesting and expiration dates, which must be met before the stock can be issued. Legally, stock options must be granted with a strike price at or above the current stock price. If an option exceeds the strike price, they are usually exercised by the option holder and become common stock, thereby increasing the number of shares outstanding. This is called dilution.

Note: If someone is given stock options, normally they have to wait a period of time. First, they might have to wait for the strike price to be reached. Second, they might have to wait until a vesting period has been reached (vesting periods are generally only used to keep employees from leaving the company). Third, if the expiration date occurs before these dates are reached, then the options expire worthless.

Note: If someone owns options that are at or above the strike price, at or above the vesting date, and before the expiration date, then they have the right to purchase the stock at the strike price (also called the exercise price). Essentially, they will likely be purchasing the stock at a discount. Once they own the stock, they can either hold it or sell it.

Warrants: These are essentially options owned by private investors that can be used to purchase stock at a fixed price. Private investors can obtain warrants by participating in a private share offering. This is quite common in the mining business. Companies use warrants as an incentive to get investors to participate in a private share offering. Generally, when an investor agrees to participate in a private share offering, they will receive either a half or full warrant for each common share they purchase. Investors can then hold the warrants and purchase the stock directly from the company at a later date at this fixed price (before the warrants expire). If a warrant is exercised and stock is purchased by an investor, these new shares become common stock and increase the number of shares outstanding.

Note: Warrants and options are also a source of capital for companies. Warrants are an option to purchase common stock at a fixed price. If they are exercised, then the company is paid. If warrants are "in the money," they are usually exercised. For instance, if you own a warrant with a strike price of $1, and the share price rises above $1, you will likely exercise it to obtain the profit, as long as it has not expired. Moreover, when options and warrants are exercised, they become common stock, which creates dilution to the existing market cap.

Fully Diluted Shares: These are the combined total of shares outstanding, along with options and warrants that have not expired.

Note: It is a good practice to use this fully diluted number for calculating valuations instead of the shares outstanding, if you wish to use more conservative numbers. I always use FD (fully diluted) shares in my valuations.

Float: The float is the number of shares that can be traded. All shares outstanding are not traded. Normally, there is a small percentage of stock held by company insiders who are long-term investors. Also, there can be shares that are restricted from trading. For these reasons, companies with tight share structures can have a small float. Moreover, a company with a small float can have a highly explosive share price, because there are fewer shares available to be traded.

Tightly Held: When there are a small number of Fully Diluted shares, a company's share structure is said to be tightly held. I consider anything less than 100 million shares as tight. But some investors prefer to define tight as closer to 50 million shares.

Dilution: When additional common shares are issued, the Outstanding Shares total increases. This is called share dilution. And because the market cap (value of the company) is the share price multiplied by the number of shares outstanding, the market cap tends to decrease. Additional shares also reduce the earnings potential of each share (see EPS example below) and reduces the value of each share.

This is easy to comprehend. If there are 100 million shares outstanding and a company's profit is $100 million, then the profit is $1 per share. But what happens if they issue another 100 million shares? The effective worth of each share has dropped by 50%. In all likelihood, the stock will also drop by 50%. Thus, dilution is bad.

$$\text{EPS (Earnings Per Share)} = \frac{\text{Net Profit}}{\text{Shares Outstanding}}$$

Note: When you think of share structure, think fully diluted shares. Why? Because the stock market is aware of the number of fully diluted shares, and the stock price will reflect this potential dilution.

Importance of Share Structure

Share structure plays an important role in stock price valuation. Let's look at the example below. Both companies have the same size market cap, but Company A has a much larger share structure. If the stock price for both of these companies rises 500%, what happens?

Ounces Per Share = Resources / Shares Outstanding

Company A	*Company B*
Resources 100 Million oz.	Resources 100 Million oz.
Shares 500 Million	Shares 100 Million
oz. per Share 20 cents	oz. per Share $1

Company A, because it has a large share structure, only increases to $1, while Company B increases from $1 to $5. It is the same percentage growth, but psychologically it has a big impact on investors. They see the stock growing from $1 to $2 to $3… This gets investor's attention, and they often will buy the stock to ride the trend. In fact, this psychological effect can cause the stock to grow faster than if it were highly diluted. This is the main reason people avoid stocks with large share structures, and why smart investors prefer companies with tight share structures. The takeaway is that the stock price can be explosive for companies with tight structures because of psychology.

Ironically, the opposite happens when a share price gets too high. People will not buy stocks that are valued in the hundreds of dollars because they are perceived as too pricey, regardless of their fundamentals. For this reason, companies do stock splits to get stocks into a more palatable psychological price point.

Reverse Stock Split

Another reason to avoid highly diluted share structures is that they are vulnerable to reverse stock splits. This is when companies reduce the number of shares by a specific ratio, generally 5 to 1 or 10 to 1. A reverse split can be painful for shareholders because, after the split, the stock price often drops, and you can never recover from the reduced share count. I have been decimated on occasion by companies doing reverse splits. Give me a tight structure anytime! Anything over 500 million shares can be vulnerable to a reverse split, although I have seen some companies do reverse splits under 300 million shares to increase their share price.

Because many investors avoid highly diluted companies, you have to discount the future value of a company if it has a large number of shares outstanding. This is not always true for large caps, where investors tend to ignore the share structure for Majors. However, for mid-tiers and juniors, the share structure impacts the valuation. This will prevent or hinder the stock price from rising at the same rate as its peers. Conversely, the stock price of a tightly held stock can increase dramatically as the market cap rises.

As I have explained, share structure is important for both psychological and valuation reasons. Because it is important, you want to count all potential shares and use the number of fully diluted shares in your valuation formulas. Companies often have stock options or warrants that could eventually become outstanding shares. You need to research these. How many there are, the expiration dates, the strike price, etc. Note that most financial websites only display total shares outstanding and ignore options and warrants. This understates the fully diluted total. You will have to go to the company's website, or to its financial reports, to get the total diluted shares.

Cash Flow Multiple

The next thing to look at is how the stock market is valuing a company's cash flow. Earlier, we compared net debt to cash flow. Now we are going to compare cash flow to the market cap. This is done using the following calculation:

Cash Flow Multiple = Market Cap / Cash Flow

I already showed you how to do a no-frills cash flow (under the Debt Coverage section), so this calculation should be easy to understand. Market cap is simply the number of shares outstanding times the current stock price. The market cap is what the stock market thinks the company is worth. Often this is something like 5 times cash flow or 10 times cash flow. The industry average is approximately 10 times for quality producers, with most Majors higher than the average, and most Mid-Tier and Junior producers lower.

You could use this calculation for each stock you are considering, and see how they are valued versus their actual or potential future cash flow. Try to find a company with strong cash flow (or projected strong cash flow) that is not being rewarded with a high stock price. This will often be an undervalued stock. I try to find stocks with fully diluted market caps valued at 1 times potential future cash flow or less.

On the GSD website, it displays both the current CFM and the future CFM. I will look at both, but the number I am much more interested in is the future CFM. I want to know what the stock could be worth in the future. For instance, earlier we found that Pan American Silver appeared to be somewhat fairly valued (in 2019). When I look at its future CFM, it is 1.5 (see below), with future cash flow estimated at $1.5 billion (using $100 silver prices). That is very attractive if you expect higher silver prices.

Cash Flow Multiple = Market Cap / Cash Flow

1.5 = $2.3 billion / $1.5 billion

You can also use this calculation to monitor a producing company. Using this calculation, you can monitor the current cash flow multiple and see if the market cap increases. If the market cap does not rise, even though the multiple is rising (more cash flow), then it is a safe bet that the stock price is going to increase at some point. Thus, this could be a good entry point for trading the stock (expecting it to go higher).

The opposite rule is also true. Less cash flow means a lower current multiple, and that should lead to a lower market cap and the stock price heading lower. Using this multiple, you can track cash flow and see how the market cap/stock price responds.

This is an easy way to identify how the stock market rewards the profitability of a company. This calculation will expose underpriced companies. If a company has a large cash flow increase and a low market cap, then the stock price has to rise.

As an investor, what you are looking for are companies that are undervalued. If you use this calculation on all of the stocks you are interested in, the good ones will stand out.

> Note: Be careful relying on this ratio if the company has a lot of debt, and make sure to pad the all-in cost per ounce for non-producers, like I discussed earlier to get a more conservative cash flow.

Another thing you can do with this calculation is run hypothetical models. What happens to future cash flow if the gold price rises to $2,500? You can do this on the GSD website to get an idea of future valuations at higher gold prices. We have a cash flow calculator that makes it very easy to simulate different gold prices, all-in costs, and production levels.

In addition to the gold price rising, there are several other hypotheticals. What happens if production increases, thereby increasing cash flow? What happens if costs rise, thereby reducing cash flow? All of these factors can be monitored or simulated. Professional stock traders run these numbers all the time. They anticipate how the stock market is going to value the company in the future. They anticipate how changes can affect a company's cash flow. For instance, if you know a company is going to add 100,000 ounces of gold production next year, you can use this calculation to do a quick check. Is that additional cash flow already reflected in the stock's price? Very likely, it is not.

The variables in the cash flow multiple are constantly changing (i.e., production ounces, shares outstanding, mining costs, metal prices, and the stock price). So, you can keep a history, and see how the valuation and stock price move. This ratio should be fairly consistent: more cash flow = higher stock price = higher market cap. Over time, you can get a good feel for what affects the stock price. This is what professionals do. And this is why you want to pay attention to what the professionals are saying. They know these stocks very well, and so can you.

Other Valuation Methods

There are several valuation methods that professionals use, such as net present value using discounted cash flow, the weighted average cost of capital, and economic value added. All of these are complicated accounting ratios that are a pain to understand and mock-up. For mining shares, I think it is more than adequate to use simple formulas, along with the rising trend of gold/silver.

For gold/silver mining companies, I don't think the PE (Price/Earnings) ratio is important. This ratio is used by a lot of analysts, but I think it is worthless for miners. If a company has a low PE or a high PE, that doesn't mean anything, in my opinion. Because mining companies are valued on their location, management team, recovery rate, ore grade, share structure, costs, debt, reserves, production growth, and the price of the metal, it makes much more sense to focus on these factors. These variables are going to tell me much more than their PE ratio.

The current PE doesn't mean much if several of the valuation factors (listed in the previous paragraph) are changing. Most gold and silver investors aren't going to be concerned with past and current PE ratios. Instead, they are going to be analyzing all of the valuation factors. Moreover, as we have seen with technology and Internet stocks, a high PE does not mean that the stock price can't go higher.

The mining business isn't that complicated for calculating future profits. You mine ore at a certain cost, and then you sell it at the going market rate. If you are lucky enough to have a large gold or silver deposit with moderate to low costs, it is like printing money. This is why investing in mining companies can be very lucrative in a bull market. These companies can be exceptionally profitable at higher metal prices, with very high margins.

My favorite valuation method is one I identified from ideas generated while writing this book. It is a simple formula of calculating future market cap growth. I found this formula realizing that we can simulate future gold prices and future reserves for a company. This calculation is an easy way to find an investment opportunity. After I have calculated the future market cap growth, I then use all of the other valuation factors to adjust down the future market cap growth. The result is a company rating. I will be discussing this in Chapter 10 - How to Value Mining Stocks.

Here is the formula.

Annual Future Production Ounces x (Future Gold Price - Future All-In Cost Per Oz) x Multiple = Future Market Cap

I use either 5, 10, or 15 for the multiple based on the quality of the company.

(Future Market Cap - Current Market Cap) / Current Market Cap = Future Market Cap Growth

Note: The future market cap is the theoretical maximum value a company can obtain using an estimated future gold/silver price.

Note: I prefer to invest in stocks (not counting mutual funds of ETFs) that have a theoretical future market cap growth of at least 500%. What do they say? Go big or go home? If you want to be less aggressive and focus on strong companies with less potential returns, that is an acceptable strategy. I have found that dropping my required market cap growth rate to at least 300% has improved my portfolio by adding more quality stocks.

Partnerships / Joint Ventures

In the mining business, Majors and Mid-Tier mining companies are always looking for Juniors to partner up in a joint venture (JV). Thus, they let Juniors do most of the exploring, and then they create a partnership when the Juniors discover a deposit. The larger company then takes over the property and builds and operates the mine. The Junior remains a silent partner with a percentage of ownership, usually around 20% to 30%.

I've seen JV deals as low as 20% ownership and as high as 50/50. Often, a Junior will take cash, stock in the acquiring company, or keep a small NSR (Net Smelter Royalty). These NSRs are small royalties on production, usually around 1% to 2% of production. This is a net amount, without any cost to the NSR holder. For instance, if a mine has 100,000 oz. annual production and a 2% NSR, that would be 2,000 oz. At $1,500 gold, the NSR holder would receive $3 million in annual income.

Many of the Majors and Mid-Tier mining companies have partnerships (either JV deals or small ownership stakes) with Junior mining companies. Don't ignore these partnerships. Take some time to see what their Juniors partners have drilled and what they have planned. The chapter on Junior Explorers will help you to research them.

Takeovers / Acquisitions

Takeovers are common in the mining business. This happens mostly when larger companies consume smaller ones in an effort to grow. This is currently a curse for junior mining investors. The reason why is that once a Junior finds a large deposit, the Majors or Mid-Tier companies swoop in like vultures and steal these properties for small premiums. This has happened to me several times, and I now consider it part of investing in this sector (I don't expect it to change).

The ugly thing is that Junior companies are often willing to give their properties away for small premiums, regardless of the potential future valuation. In fact, executives often get rewarded with payouts for selling their company. These are analogous to golden parachutes in the corporate world. While the executives and board members are often paid a significant sum, the shareholders usually get the short end of the stick, with a small premium that does not reflect the true value of the stock.

While executive payouts do occur for company buyouts, the other reasons acquisitions are happening today are the difficulty in getting financing, and the fear on the part of investors and corporate board of directors that without the deep pockets of a larger company, their project could not get developed.

Most investors seem to be welcoming takeovers if it helps Juniors develop their deposits, even if that means low investment returns. Recently the premiums for Juniors have been about 40% over the current share price. But when you factor in the recent drop in most shares prices, the premium is well below where the stock recently traded. In effect, the takeover company is buying the dip in the share price. They are actually buying at a large discount.

For instance, in 2013, Volta Resources agreed to a friendly takeover by B2Gold for 42 cents a share. The premium was 100% of their share price, which seemed fair. However, the premium does not tell the whole story. Volta had a 6 million oz. advanced project ready for construction and a market cap of only $31 million. Thus, at the time of the deal, they were selling for only about $5 per oz. in the ground. Selling to B2Gold for $10 per oz. was a bargain for the buyer. The fact is this was a significantly discounted sales price. The premium did not reflect the value of the gold in the ground.

Takeovers for $10 to $20 per oz. in the ground have been quite common. Wits Gold agreed to a takeover by Sibanye Gold for less than $1 per oz. of gold in the ground. This is the lowest purchase price of gold in the ground I have witnessed. When it requires about $25 to $35 per oz. to find gold in the ground, buying it for less is a steal, especially when the project is advanced. It wasn't too long ago when gold in the ground was selling for $75 to $150 per oz. I expect those valuations to return with higher gold prices.

One final word about takeovers. If you own a junior, recognize that it is always vulnerable to a takeover unless there are enough insiders who refuse to sell. I like to find juniors, where management and insiders own at least 40%. Under these scenarios, the management team can fight against a takeover that is not in their shareholder's interest.

Companies know that insider ownership is valuable. They tend to publicize it in their company website presentations. You can also email their investment relations person and ask them if they have enough votes to prevent a hostile takeover, and if management is against any possible takeover offer. Some management teams are smart enough to know they have the potential for incredible returns if gold prices rise.

Analysts / Web Forums / Web Sites

I always want to know what investment analysts or other investors are saying about a company that I am interested in. For instance, are there any red flags? There is so much information on the Internet that it makes no sense to purchase a stock without first reading about it. Most of the material available about a company comes from their website. The other places are web forums, analyst's websites, and gold/silver websites. This is the information that uncovers the details about a company that truly identifies its strengths and weaknesses. If you did a good job researching a company by checking all the areas I have outlined in this chapter, then your conclusions should match what the analysts are saying.

Don't dismiss web forums and think there is no useful information to be found on a forum of amateur investors. Some of the best news originates on Internet sites like Twitter, Yahoo Finance, Google Finance, Stockhouse.com, and CEO.ca.

If you're new to website investment forums, make sure you don't jump to conclusions or believe everything you read. Remember that people have their own motives and biases, and that you should approach these sites with a healthy dose of skepticism.

On forums you can get firsthand information from people who have followed these companies for years. Some of the best information is on Internet forums. It is often more timely than paid information. And all the latest news about a company is usually available (the good, the bad and the ugly).

The best thing about investing in Majors is that a lot of people invest in these stocks. So there is a lot of information available. With just a little bit of effort, you can find the best stocks, and everything you need to know about them: their strengths, weaknesses, and potential.

Gold/Silver Websites

In addition to stock research, you should also read about gold/silver in general. These are sites that are more oriented to news articles that pertain to gold/silver. Many of them are written by analysts who recommend stocks, but the majority of them are economic in nature. I think it is imperative to read these sites if you are a serious investor. It is the only way to time the market for identifying good entry levels. My favorite sites that I have read in the past include Zerohedge.com, 321gold.com, TheAuReport.com, and Kitco.com (especially their daily news releases section). These sites are biased towards gold (except ZeroHedge), but the quality of the material is excellent.

Here is a list of gold/silver web sites to visit:

- 321gold.com .... Excellent daily news articles
- TheAuReport.com........................... Daily analyst interviews
- Kitco.com .... Daily news releases
- Zerohedge.com.................................... Daily economic news
- FinancialSense.com........................ Free Internet radio show
- Goldseek.com .... Free Internet radio show
- Kereport.com .... Free Internet radio show
- MiningStocks.com........................... Free Internet radio show
- SilverAxis.com... Excellent links
- Infomine.com
- Jsmineset.com
- Mineweb.com
- ResourceInvestor.com
- Silverseek.com
- Silver-Investor.com
- SilverStrategies.com
- KitcoSilver.com

Books / Newsletters

Generally, the above material is sufficient, but if you are a stickler for doing research, there are a few more sources of information. I would recommend the CPM Gold Yearbook and CPM Silver Yearbook.[54] These books cost $150 each and are published annually. Try to get a used edition on Amazon (generally around $100). They will tell you quite a bit about each of the Majors.

There are also many good newsletters on the market. For Majors, I would recommend John Doody's newsletter at *www.goldstockanalyst.com*. If you want to do a thorough job of analyzing the Majors, his newsletter can add the missing details and give you a professional's opinion. It's expensive at about $1,000 per year and is directed at professional investors. However, if you are going to invest a large amount in specific Majors (he also covers Mid-Tiers and a few Juniors), a subscription might be worth it. You can download a sample newsletter from his website.

For Juniors, I like Brien Lundin's newsletter at *www.goldnewsletter.com*. It is about $200 per year and provides a nice list of stocks he recommends. My personal bias is that his analysis and supporting data is a bit thin, but you might want to try it. I also recommend that you read a few samples from other newsletter writers and try to find one you like. They are generally priced between $200 and $500 per year. And if you join my website (GSD), you get the monthly newsletter for free. It currently includes the following: Top 10, Top 25, 1 Bagger List, 2 Bagger List, 3 Bagger List, 5 Bagger List, 10 Bagger List, Exploration Stock List, plus a wide range of information..

Here is a link to an excellent web page with a list of newsletters:

www.theaureport.com/pub/htdocs/newsletters.html

Majors Defined

I categorize a company as a Major differently than the professionals. They define a company as a Major from a production standpoint. To them, a Major must have production that exceeds 500,000 ounces per year (gold equivalent). My definition is a gold/silver producer with a market cap of over $3 billion.

I'm more concerned about how much money I can make. If a company has a market cap greater than $3 billion, how much upside is left? As a rule of thumb, the greater the market cap, the less the upside. So, if I define a company as a Major, I see it as having a small likelihood of having significant upside.

I might miss some great companies who happen to have a market cap greater than $3 billion and a lot of growth potential, but that is the risk I am willing to take. I prefer to spend my time analyzing and watching companies with market caps below this threshold. However, if you are looking for safety, and have less aggressive investment goals, then spending time analyzing these companies might make sense.

Profit is profit. And many of the Majors will make a lot of money in this bull market. It is not foolish to focus on companies with market caps greater than $3 billion, especially if you after income stocks. You will do very well. Companies like

Kinross Gold, Newcrest Mining, and Newmont Mining all have incredible properties and growth prospects. I don't see how these companies could fail to triple in value from today's valuations. That said, this is not where I spend my time doing a lot of analysis.

Emerging Majors Defined

These are gold/silver producers (my definition) with a market cap between $1.5 and $3 billion.

There are a lot of really solid companies in the group, such as IAMGold, and a few of the large silver producers. These are stocks that can both grow substantially and provide dividends to reduce your cost basis. Even as an aggressive investor, I take a close look at large-cap stocks with market caps under $3 billion. Many of these stocks have an excellent risk/reward profile and could become five baggers (my lofty target).

CHAPTER 7

MINING COMPANIES: MID-TIER PRODUCERS

Mid-Tier Producers are the sweet spot from a risk/reward perspective. They offer substantial returns, and the risk is generally moderate (as long as you buy an undervalued stock and the bull market marches onward). If I were starting out investing in gold/silver mining stocks, I would be tempted to focus most of my investment dollars in this area. If you pick ten Mid-Tier Producers, you should do very well. Returns likely will exceed 300%. Many Mid-Tier Producers are undervalued versus their growth potential. These are the stocks that can grow production at a rapid pace through acquisitions and development, and can bring substantial value to shareholders.

Van Eck Junior Gold Miners ETF (GDXJ)

One easy way to invest in Mid-Tier Producers is by using the ETF that trades with the symbol GDXJ. It began trading in late 2009. It is called a Junior Gold Miners ETF, although it no longer has any juniors and also includes several silver miners. Most of the stocks in the fund are large-cap Mid-Tier Producers, with nearly half of the stocks having $1+ billion market caps. The fund has gotten so large that most of its larger holdings are Majors.

Because GDXJ has grown into 72 stocks that are mostly large cap, the upside potential has dropped from what it once was. For this reason, it makes more sense to pick your own mid-tier producers if you want higher returns. However, if you are content with a good risk/reward stock that will track the HUI index, then GDXJ makes a lot of sense. It's a good way to allocate a significant portion of your portfolio without assuming the risk of a single stock.

Global X Silver Miners ETF (SIL)

Another Mid-Tier ETF is the Global X Silver Miners fund, which trades with the symbol NYSE:SIL. This fund was started in 2010 and includes most of the silver producers and some of the Juniors. It is a good way to reduce risk and get exposure to silver's potential rise in price. I think this fund very well could be one of the better performers over the next few years. While I am categorizing SIL as a Mid-Tier fund, it also includes Majors and Juniors.

Mid-Tier Producers Defined

Mid-Tier Producers are gold/silver companies with a market cap between $150 million and $1.5 billion (my definition). They also must produce significant amounts of gold/silver. For gold producers, this would be more than 80,000 ounces per year. For silver producers, this would be more than 3 million ounces.

These market caps and production numbers are just general guidelines, and if a company is near these numbers, you can easily put it in this category.

> Note: Professionals define Mid-Tier Producers differently. The general consensus is that a gold mining company must produce at least 200,000 ounces of gold per year to reach this category. I have reduced that total because once a company reaches 80,000 ounces of production, the risk drops dramatically. Thus, I want to capture that risk point and invest above it for risk aversion.

Emerging Mid-Tier Producers Defined

Emerging Mid-Tier Producers are companies forecasted to become Mid-Tier producers within three years (my definition). These are usually companies that have given guidance of increased production.

Growth Companies

One advantage of investing in Mid-Tier Producers and Emerging Mid-Tier Producers is that they are usually young companies with excellent growth prospects. Moreover, the stock market is reluctant to give youthful companies value for projected growth. Thus, they are likely to be undervalued when factoring in their growth potential.

Another advantage of investing in Mid-Tier Producers is that they benefit immediately when the price of gold and silver rises. I call this leveraging your investment dollars because the risk is rewarded. By investing in a Mid-Tier Producer, instead of bullion or a Major, you have accepted additional risk. I think this risk is minimal, but the upside can be amazing. Watch what happens when gold/silver prices rise. These stocks usually jump in value.

The reason these stocks jump in value is because the stock market does not value mining companies on the projected price of gold/silver. Instead, it values them on the current price of gold/silver. This is why when the price of gold rises, the mining stocks rise in tandem.

The last advantage I will mention is cash flow. These companies have cash flow and can use it for growth. They can explore (drilling exploration), expand production, and build additional mines. Plus, they can purchase smaller mining companies, usually for very low valuations. In the current economic environment, smaller companies are extremely vulnerable to financing issues and the potential for bankruptcy. This makes companies with cash, such as the Mid-Tier Producers, at a significant advantage.

Taking Advantage of Risk Leverage

Because mining stocks are valued at current gold/silver prices, this is a good thing for investors. It allows you to find undervalued Mid-Tier Producers, which will eventually get revalued higher when the price of gold/silver rises. There are a lot of undervalued companies that own significant gold and silver resources which will eventually be revalued higher. Each time the price of gold/silver goes up, these companies become more valuable. This increased valuation comes from three sources. First, their profitability improves from higher income. Second, the resources in the ground increase in value. And third, their risk level diminishes because they have more cash flow.

One important thing to understand is that, as the price of gold/silver rises, the market doesn't just add value to a stock because it has more income. The market also increases the value of the company for having increased growth prospects, reduced risk, and higher valued resources. This is why Mid-Tier Producers can be so lucrative.

Whereas Majors are too big to grow at a rapid pace, and Juniors are inherently risky, Mid-Tier Producers sit right in the middle (the sweet spot).

Production / Market Cap Correlation

Generally, Mid-Tier producers are valued somewhat closely to their production numbers (see chart below from 2012). At $2,000 gold prices, a high quality 100,000 ounce producer is generally valued at approximately $1 billion, a high quality 200,000 ounce producer at $2 billion, etc. Note that this correlation can be impacted by many factors, such as location, management, debt, cash costs, etc. Currently, due to the low sentiment for mining stocks, these valuations have dropped, but I expect them to return.

Company	**Forecasted 2013 Production**	**Market Cap 2012**
Argonaut Gold	100,000	$1.4 Billion
B2Gold	160,000	$1.4 Billion
CGA Mining	200,000	$914 Million
Perseus Mining	200,000	$1 Billion

Another valuation that tends to fit Mid-Tier Producers is the market cap value of the ounces in the ground (excluding inferred). Generally, a high-quality Mid-Tier Producer can be valued at approximately $500 per ounce. In 2019, the average for Mid-Tier producers was well under $100 per ounce. My database had 43 Mid-Tier producers, with an average of approximately $70 per ounce, and only eight stocks valued over $100 per oz. I think this will change as gold prices rise, and then we will see high-quality Mid-Tier Producers once again reach a $500 per ounce valuation.

The bad thing about Mid-Tier Producers is that usually, the best entry price was available before they became Mid-Tier Producers. For instance, Pure Gold Mining had a share price of 10 cents in 2015, several years before they began producing Thus, many of the strong Mid-Tier Producers are usually not cheap, but that does not mean they won't triple or more as the price of gold heads to a new ATH.

Finding Value

When you go looking for Mid-Tier Producers, you will generally find that most of them are not highly undervalued. The reason for this is that they have significant cash flow and substantial gold/silver reserves, which are reflected in their share price. Your job is to find the ones that are undervalued in relation to their growth prospects.

Chapter 10 was specifically written to help you to find value in mining stocks. It includes a ten-step method for analyzing stocks and finding value. After you read it, you will be much better at valuing stocks.

Categories

I have created my own mining company categories to differentiate companies and for managing risk. My definitions do not match how most professionals define companies, although they are quite similar. This book is from my viewpoint as an investor, so I have simplified company definitions to know what I am looking for, and for managing risk.

To review, I have split companies into three main categories: 1) Majors, 2) Mid-Tier Producers, and 3) Juniors. My definitions of Majors, Emerging Majors, and Mid-Tier Producers are very basic: I use current market cap and production levels for the criteria. These numbers help me to understand the upside potential and risk levels of a company.

For Juniors, I have broken them into eight different categories. Again, the purpose is to understand the upside potential and risk levels of a company. Each of these Junior categories will be explained in detail in the next chapter.

Refer to the chart below for my definitions:

Major	Greater than $3 billion Market Cap.
Emerging Major	Market Cap between $1.5-3 billion, with gold production >80,000 oz., or silver production >3 million oz.
Mid-Tier Producer	Market Cap between $300 million and $1.5 billion, with gold production >80,000 oz., or silver production >3 million oz.
Junior: Emerging Mid-Tier Producer	Forecasted to become Mid-Tier producers within three years. These are usually companies that have given guidance of increased production..
Junior: Small Producer	Producer that does not qualify as an Emerging Mid-Tier Producer
Junior: Near-Term Producer	Production forecasted to begin within two years.
Junior: Late-Stage Development	Production forecasted to begin within three to six years.
Junior: Early-Stage Explorer - enough reserves for a long life mine	Development company with enough reserves have been found for a long life mine.
Junior: Early-Stage Explorer - almost enough reserves for a long life mine	Development company with almost enough reserves have been found for a long life mine.
Junior: Project Generator	The objective of these companies is not to mine gold, but to find it and sell it in the ground to another company.
Junior: Potential Exists	If a mining company does not fit any of the other categories, then they go here - all they have is potential.
Royalty Company	Owns royalty streams.

From a risk perspective, this chart is broken into three parts, the three main categories. I know the Majors because they are the big caps. I know the Mid-Tier

Producers, because they are producing significant quantities, but are not yet Majors. Everybody else is a Junior. The Junior level is a whole other ballgame, which we will get to in the next chapter.

The Sweet Spot

I mentioned earlier that Mid-Tier Producers are the sweet spot for investing in mining stocks. However, there is also another sweet spot. A favorite sweet spot for many professional investors is finding an undervalued company with a market cap between $100 million and $300 million. The reason why it is the sweet spot is that below $100 million, and a company carries higher risk. Above $300 million, and the valuation carries less upside potential.

You will find that most quality Mid-Tier Producers do not fit into this range. Why? Because they already passed that level once they began producing. Once a company begins to produce significant quantities, the stock market immediately revalues their future reserves (gold/silver that is likely to be mined) higher. This is why mining investors are always searching for future reserves that have not yet been revalued.

Professional investors know that a market cap between $100 million to $300 million is the sweet spot for high returns, and they grab these companies when they hit this range. Gold Resource Corp. (GORO) is a good example. They zoomed through this range once production neared. Anyone who saw the potential in Gold Resource Corp., when it had a market cap under $150 million, made a very good investment (see chart below).[55] The chart trends up immediately after they announced in the last quarter of 2009 that production was ready to commence.

It turns out that the smartest investors sold at the top, when GORO reached $30 in 2011. Today, it trades for $2.70, and probably will never reach $30 again. Why did this happen? They couldn't show production growth. This is why you always want to own companies with enough resources and exploration potential to grow production.

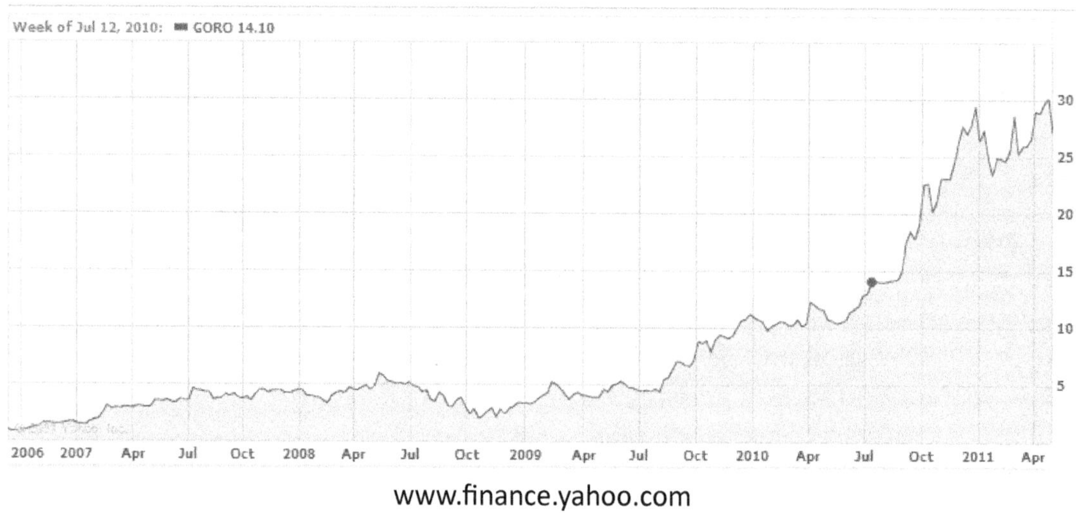

www.finance.yahoo.com

You can look at the charts of Mid-Tier Producers, and you will see where their share price zoomed into or through this range once production neared or commenced. Most of these companies will not come back down in price. You missed it, the low entry price.

The difference between a $300 million market cap Mid-Tier Producer and a less than $100 million market cap Junior, is not that much in dollar terms. However, how their M&I resources are valued by the stock market is very different. It's possible that these two companies have the same amount of M&I resources, but the Junior often does not get any credit for theirs.

It is quite common for a Junior's valuation to languish until they can get close or into production. Moreover, it is very difficult for a Junior to become a Mid-Tier Producer. In fact, it takes years. For this reason, once a company is on the verge of becoming a Mid-Tier Producer, the investment community will be watching the stock very closely.

While I say that the sweet spot is between $100 million and $300 million, I prefer to find opportunities when a company is valued around $150 million (fully diluted market cap). From experience, this seems to be an ideal Mid-Tier entry point for large returns. So, you can consider the range of $125 million to $175 million to be the sweet spot within the sweet spot.

Risk Levels

The difference in risk level between a Junior and a Mid-Tier Producer is huge. Conversely, the difference in risk level between a Mid-Tier Producer and a Major can be slight.

A good analogy is the restaurant business. Every large town has a handful of large, popular restaurants (these are the Majors). At the next level below them, there are many successful, highly profitable, mid-sized restaurants (these are the Mid-Tier Producers). It doesn't matter if you are a business owner on either of these levels, because your business is likely highly profitable and moderate risk. However, the level below them contains all of the small, risky restaurants that have low cash flow and could easily go bankrupt.

The small risky restaurants cannot grow until they reach the successful mid-sized level. Moreover, once they get to that next level, the sky is the limit. They can then open new restaurants and grow to their hearts' content. Under this scenario, the restaurant business is dependent on the economy being strong. For gold/silver mining companies, they are dependent on the price of gold/silver rising or staying high.

If you understand this analogy, you will understand why investing in early or Emerging Mid-Tier Producers is a sweet spot of investing in gold/silver mining companies. As further evidence of this fact, any Junior that shows signs of potentially becoming a Mid-Tier Producer will see its market cap rise to approximately $100 million. This is a signal to investors that the stock market has taken note that a Mid-Tier Producer is on the horizon. It is very rare for a mining company to reach this market cap level without some evidence that they have the potential to achieve the Mid-Tier Producer level (my definition).

Most savvy investors like to catch these potential Mid-Tier Producers when they are still Juniors and have a low market cap. But the risk level really jumps at these lower valuations (below $100 million), since these are Juniors.

It is smart to focus on near-term Mid-Tier Producers. The market caps for these companies will likely be around $150 million or even higher. Once you have a few solid Mid-Tier Producers, then you can play the Junior risk game and try to find the gems in the sweet spot, or at lower valuations below the sweet spot.

Catching the Right Stock

This next paragraph is one of the most important things I have learned as a mining stock investor. The difference between a $25 million market cap Junior and a $150 million market cap near-term Mid-Tier Producer is like night and day from a risk perspective. Catching a $25 million Junior that is going to grow to $125 million, versus catching a $150 million near-term Mid-Tier Producer that will grow to $750 million, is not a valid comparison. One has high risk and long odds, while the other can have low risk and short odds. The difference in risk can be huge.

Finding undervalued $25 million market cap Juniors is easy; however, finding undervalued $150 million near-term Mid-Tier Producers is not so easy. When you find those, you invest in them. Are you catching on to this game? To catch an early Mid-Tier Producer, you have to anticipate that a company is going to become one. Once you recognize the potential, you jump on board. Yes, this is risky, but this is how you get the low entry prices and make a large return. This is how the professionals do it, and I'm telling you the secrets of the game. I had to learn them on my own. But anyone who is investment savvy can take these secrets and make a lot of money (as long as this bull market continues).

The professionals often invest in potential Mid-Tier Producers years in advance. Companies like Pure Gold Mining signaled their potential through drill results and development efforts, years before production takes place. I will be explaining this in the next chapter on Juniors. For Mid-Tier Producers, you want to find undervalued producers or companies that are very close to becoming Mid-Tier Producers. You want to find companies that are undervalued (using my simple valuation formulas) and have a low market cap (start small and grow big), good properties, an economic project (with low cash costs), good management, good location, tight share structure, and growth prospects (production and resources). They are out there, and you can find them.

Majors vs. Mid-Tier Producers

Some of you may be asking, why invest in Majors when Mid-Tier Producers are reasonably safe with solid returns? That is a good question. Often, the only difference between a Major and Mid-Tier Producer are the dividends that Majors pay, although many Mid-Tier Producers also pay dividends. Some analysts will say that a Major has less risk, but you could argue that point. I feel just as comfortable owning a high-quality Mid-Tier producer as a Major.

It doesn't matter if a company owns multiple mines. All it will take to hurt the stock price is a problem at one of their mines. Those extra mines aren't going to help their stock price if production falls. A good example of this is Hecla Mining, which lost production at one of their mines in 2018 and their stock got slammed. Thus, a company with a single producing mine offers no more risk than a company with several (unless, of course, their single mine has a problem).

Let's face it, investing in mining companies is risky. This is why it is important to use diversification. If you create a balanced portfolio of bullion, Majors, Mid-Tier Producers, and Juniors, then you will reduce your overall risk. And never invest too much in a single stock. Always be able to lose a single stock without a significant loss to your portfolio.

I never invest more than 3% of my total portfolio cost basis in an individual mining stock. I only exceed 3% for bullion, ETFs, or mutual funds. The majority of my individual mining stocks are below 1% of my total portfolio cost basis, with a minority between 1% to 2%, and only a few between 2% to 3%.

If I have a stock with a cost basis above 2%, it makes me concerned. This generally only happens because of a merger between two stocks that I own, or if I bought more shares to lower my cost basis. Conversely, if I own a stock with a cost basis below 1%, I have much less concern.

Getting the Right Entry Price

If you get a good entry price for a Mid-Tier Producer at a low valuation in this bull market, you are likely going to get a 300% return. And that investment will be relatively safe (as long as it passes all of the factors I have mentioned). Currently, mining stocks are depressed and getting a good entry price is fairly easy. It seems as though most stocks are significantly undervalued. And by reading this book, you now have the tools and knowledge necessary to go looking.

Most of your home runs (1,000% return) will come from Juniors who are on their way to becoming Mid-Tier Producers. However, in this bull market, it will not surprise me to see several Mid-Tier Producers become home runs.

A good entry price for a Mid-Tier Producer is primarily based on three things:

1. Resources are being valued cheaply by the stock market.
2. Production is going to increase significantly in the future.
3. Resources are likely to grow because of exploration potential.

While these are the primary factors, the company has to have passed the previous factors mentioned in the last chapter. I could have also included an increasing price for gold/silver in this list, but that is an underlying assumption.

Gold/Silver Mining Sector is Being Ignored

I don't know if the demand for mining stocks will increase in the near future. But today, the gold/silver mining sector is largely being ignored. I think this is because people don't understand it and are afraid of the risk. For this reason, there are a lot of opportunities.

For instance, in 2019, the total global market cap for silver mining stocks was about $30 billion, and for gold mining stocks it was about $225 billion. This is tiny compared to the value of all global stocks and bonds. The global bond market is over $75 trillion, and the global stock markets are over $50 trillion. When you compare these huge asset values to gold mining stocks, it is less than one-tenth of one percent. At some point, I expect this percentage to increase, and potentially quite dramatically.

Ideal Emerging Mid-Tier Producer

The ideal Junior that is close to becoming a Mid-Tier Producer would look something like this:

- Right market cap ($100 million to $150 million)
- Right valuation ($50 per oz. gold or $2 per oz. silver)
- Late-Stage Development (Production scheduled to begin within three years)
- Large resources (2 million oz. of gold or 40 million oz. of silver)
- Additional properties (Growth prospects and drilling programs)
- Low cash costs
- Economic project
- Good management
- Good location Tight share structure
- Low debt
- Good drilling results (Expanding resources)
- Significant cash on hand
- No hedging
- 100% ownership of properties
- All licenses obtained
- Financing obtained

Note: When you are analyzing whether to invest in a company, don't pay attention to the price of the stock. (Notice that is not one of my criteria.) This is a mistake that many investors make.

Ideal Mid-Tier Producer

The above criteria would bring some risk to your portfolio, since this is not truly a Mid-Tier Producer. And something could go wrong, thereby delaying or cancelling production. For this reason, you only want to select a few of these near-term, Emerging Mid-Tier Producers.

For maintaining less risk, you can initially focus on solid companies, such as Lakeshore Gold, Timmins Gold, or Argonaut Gold who have significant resources and growth potential. These are relatively low risk, solid companies.

For these companies, the criteria is a little bit different:

- Right market cap (Less than $1 Billion)
- Significant production (100,000 oz. of gold, or 3 million oz. of silver)
- Large resources (2 million oz. of gold, or 40 million oz. of silver)
- Good drilling results (Pointing towards expanding reserves)
- Growth prospects (Another property scheduled to begin production)
- Economic projects
- Good management
- Good location
- Tight share structure
- Low debt
- Significant cash on hand
- No hedging
- 100% ownership of properties
- Low to medium cost structure

Stock Valuation

Valuation for Mid-Tier Producers can be done using the criteria from the preceding chapter. However, quite often they are just now ramping up production, and cash flow may only be an estimate. One nice thing about the Internet is that you can often find what you need to perform a valuation.

Let's look at Argonaut Gold for a valuation example:

Argonaut Gold Valuation (2013)

Debt Coverage

Cash Flow = Production minus Costs
(Production oz. x Current Metal Price) - (Production oz. x Cost Per oz.)

Debt = Debt - Cash
(Always subtract cash, since it could be used to pay off debt.)

Debt Coverage = Cash Flow / Debt

Production = 200,000 equivalent ounces of gold (estimated)
Cost Per Ounce = $1,150 ($750 cash cost, plus $400 padded operations costs)

Current Gold Price = $1,300

Cash Flow = (200,000 x 1,300) - (200,000 x 1,150) = $30,000,000
Debt = $8,000,000 (debt) - 21,000,000 (cash) = -$13,000,000

$30 million   Cash Flow, divided by

----------------   = No Debt

$-13 million   Debt

Argonaut does not have any debt when you subtract their cash. Their cash position is very strong and allows them to grow organically.

Market Cap Valuation Per Resource Ounce

$243 million   Fully Diluted Market Cap, divided by

----------------   = $30 Market Cap Value Per Gold oz.

8 million   Resource Ounces (excluding inferred)

Each ounce in the ground is valued at $30 by market cap.

This is very low for a company of Argonaut's quality and is reflection of the gold price correction.

Share Price Valuation by Resources in the Ground

8 million Resource Ounces, divided by

---------------- = .04 Ounces

183 million Shares Outstanding Fully Diluted

Each share represents .04 ounces of resources.

Each share is worth $56 of gold in the ground ($1,300 x .04 oz.)

This is very cheap. Ideally you want to buy below $100. This is not a crucial valuation criteria, but is good to use to find red flags or highly undervalued stocks.

Resource Valuation as a Percentage of Market Cap

Step 1: Value of Resources:

8 million (Resource Ounces) x $1,300 (Current Gold Price) = $10 billion

Step 2:

$243 million Market Cap Fully Diluted, divided by

---------------- = 2.4%

$10 billion Value of Resources (excluding inferred)

The market cap is currently valued at 2.4% of the resources in the ground. This is very cheap, and another indicator that is highly undervalued. We are trying to find valuations around 10% or less.

Quick and Dirty Market Cap Valuation

Step 1: Current Value of Resources (excluding inferred)

8 million (Resource Ounces) x $1,300 (Current Gold Price) = $10 billion

Step 2: Current Value of Resources at 15% (I would use 10% for a non-producer)

$10 billion x 15% = $1.5 billion (quick and dirty valuation)

Actual market cap fully diluted: $243 million

The current valuation of the market cap appears to be undervalued (when compared to the quick and dirty valuation). Moreover, if you use a future perspective of 8 million ounces of minable resources, you get this:

Step 1: Future Value of Resources (excluding inferred)

8 million (Future Reserve Ounces) x $2,500 (Future Gold Price) = $20 billion

Step 2: Future Value of Resources at 15% (I would use 10% for a non-producer)

$20 billion x 15% = $3 billion (quick and dirty valuation)

When you compare $3 billion to the current market cap, it appears to be highly undervalued. This is only a theoretical future market cap, but if gold prices take off, a market cap of this magnitude is possible.

Cash Flow Multiple

Market Cap = $243 million

Cash Flow = Production minus Costs

(Production oz. x Current Metal Price) - (Production oz. x Cost Per oz.)

Cash Flow = (200,000 x $1,300) - (200,000 x $1,150) = $30,000,000

$243 million   Market Cap Fully Diluted, divided by

---------------- = 8

$30 million   Cash Flow

In this instance, the market cap is 8 times the cash flow, which is not undervalued. A good Mid-Tier Producer should be valued with a market cap approximately 10 times the cash flow. However, this cash flow reflects current gold prices, which I think are heading higher.

Valuation: It's All About the Market Cap

From an investor's standpoint, it's all about the market cap. How big can it get? To move it higher, you need increased cash flow. That can happen mainly from two factors: 1) An increase in the price of gold/silver, or 2) An increase in production. If you get both, you have hit the lottery. The one big factor that can work against you is costs. As I said earlier, beware of energy costs. Spikes in oil prices are not beneficial to the mining industry, which use a lot of diesel and electricity.

As you have seen from my valuation methods, I tend to keep it simple. A good investment should stand out. You shouldn't have to get into the details and worry about the net present value of a project or what the project is supposed to pay out on a discounted basis. There are too many variables to worry about in the mining business. It's best to get your head around simple cash flow expectations if everything goes according to plan. The one exception is the IRR. This is the rate of return of a project. You don't want to invest in projects with low IRRs. I prefer an IRR of at least 25% after-tax, but I will go down to 15% if I like the stock (these are usually optionality plays).

> Note: Companies release the IRR of a project when they produce their mining plans. The first IRR is released with the PEA (preliminary economic assessment). I will discuss this in more detail in the next chapter.

The IRR is important for two reasons. First, it is a good indicator of cash flow and the profitability of a project. Second, the higher the IRR, the easier it is to finance a mine. Any project with an after-tax IRR above 35% usually can get financed. The exceptions are generally small projects with a short mine life. The other exception is small companies with a large capex. Even if the project is economic, bankers generally do not like to give small companies large loans.

The previous case of Argonaut Gold is a good example of using simple valuations techniques to spot undervalued stocks. They have everything in place to take advantage of this bull market. As the price of gold/silver increases, so will their stock, because their resources and profitability will get revalued higher. And if they continue increasing production and resources, that will also benefit the stock. Companies like Argonaut Gold are leveraged for higher gold prices. The coming higher gold prices will go right to their bottom line and right into their share price.

Future Market Cap Valuation

Let's do a future market cap growth calculation for Argonaut Gold using $2,500 gold and 8 million ounces of future reserves (minable resources).

> Cash Flow - (Future Production oz. x Future Metal Price) - (Future Production oz. x Future Cost Per oz.)

Cash Flow = (300,000 x $2,500) - (300,000 x $1,200) = $390,000,000

Future Market Cap Method #1

Future Cash Flow x Cash Flow Multiplier = Future Market Cap

$390 million x 5 = $1.9 Billion (5 is conservative)

Future Market Cap Method #2

Future Reserves x Future Gold Price x 10% = Future Market Cap

8 million oz. x $2,500 x .10 = $2 Billion (10% is conservative)

Future Market Cap Growth Rate

(Future Market Cap - Current Market Cap) / Current Market Cap =
Future Market Cap Growth

($2 billion - $243 million) / $243 million = 700% Return

Argonaut Gold might not reach this future market cap estimate. But if gold prices do rise to $2,500, and they can increase production to 300,000 ounces, the odds are very good that they will become at least a five-bagger, and possibly a 10+ bagger. I currently have them with an upside rating of 3. That rating projects a potential five bagger (see ratings chart below). I will be explaining my ratings in Chapter 10..

Ratings Chart

Upside

1	Lowest Rating
1.5	Potential 2 Bagger
2	Potential 3 Bagger
2.5	Likely 3 Bagger
3	Potential 5 Bagger
3.5	Likely 5 Bagger
4	Potential 10 Bagger
4.5	Likely 7-8 Bagger
5	Likely 10 Bagger

Downside

1	Lowest Rating
1.5	Very poor risk/reward
2	Poor risk/reward
2.5	Marginal risk/reward
3	Good risk/reward
3.5	Excellent risk/reward
4	Tremendous risk/reward
4.5	Stellar risk/reward
5	Rare risk/reward

Cash Flow Will Fund Growth

The way the mining business works is that the successful tend to get more successful. They use their strong financial position to make acquisitions (usually undervalued Juniors). In other words, they can finance their growth once they get going. This is why you want to jump on Mid-Tier Producers who are just starting out. These companies can turn into Majors and have their stock prices explode in value. Of course, this does not happen overnight. It can take years.

I have a saying, "You don't make your big money on the first mine." It usually comes later, on the second or third mine. My hope with Argonaut Gold is that they build their cash and then use it to purchase another company or two. If they pursue this strategy, they could grow into a large company with a much larger market cap.

A good investor buys a stock once they see an opportunity, even if it could be a long-term investment. In the mining sector, a typical investment is 3-5 years. Of course, there are a lot of short-term investors who like to chase drill results and trends. However, I don't think it is smart to invest for the short term with mining companies. If you try to focus on the short term, you are going to be playing a risky game. Of course, if we do have a mania phase, which I expect, a short-term investment could be lucrative.

CHAPTER 8

MINING COMPANIES: JUNIORS

Investing in Juniors is a completely different animal than investing in Majors or Mid-Tier Producers. The difference in risk is so substantial that it is almost like investing in a completely different asset class. To give you an idea of the difference, consider the number of gold and silver mining companies in each of the three main categories. Currently, there are approximately 1,000 Juniors, but only 24 Majors, 4 Emerging Majors, and 62 Mid-Tier Producers.

As you can see, it is not easy for Juniors to move up to the next level, which is a very exclusive club of about 90 mining companies. In fact, most analysts would consider about one-third of my Mid-Tier producers to be Juniors. So, the true club of large-cap and mid-size producers is only about 55 mining companies.

Because it is difficult for Juniors to succeed, there is enormous risk in this sector. However, with high risk comes high return, and that is the allure of Juniors. By managing risk and allocating investments into the various Junior categories, you can have lucrative returns. As you will learn in this chapter, managing risk while investing in Juniors is possible (as long as you know what you are doing).

Taking Advantage of Opportunities

I remember when the stock market crashed in 2008 and mining stocks collapsed. I looked around like a kid in a candy store. What to buy? I put at least 20 stocks on my buy list. However, I could not buy them all until I accumulated more cash.

One of the first stocks I bought was First Majestic Silver, which was trading around $1. I knew at that time it would easily be a $10 stock before this bull market was over and likely a $20 stock. I quickly snatched up 10,000 shares and couldn't believe the market was pricing it this low. It was an easy trade to figure out (after you read this book, you will know why it was undervalued). Amazingly, this stock stayed under $2 for nearly another year (see chart below).[56]

www.finance.yahoo.com

For First Majestic, my expected return (based on my entry price) is 5,000% at $100 silver. Where else can you find those kinds of returns? Back in 2008, First Majestic was projecting 10 million ounces of annual silver production by 2012 at low cash costs, so this was a low-risk trade. While low-risk trades with 50 times returns are not the norm, today there are dozens of Juniors that are extremely undervalued. The opportunities for large returns in gold and silver mining stocks are there for the taking.

First Majestic was a Mid-Tier Producer, so the risk/reward was excellent after the share price crashed. Generally, you will not find those types of risk/reward opportunities for Juniors. However, what you will find is high return potential with higher risk. Sometimes, Juniors will rise rapidly in a very short time frame. For instance, take a look at what happened to Aurelian Gold in 2006.

Aurelian was a small gold explorer trading around 50 cents. Then they released drill results for a new mine in Ecuador. They hit 4.4 grams of gold per ton over 200 meters at the surface. This was a monster hole, but not proof that a large deposit was discovered. After the results were released, the stock price barely moved. Then they reported another hole of 200 meters with an average of 8 grams per ton! This confirmed that the first drill result was not an anomaly, and the high grade was stunning for a surface mine. The stock price exploded.

Those who heard about these two news releases were very lucky. I wasn't one of them. I didn't hear about it until the stock was at $7. The stock zoomed from 50 cents to $37 in just a few months (7,400% return). That one mine found 13 million ounces of gold.

While the Aurelians of this world are extremely rare, Juniors with excellent properties can be found and leveraged for maximum benefit. The one thing most Juniors have in common is they generally have significant upside potential. Most of them have a market cap under $100 million. I have 728 Juniors in my database, and only 125 have a market cap over $100 million.

If gold prices increase as much as they did during the last gold bull market (1971 to 1980), when gold rocketed from $35 to $850, many Juniors are going to be 10+ baggers. That bull market saw gold prices rise 23 times from start to finish. This bull market began at $250 gold in 1999. Using a 23 multiple, that would place the projected high at $5,000 per oz. to exceed the last bull market.

Dismal Winning Percentage

The first thing to know about Juniors is that it is extremely difficult to find new mines. For every drill target that an experienced, knowledgeable geologist picks, only about 1 in 100 will find significant mineralization that is economic to mine.[57] Thus, 99% of new mine drilling targets are dry holes!

And that 1 in 100 mineralized hole discovery doesn't mean they found a mine. It just means that this single hole found mineralization that is economical to mine. They still have to find enough ounces nearby. It is estimated that only about 1 in 500 drill targets results in a producing mine. Can you imagine the difficulty?

What an incredibly dismal winning percentage. And these drilling programs are not cheap. It can cost millions of dollars to fund one drilling program. Usually, Junior Exploration companies will spend anywhere from $1 million to $20 million annually on exploration. With these large outlays and the likelihood of finding a large mine nearly impossible, the risk is enormous.

So, if you are a Junior Exploration company, your odds are dismal of ever bringing a mine into production, let alone becoming a Mid-Tier Producer. Most Junior Exploration companies can get enough funding for several drilling programs. And if they are lucky enough to find a few good holes of mineralization, they can go back and get additional financing to continue their exploration. It is always a race against time and money to find a property that is economically viable for a producing mine. The odds are so slim that it is amazing these exploration companies get any financing at all.

Junior Risk Levels

As you can imagine, funding one of these Junior Explorers is about as risky an investment as one can make. For most of us savvy investors, we don't buy a single share until they release their drill results. This is when the potential of the property comes into play. For Juniors, it's always about potential. Do they have a shot at finding a producing mine? And if they do, will it become an operating mine?

Investing in Juniors is all about identifying and understanding the risk, and offsetting that with the potential upside. The key for Juniors is their properties, although the management team can be just as important. Once a property reveals its value, the risk level begins to diminish.

Nearly all Juniors (because the risk level is so high) begin with a very low market cap. These market caps are generally less than $5 million, which is enough to fund a few drilling programs. Normally, any company with a market cap under $5 million has not yet found any significant mineralization (1 million oz. of gold or 20 million oz. of silver). They are either drilling to find some or trying to raise money for drilling. There are some micro-cap companies that have found significant mineralization, but they are the exception.

Once a gold/silver Junior reaches a market cap beyond $10 million, they usually have found (or own) mineralization that could be a mine. These are companies that have proven their potential by releasing good drill results or resource estimates. However, until they approach the $50 million market cap level, they likely have not yet proven the economic viability to potentially produce a mine. Once companies start inching towards a $100 million market cap, the risk level begins decreasing. At this point, the project has either reached a level where a mine has become viable, or the odds of this occurrence have increased dramatically.

My personal sweet spot for investing is the $50 million to $150 million market cap range. This is a risky range but offers enormous rewards if you pick the right companies. Risk begins to decrease significantly around the $150 million market cap level. For this reason, many savvy investors focus on the $150 million to $300 million market cap range. That's as low as they will go, in order to reduce their risk exposure.

While my preference is to buy companies with market caps between $50 million and $150 million, that does not stop me from buying stocks with market caps much lower or much higher. I prefer the sweet spot companies because they tend to have a better risk/reward profile. I also know from experience, that buying companies with an FD market cap under $50 million has led to a lot of losses. In hindsight, I probably should have just avoided micro-cap stocks. But where is the fun in that?

43-101 Report

Once a company finds a property with gold/silver on it, they will expand their drilling program. Steadily, as a company releases drill results, the market cap will rise to match their increasing potential. As they drill and find more mineralization, they will continue to add tons of mineralization at specific ore grades.

At this early stage of exploration, a 43-101 report most likely has not yet been issued. This is the legal report that validates and defines the Measured and Indicated (M&I) Resources, as well as the Inferred Resources. Once this report is issued, if there are enough ounces in the ground for a viable mine, the stock price will normally rise above $10 million, and perhaps above $100 million, based on the number of ounces that were found.

As an investor, you will have two choices: 1) Wait for the 43-101 to confirm the viability of a mine. 2) Invest prior to its release and take a gamble that it is going to be a good report. Once a good report is released, the company will then begin the development phase (unless more drilling is necessary), which will take three to 10 years (refer to the Mining Life Cycle in Appendix C). The development phase nearly always begins with a PEA (preliminary economic assessment), followed by a pre-feasibility study, which is essentially the blueprints for building the mine. If it is an economic project, it will then be permitted and financed, culminating in construction of the mine.

There are many variables that affect the timeframe for developing mines. Often permits are delayed for years at a time. In some mining friendly countries, a mine can be permitted and built in three years, but that is not the norm. I would estimate that it takes on average about five to seven years from the time a company decides to build a mine until completion. Of course, small mines take less time to build, and large mines require more time. Also, permitting varies from country to country, with the USA being the slowest.

Another good rule of thumb is that it will generally take at least five years to begin production from the time the PEA (preliminary economic assessment) is released. Some small projects can get built in three or four years, but these are not the norm.

After the pre-feasibility study (the mine plan) is released, the stock price will often surge (if it is a good report and matches expectations). However, from that period until the project receives financing and begins construction, the stock price will often languish. Investors usually will refuse to give a company credit for future production. The attitude will be, "Prove it!" Once financing and all of the permits are obtained, the stock will begin to surge again as construction nears. Then, after production begins, the stock will make its last surge when reserves are finally valued at their fair market value.

Financing / Working Capital

Before I begin explaining each of the eight junior categories, a word about financing. Most Juniors are not well capitalized, and subsequently, are constantly raising money. Moreover, the few rare juniors that have $10 million or more in the bank, never seem to have enough. Why? Because most of them do not have any cash flow. And even those that do have cash flow have ambitions to grow.

The mining business is very cash intensive. Production, exploration, development, and expansion all cost money. Conversely, it is rare for a junior to be able to organically fund their needs. From my research, I have found that most Juniors raise money on an annual basis, and some of them do financings twice a year. These can be public equity financings, private equity financings, debt financings, or forward gold sales. Any way they can raise money, they will.

Because Juniors are so dependent on a consistent inflow of money from outside investors, they are extremely vulnerable to cash flow problems. If gold prices drop, or if their projects lose their appeal, they can quickly be shutout of financing options. Even if gold prices are high, there will always be companies that are languishing and heading toward bankruptcy because of financing issues (lack of working capital). This is always a threat when you invest in a Junior.

The ugly part of financings is share dilution. It is not uncommon for Juniors to dilute their share price substantially. I do not mind when a company dilutes 5% of their shares, but when they dilute 25% or 50%, that is painful for shareholders. I have seen instance after instance of Juniors doing reverse splits after diluting millions of shares.

Junior: Near-Term Producer

Junior: Near-Term Producer defined (my definition): Production forecasted to begin within two years.

The key for these stocks is the size of the mine they are building. If it is a small mine with low resources, then I am rarely interested. I'm chasing cash flow, and how much will a small mine provide? However, there are exceptions. Sometimes a company with a large mine will build the small mine first to finance development of the larger mine. I like those types of situations since I am a long-term investor. The other exception is when the small mine has the potential to grow into a larger mine.

If a company is building a potentially large mine (approximately 2+ million oz. of gold or 40+ million oz. of silver), then I am always interested to analyze the upside potential. I want to get in early if I like the project, because the market refuses to value future production, and these stocks are usually undervalued. The key is how much are they undervalued? This is where the valuation methods that I have already discussed come in handy.

If a company has made it to this category, then it likely has obtained financing and has either began construction or is close. The risk of buying these stocks is that there is always a chance that they will get acquired by a larger company. Thus, you will tie-up your capital, and all you will get in return is a small premium.

I should mention that nothing is better than when you own a stock that is building its first mine and it makes its first pour. That is when then risk diminishes for the stock, and now they are on the road to growth. Of course, the key to that growth is that the company making the first pour has a quality project. Also, it might take another three to five years until they build their second mine. These are the stocks that you get in early and hope they build two or three mines and become a large company.

Juniors that are near production are not necessarily home runs, and they are much riskier than Mid-Tier Producers. For instance, I would rather own a Mid-Tier Producer because they have less risk. A Near-Term Producer might perform well, but there is also a lot of risk. They still have to prove they can bring the mine into production and achieve their guidance targets. Plus, they have to find a way to grow production.

I buy Near-Term Producers because I like to diversify my risk-reward opportunities. And these stocks can offer large potential returns. The key to building a portfolio is having the right balance of risk and safety that matches your investment goals. The more risk-averse your temperament, the less Junior exposure you want to have, especially high-risk Juniors. However, if you are a gambler at heart, then Juniors are a lot of fun.

Stock Price Volatility

You might think that a Junior near production should hold its value. However, this is not always the case. The primary things that impact the volatility of the share price are the price of gold/silver, production expectations, share dilution, and drill results. Any of these can impact the price prior to production.

Stock price volatility is the bane of gold/silver mining investors. It's not uncommon for the share price of a company to drop 50% or more in a single year. The large drops are usually due to a drop in gold/silver prices, and all it takes is a small drop in the gold/silver price to have a big impact on the share price. The "market" tends to price-in the perfect scenario for a stock, and any deviation from that expectation is often sold off.

Risk Levels

I categorize companies into four different risk levels: extreme, high, moderate, and low. You can think of this as a chart, with the least risky stocks on the left side, and the high speculation risky stocks on the right. On the left, you will have most of the Majors and the strong Mid-Tier Producers. However, you will also have some Juniors if they have all of the right factors, such as strong management, good location, flagship property, strong balance sheet, cash flow or financing for production, growth prospects, etc.

A low-risk stock can be defined as a stock that has a low probability of falling dramatically in value or going bankrupt. These are strong companies because they have profitable properties in good locations, and investors are unlikely to abandon them. These are companies with proven management teams that have shown they know how to execute.

> Note: I have come to believe that it is a rare occurrence for a gold/silver mining stock to have low risk. This is because they are impacted so dramatically by the price of gold/silver, as well as many other factors, such as politics. The bottom line is that gold/silver mining is a high-risk endeavor.

In the middle of the chart would be the moderate risk stocks. These are stocks that have some red flags, but overall have enough positive factors to keep them out of the right side of the chart. It is kind of easy to identify these stocks because they don't fit into the other two categories. There is always something that stands out that removes them from being either low risk or high risk.

The moderate-risk level stocks usually stand out as being a strong stock with a lot of positive factors, but not enough to make it to the low-risk level. These positive factors can be a number of things, but are usually related to their properties. This can be a producing property or a property that has a high probability of being built into a mine. Currently, I have 180 companies listed as moderate risk in my database. That might be a bit optimistic, but these are companies that I think have a good chance to succeed. Some of them might run into cash flow issues, but that is why they are not low-risk companies. Do not confuse moderate risk with no risk. These companies can fail.

On the right side of the chart are stocks that do not have enough factors to move them out of the high-risk category. This is usually because of potential cash flow issues. Non-producing stocks are dependent on investors to keep them solvent. If investors lose confidence in a company, they can easily be faced with bankruptcy. The biggest risk in the mining business is running out of cash. However, there are other risks besides cash that can make a stock go down. For instance, many stocks are valued based on expectations, and when these expectations are not met, they can fall in value, often dramatically. If drill results, cash costs, profitability, ore grade, recovery rates, etc., do not meet expectations, it can be detrimental to the stock.

Most stocks are high risk because of the potential for not meeting investor expectations. A lot can go wrong in the mining business, and unless a company is positioned to avoid these missed expectations, they will fall into the high-risk level.

The final risk level is extreme. I reserve this for stocks with a high likelihood of bankruptcy. If I give a stock a downside rating of 1 (the lowest), then it also gets labeled with extreme risk. If a stock has very high risk, but it is not extreme, then I give it a downside rating of 1.5 and label it high risk. My downside ratings of 1 and 1.5 are red flags to stay away.

All of these risk levels have different degrees. For instance, if two companies are both listed as high risk that does not mean they have the same degree of risk. One high-risk company can be a very high-risk speculation stock, while another could be close to the moderate-risk level. It is your job to analyze a stock and understand its risk level. That is perhaps the best value of this book. As we go more into these Junior categories, you will get a better understanding of these degrees of risk.

Junior: Late-Stage Development

Junior: Late-Stage Development defined: Production forecasted to begin within three to six years (my definition).

This category includes many stocks with huge upside potential. Often investors will ignore these stocks if they are several years away from production, even if they have large resources. I often invest in these companies, even though they have substantial risk. I try to find companies that will begin construction within three years and have a path to production. Once construction begins, these stocks tend to begin rising in value as they approach production.

The highest risk with this category is that the mine doesn't get built and the stock price languishes. Also, there is always the threat of a takeover (or a joint venture) by a larger company. When a company gets acquired, instead of a huge potential return, it usually ends up being less than 50%. Some people like instant 50% returns, but I don't. I buy these highly undervalued stocks to get big returns, and when a larger company steps in, which happens quite often in the mining business, it is frustrating. It often feels like the takeover company is stealing from you because they are the ones who will get the big returns.

Another risk with this category is financing. If a company has a solid project but can't get financing, they are often forced to seek a JV partner or sell the project. If a project is not moving forward, the board of directors often has little patience to wait. This is why when during this recent gold and silver price correction from 2011 to 2018, so many development projects were sold at cheap prices. Revett Mining, Gold Canyon Resources, Sunward Resources, Mega Precious Minerals, Kaminak Gold, Truegold Mining, Mines Management, Dalradian Gold, Brazilian Gold, Bellhaven Gold, Kiska Metals, and Northern Gold all sold their large projects for small premiums.

Shareholders of these companies became victims of a takeover and were not allowed to wait for higher gold and silver prices. Who knows how valuable these companies could have become at much higher gold and silver prices?

My Favorite Place to Find 10 Baggers

There are many stocks in this category with huge potential upside. When you research companies that are getting close to becoming producers, you will recognize the potential upside. The key will be, how do you decide if it is a good investment?

This is where investing in Juniors is difficult and often a crapshoot. Which ones are going to pay off? If you choose the right stock, the upside can be tremendous. If you invest in companies before they begin production, you can follow them all the way to production and beyond. Many people who invested in Kirkland Lake Gold at $2 or Silver Standard (now SSR Mining) at $1 still own their stock and will likely watch them reach new highs.

Late-Stage Development is my favorite place to find 10 baggers because you can find some great opportunities. However, I do not take my eye off having a balanced portfolio. I understand that there is significant risk in this category and that I will have a few disappointments. My strategy is to invest in enough stocks in this category to find a few big winners. In this bull market, one stock could take you close to retirement.

Managing risk in my portfolio is always in the back of my mind. But taking some calculated risks is part of creating a balanced portfolio. If you only play it safe, you will never find those big winners, and this is a category that is going to produce a lot of home runs in the long term.

While Late Stage Development might be my favorite place to find 10 baggers, I know that Mid-Tier producers have the best risk/reward profile. However, it is not easy to find high returns for Mid-Tier producers unless you get a good entry price or the company becomes a growth stock.

Sometimes you have to take a risk to get a big return. When you find an undervalued advanced-stage project that has a path to production in 3-5 years, along with all of the factors that I have mentioned, then buy it and hold it.

You will have to decide how much timeline risk (the time until production) you want to assume. Can you wait five years until production, or is three years your maximum? These stocks tend to languish until they finally get close to production, so stock price volatility comes into play.

The key for big returns (which I discuss in the next chapter) is finding upside potential. This is the difference between the current market cap and your projected future market cap. Just about every company I invest in has significant upside potential, otherwise, what's the point? You want a company that has a solid property (or properties) that is going to generate increasing cash flow. Not all of your stock picks will provide a huge payoff, but if you find enough of these companies, you increase your odds. What is the saying? "You create your own luck."

Junior: Emerging Mid-Tier Producer

Emerging Mid-Tier Producer defined: These are gold/silver companies forecasted to become Mid-Tier producers within three years (my definition). These are usually companies that have given guidance of increased production.

This category offers excellent opportunities. There is a degree of risk because they have not yet obtained Mid-Tier Producer status, but they are on the threshold. If you can find one of these companies that is undervalued and has growth prospects, it can be a very good investment. This is one of the best risk/reward opportunities if you can find a highly undervalued stock in this category. You analyze these companies the same way you would a mid-tier producer. The only thing that is different is that they are little bit smaller.

Junior: Small Producer

Junior: Small Producer defined: Producer that does not qualify as an Emerging Mid-Tier Producer (my definition).

The key to Small Producers is their growth potential. However, they usually have resource issues and limited upside potential. If a company is producing and is not an Emerging Mid-Tier Producer, the reason is usually low resource properties. If you can find a small producer that does not have resource issues and appears to have a good chance of becoming a Mid-Tier Producer, then you have probably found a good investment. Sometimes Small Producers can be so undervalued that it simply makes sense to buy them.

From experience, I have learned that small producers often carry more risk than anticipated. The reason why is because they generally do not have very much cash flow. They can get into trouble with their balance sheet if gold/silver prices drop. I have witnessed several small producers get into trouble. For this reason, I am now very careful when picking small producers.

The key factor for me with small producers is their exploration and production growth potential. If a Small Producer is valued around $50 million and passes all of the factors that I look at, plus it has the potential to become a Mid-Tier Producer, then I might take a chance. If my gut says that it will always be a Small Producer, then I likely will pass.

Valuation Factors: A Review

Okay, we have covered the Juniors that are relatively easy to value: Near-Term Producer, Late-Stage Development, Emerging Mid-Tier Producer, and Small Producer. If you use the methods I have described to value these stocks, then you will get an idea of what the stock price should do over the next few years, as gold/silver prices increase. Let's review some of the factors to check, other than stock price valuation, before we move on to the really risky Juniors: the Explorers.

Management

Management is crucial in the mining business. The reason for this is that mining is difficult, and experience is required to succeed. I have found that many management teams are more concerned with paying themselves and the board of directors through continuous stock options, rather than focusing on finding and developing mines. It is tempting to take from the cookie jar when you are in a position to do so, and in the mining business, this is quite common.

There are certain CEOs who have a stellar reputation and are focused on providing investor value. Three of these are Ross Beaty at Equinox Gold, Keith Neumeyer at First Majestic Silver, and Rob McEwen at McEwen Mining. While it is not always easy to find these types of people when you go looking for undervalued companies, try to get an idea of the type of CEO or management team in which you are investing.

For small market cap Junior Explorers, management is not as important as it is for companies that are producing or building mines. Management teams that operate mines have to focus on growth and hitting their forecasts, which is not easy to achieve in mining. A management team that is successful at growth is rare and will return significant returns to shareholders. Juniors who have small market caps are trying to prove up a mine. What is important here are the drill results. Thus, for small market cap Juniors Explorers, you are often betting more on the geology and geologist than the management team.

It is my opinion that you shouldn't invest in any Junior that doesn't already have excellent drill results or a significant discovery. I have heard many gold analysts speak highly of stocks because of the management team, regardless of whether they already have a solid property. However, it is almost impossible to find large economic mines. It is much smarter to bet on companies who have already found a quality project or a potential flagship project60, than on companies with excellent management teams that currently have nothing.

The first thing to check for on the management team is experience. Have they done it before? Ideally, you want a management team with a good track record, whose managers are respected. It's a good idea to listen to an interview with the CEO, and see if you are comfortable with what the CEO has to say. I also like to find out what other stockholders have to say about management. The place for this is on company web forums.[61]

I analyze management teams from a red flag and green flag perspective. Lack of experience building and operating mines is a red flag. If the CEO has never built and operated a mine, then that should give you pause. I prefer management teams that speak highly of their shareholders and publicly have an aversion for stock dilution. This would be a green flag. I also like to see management teams who own a significant quantity of the stock. This is another green flag. For those companies that do not have these attributes, it would be a potential red flag.

One of my favorite places for finding information about management teams is from podcasts on YouTube. Most CEOs do podcasts where they are interviewed. You can learn a lot about a CEO listening to how they explain their properties and strategies. I've listened to hundreds of these podcasts and they have impacted many of my investments.

This may sound odd, but I respect management teams who do a good job marketing their companies. In my opinion, their best marketing tool is their website. A good web page should be up to date with the latest information. So if management teams do a poor job of building and managing their web page, consider that is a red flag. If you go to analyze a stock and the company does not have a company presentation, then that a red flag. Nearly every quality management team has an up-to-date company presentation, or perhaps it is three months old. This has become an industry standard for communicating with investors.

Always check for any hedging and streaming deals. Often Juniors are forced to hedge their initial production to get financing from a bank. This is okay for a small portion of production and a short duration. However, if a company hedges or sells a large portion of its production at a fixed price, this is not shareholder friendly.

Producing Properties

We have already discussed what to analyze for producing properties. You can go back to the more detailed explanations in the chapter on Majors. Here is a much more condensed list of items to check.

Size: Production ounces, reserve and resource ounces, acreage/hectares for exploration/expansion.

Location: Safety (investment risk), environmental issues, native issues, accessibility, politics, taxes, infrastructure, mining friendly, etc.

Ore Grades: It's always nice to have high grades, but that's not a necessity. Low grades can be very profitable if you have enough reserves. Moreover, even if the grade is high, you still need adequate reserves. If you can get the best of both worlds - high grades and high reserves - that is the jackpot.

Cash Costs: The cash cost per ounce and the all-in cost per ounce will determine the profitability of the mine. Also, the recovery rate can be a big factor.

Grades of Metals

High grades will keep costs down because you don't have to process and move as much ore per ounce. However, today gold can be economical with as little as .5 grams per ton (gpt) for surface mining. If you have enough tonnage, you can still have a profitable mine. Silver must have about 3 ounces per ton (opt) to be economical for surface mining. It's possible to mine lower grades if the deposit includes other metals, such as gold, lead, zinc, and copper (also called offsets or byproduct production, because they offset the cash costs). Sometimes a mine will include all of these metals, plus a few more such as nickel and moly.

These minimums of .5 gram per ton gold and 3 ounces per ton silver are unusual and not generally economic. Most mines have higher grades. Those companies that can mine at these lower grades usually have very efficient operations. The more common mining grades are closer to 1 gpt gold, and 5 opt silver, unless they have offset metals to lower their cash costs.

I'm leery of projects with low grades because the cash costs can be high to move and process that much mineralized ore. However, the economics on some of these mines is very good at higher gold prices. Currently, anything above 1 gpt gold or 5 opt silver is usually economic for surface mining. Plus, if they have any offsets that increases the economics of the mine.

I prefer mines that are economic without base metal offsets. That way the risk is reduced if the demand for the base metal decreases. For a long life mine, you don't want to be dependent on a base metal for the economics.

I try to keep an open mind with regards to grade, especially if there are significant offset metals to lower the cash cost per ounce. In other words, I don't get scared off if the grade is low. I wait to see the cash costs and to see if it is economic (25% after-tax IRR). A lot of investors are much more conservative and want the mine to be economic at lower gold prices. As you have probably come to surmise, I have a higher risk appetite. Also, economics is only one factor in a stock purchase decision.

If I do buy a stock with low grade, I understand and accept the risk. Also, because these are high-risk stocks, I keep my cost basis low. Plus, I only buy a few of these low-grade stocks, always keeping in mind the risk balance of my portfolio. It's okay to buy a few low-grade stocks that are not economic today, but will become economic at higher gold/silver prices.

Grade Chart

This chart shows the range of grades and their values at one million tons. Thus, one million tons of high-grade surface gold at $1,500 per oz. is worth approximately $225 million dollars.

Surface Gold

High ....15 oz. / 5 grams per ton.... (1 million tons = $225 million @ $1,500/oz.)
Good...........07 oz. / 2.5 grams per ton. (1 million tons = $105 million @ $1,500/oz.)
Okay...........50 oz. / 1 grams per ton...... (1 million tons = $50 million @ $1,500/oz.)
Low.............5 grams per ton .... (1 million tons = $25 million @ $1,500/oz.)

Underground Gold

High ....50 oz. / 15 grams per ton.. (1 million tons = $750 million @ $1,500/oz.)
Good...........15 oz. / 5 grams per ton.... (1 million tons = $225 million @ $1,500/oz.)
Low.............07 oz. / 2.5 grams per ton. (1 million tons = $105 million @ $1,500/oz.)

Note: The cutoff grade is generally .35 grams for gold surface mining, and much higher for underground mining, approximately 2.5 grams per ton. However, as gold prices rise, it will likely become the norm to use cutoffs of .3 grams per ton for gold surface mining, and 2 grams per ton for underground mining.

Surface Silver

High ....10 oz. / 300 grams per ton...... (1 million tons = $300 million @ $30/oz.)
Good..........5 oz. / 150 grams per ton........ (1 million tons = $150 million @ $30/oz.)
Low............1 oz. / 30 grams per ton............ (1 million tons = $30 million @ $30/oz.)
Very Low..5 grams per ton .... (1 million tons = $5 million @ $30/oz.)

Underground Silver

High ....10 oz. / 300 grams per ton...... (1 million tons = $300 million @ $30/oz.)

Good..........5 oz. / 150 grams per ton........ (1 million tons = $150 million @ $30/oz.)
Low............1 oz. / 30 grams per ton............ (1 million tons = $30 million @ $30/oz.)

> Note: The cutoff grade is generally about 5 grams for silver surface mining, and much higher for underground mining, approximately 1 ounces per ton. These cutoffs will fall as the price of silver rises.

As you can see from the chart, the real key is tons. You want a lot of tons. The grade is secondary, as long as it is economical to mine. Any way you look at it, the end result is the *total* amount of resource ounces, which are then valued by the stock market.

Drill Results

The lists of ore grades above can be called assay charts. After a while, you will know a good drill result when you see one, because most of them are mediocre, at best (usually low grades and short intervals).

For instance, when they report 1 gram of gold over 10 meters you will be disappointed. However, when they report 5 grams over 30 meters, you will take notice. And if they report 5 grams over 100 meters, you will do some serious research. Anything around 5 grams or higher with good widths are excellent drill results for gold. Most results will be closer to 1 gram or less, which coincides with global production. The average grade mined today is 1 gram per ton. That is the average!

When they find 5 grams per ton, you will see the words "high-grade deposit" in the news release. But, remember, it's all about tonnage. If they find a few high-grade holes, but not enough tonnage, those holes will never be mined. I invested in one company that reported 56 ounces of gold in 1 ton. However, they didn't find enough gold for a mine, and the stock crashed. So, sometimes it is better to wait for follow up drill results that confirm a discovery.

I've been doing this for so long that I created a simple method to identify good drill results. The method is to multiply the width (meters) by the grade (gpt). For gold, use these definitions. While they won't be perfect, they will work fairly well to identify the quality of a drill hole.

Good hole: > 50

Really good hole: > 100 to 200

Excellent hole > 200 to 500

Stellar hole > 500

For silver, use these definitions.

Good hole: > 500

Really good hole: > 1000 to 2000

Excellent hole > 2000 to 5000

Stellar hole > 5000

In addition to these definitions, you need two more pieces of information for the drill holes. These are the minimum width and if it is a surface hole or an underground hole. For surface holes, ideally you want the width to be at least 50 meters. You can still get to 50/500 (the minimums for a good hole) with high-grade intercepts, but it's nice to see 50+ meter widths at surface.

For underground holes, you want the width to be at least 2 meters. For some high-grade veins, it can be acceptable down to 1 meter if the grades are huge. But anything less than 2 meters is difficult to mine and adds risk.

Another key to pay attention to is the average grade. A deposit will be valued on the average grade for the total tonnage. You will want to monitor how the drilling results are adding tonnage, and how those new resources adjust the average grade. Ideally, you want the average grade to remain constant or increase as tonnage is added to the deposit. Of course, as long as you are adding tonnage above cutoff grades,[62] then that is good (the cutoff grade is the minimum ore grade that will be mined).

Companies usually drill only part of the year. This is because it's generally too expensive to drill year round, or it's too cold in the Northern Hemisphere. These are called drilling programs, which are planned and budgeted. They usually plan to drill a specific number of holes during a drilling season. Then they will release the assay results a few months after drilling completes. Some aggressive companies will keep drills turning year round, but this is the exception.

It is not uncommon for more than 100,000 meters to be drilled before a mine is built. Normally, at least 50,000 meters is required to identify a deposit. This will generally take at least three years to complete but can take more than five years from the initial discovery. I've seen many companies drill as much as 50,000 meters in a single year, but the norm is closer to 25,000 meters. One drilling season with good drill results can double or triple the value of a stock. In 2012, Goldquest Mining exploded from 7 cents to $2 per share from good drilling results. Subsequently, the stock has come nearly all the way back (see chart below).

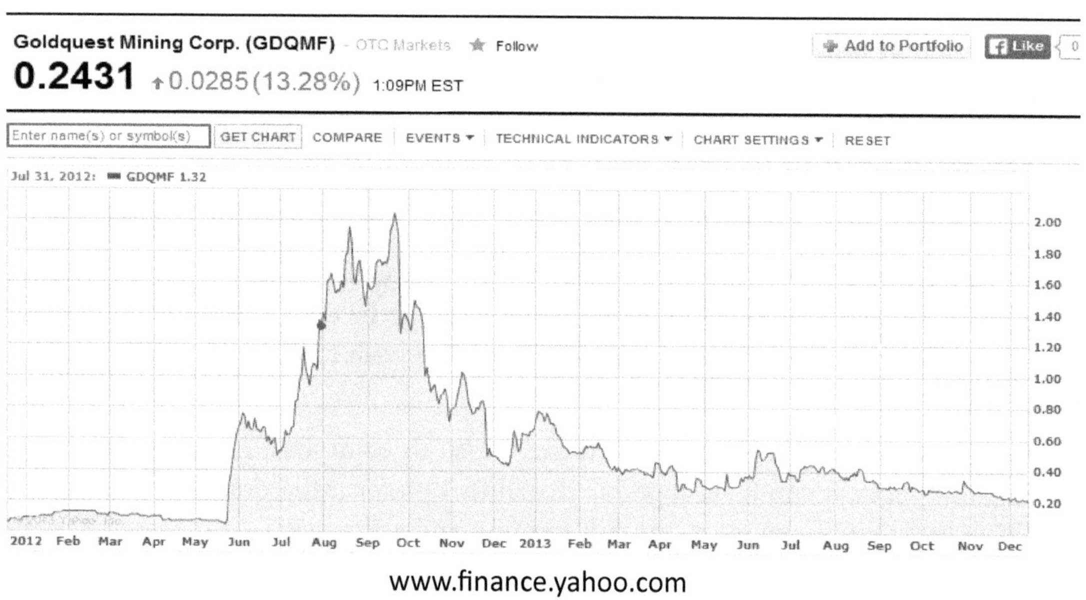

www.finance.yahoo.com

Estimating Resources Using Drill Results

Before a company releases its first resource estimate, you can do your own estimate based on their drill results. I sometimes use my knowledge of mining terminology and mining calculations to make an estimate (see below). This allows me to get a rough estimate of a company's resources, and with this information, I can do a current and future valuation.

Mining Terminology

Strike: Location of found mineralization.

Strike Length: The length of the known deposit.

Strike Width: The width of the known deposit.

Strike Depth: The depth of the known deposit.

Open at Depth: Drilling has not completed exploration at depth.

Open along Strike: Drilling has not completed exploration for the length and width.

Open in all Directions: Drilling has not completed exploration in any direction yet.

Cubic Meters of Mineralized Ore (Length x Width x Depth): This is generally converted to total tons of mineralized ore.

Cubic Meters Converted to Tons: Cubic Meters x 1.5.

In Situ Value: An estimate of the value of the resources (total ounces not counting inferred) in the ground at today's gold/silver prices. This is generally multiplied by 10% to get a conservative estimate of the company's value. Strong companies are often valued at 20%.

How to Make a Resource Estimate

Length = 1,000 meters

Width = 10 meters

Depth = 500 meters

Grade = 4 gpt

The numbers above are estimates based on reading a company's drill results. The width and average grade are generally known by the drill results, but length and depth can be hard to guess unless you have a lot of drill results. Try to be conservative and hope that your estimates are close. One of the most important factors is the grade. If you have enough drill results to get a good understanding of the grade, then your estimate for the grade is going to be close.

Cubic Meters = 1,000 x 10 x 500 = 5,000,000

Cubic Meters Converted to Tons = 5,000,000 x 1.5 = 7,500,000

At 4 grams per ton = (4 gpt x 7.5 million oz. / 31) = 1 million oz.

Current In Situ Value = 1 million oz. x $1,300 = $1.3 billion

Future In Situ Value = 1 million oz. x $2,500 = $2.5 billion

At a 10% valuation of the deposit, that calculates to a future valuation of $250 million, if we use a future gold price of $2,500. As a ballpark valuation (if my 7.5 million tons are accurate), then this deposit has a chance to be worth $250 million.

Of course, there are other ways to value it. You could take the estimated 1 million oz. and multiply it by $250 and get the same result. Based on the grade, you could guess that the annual free cash flow would be approximately 1 million oz. x $800 = $80 million. If you multiply that by 5, then you get a $400 million valuation.

As you can imagine, if you guess right on the grade on tonnage, you can get a pretty good estimate for a deposit's future valuation. After all, the value of a deposit is basically the future value of the gold in the ground. The one caveat is that this valuation is based on the assumption that this deposit will be mined and the future gold price will be realized.

Development Properties

For Development Properties, you need to check everything you did for Producing Properties. Plus, there are a few other factors to consider: What are the potential reserves that might be found? Do they have a 43-101 resource estimate, or are they close to having one? Do they have a preliminary economic assessment? If not, then production is likely at least five to seven years away. What are the drill results? Are they consistently good? Are they aggressively drilling any of their properties? Meaning, are they spending heavily on drill programs, with plans to move towards production?

One of the keys for Development Properties is guidance from management, along with a PEA (preliminary economic assessment) and pre-feasibility study. You want a company that is aggressively moving a mine toward production and is giving guidance on their plans. If a company has a large flagship property and is not forthcoming with a PEA, then they likely have no plans to move toward production.

As a rule of thumb, once a positive PEA is released the mine should be built within four to six years. This can be extended for permitting and financing delays, or large projects.

For an ideal mine, once a PEA is released, the next steps should come off like clockwork: a pre-feasibility study is released a year later; permitting and pre-development begins; the final feasibility study is released six months later; final permitting is completed a year later; financing is obtained a few months after the final permits; construction begins; the mine is completed a year later. Total time from the release of the PEA until the first poor of gold: approximately 4-6 years, depending on the size of the project.

There are situations where past producing mines are already permitted, or where new open pit projects use a nearby mill. Under these situations, they can move from a PEA to production in a very quick time frame. I've seen mines restarted in a year, and others developed in two or three years. Understanding these timelines is why management guidance is so important.

The biggest risk with development projects are delays or a lack of activity. Ideally, you don't want to buy a development stock until they have released a PEA and have given guidance of a timeframe until production. However, even with that guidance there can be delays for the various steps that have to be accomplished. These delays often cause their share price to languish.

The second biggest risk is a takeover or JV (joint venture). Often a company will give guidance that they plan to develop the mine, but then it is acquired either before first pour or shortly after. When this happens, the upside potential is significantly reduced.

Share Structure

Generally, the share structure (fully diluted shares) is going to start small and increase over time. For Juniors, you can't buy a stock with a tight share structure and expect it to remain tight. However, what you can do is try to avoid Juniors with an ugly share structure that is already extremely diluted. It's okay to hold your nose and own a few of these in your portfolio. But once a company has over 200 million shares, it begins to become highly diluted.

You want to own stocks with explosive upsides. Ideally, you want to own a producer with less than 100 million shares, who can finance growth internally with their cash flow to avoid dilution. I always consider it fortunate to own a producer with less than 150 million FD shares, because so few companies can achieve this level. So, when you buy a development stock, one of your goals is for share dilution to end up around 150 to 250 million FD shares when they begin production.

Stock Price History

Always check the stock price history of a stock when you do your analysis. If a stock has already broken out, then look for better opportunities (or wait for a correction). Today, it is still easy to find good charts with share prices off their highs. This won't always be the case. In the future, you are going to need to choose your entry spots carefully.

Check whether the chart has been volatile in the past few months. If so, you can likely wait for a dip. I'll have more to say about reading charts in the next chapter.

Project Generators

There are more Project Generators than any other category. I have 835 gold and silver mining stocks in my database, and currently 460 are Project Generators. These are mostly small companies with only a few early exploration projects. Of the 460 companies, only 46 have FD market caps over $100 million.

The objective of these companies is not to mine gold/silver, but to find it and sell it in the ground (sometimes keeping a percentage as an equity owner). These are the true explorers who only have one objective: finding gold/silver. Many investors like this business model because this is where you can get huge returns, and often in a very short period of time. These are the ultimate speculations stocks.

A successful Project Generator can use other people's money (their partners') to complete the exploration and development of new mines. All they need to do is find a potential mine and then create a joint venture (a partnership). Then they let the partner take over the property and spend all of the money to bring it to production. Often the original owner does not even need to fund development of the mine. Instead, their share of the development costs is subtracted from future shared profits.

In theory, this JV model could keep a project generator from burning through a lot of cash and keep their share dilution down. In practice, this rarely happens. Most project generators dilute their shares just like all other junior mining stocks. Some project generators have been able to keep their share dilution down, but they are the exception.

A Project Generator can obtain money from a partner in a number of ways: cash payments for selling a percentage of the property (often called an option), royalty payments from producing mines, shares of the profits from producing mines, and through equity shares from their partners.

After a few joint ventures are created, the Project Generator can benefit if the joint ventures turn into mines. This makes the profit sharing and equity interest that they hold very valuable. Many Project Generators can hold a substantial number of equity shares. The last time I analyzed Strategic Metals, they held 50 million shares in other companies. Nearly all of these shares were obtained in joint venture deals, where they traded ownership of their properties for company common stock.

This may sound like a good business model, but it has some weaknesses. First, Project Generators tend to appreciate in value slowly. The reason for this is that they generally only get a small percentage of the profits. It can take two or three producing mines for these stocks to become high-flyers. Thus, Project Generators are rarely explosive stocks. Second, it takes a long time for mines to make it into production, so new Project Generators will take a long time to pay off. Third, they are not in control of their destiny. They cannot expand a mine to increase cash flow. Instead, they must wait for their partners to succeed.

Another reason I do not like Project Generators is that many of them use a spin-out strategy. Meaning that once they make a discovery, they spin-out that project into a new company. This type of strategy prevents the company from growing. Some of you may be thinking, but don't you get free shares when they do the spin-out? Yes, you do, but generally, the spin-put is only about 10% to 20% of your share total. If you have 50,000 shares or more, then it might make sense. But generally what happens is you get a small number of shares that don't have a lot of value. Plus, your original investment declined because they divested their best property.

In hindsight, I wish I would have avoided this category. Instead of looking at the project generator model, focus on individual drill stories. Don't look at a project generator because they have several JV properties that might become mines. Instead, narrow your focus down to individual properties that have good drill results. Those are what I call drill stories. If you catch them early, they can turn into large mines and the returns can come fast and stunning. Catching a 10 bagger can be quite possible if you get in early. So, don't care about the company, or its business model, care about the property.

There is one thing that Project Generators are good for and that is making discoveries. The best way to play this category is to wait for a discovery and then ride the trend (don't make the mistake I did and buy a project generator just because they own several properties). I call this chasing drill results. Basically, you are betting that the drill results will continue to be good. It does not always work, but when it does, you can make a lot of money very quickly. It is not uncommon for early discoveries to rise more than 500% in a single year.

I have found that there are three types of gold/silver investors. First, those who buy it as a long-term asset as a hedge against fiat currencies devaluing. Second, those who are waiting for gold/silver prices to rise, and want a portfolio to take advantage of that outcome. Third, those who like to make money quickly and are drawn to trends. It is this last group who like exploration stocks and gold/silver discoveries. Some investors fit into all three types. I fit more into the second group, although I do a little bit of all three.

* * * * *

The last group is the non-producing, non-development, early-stage explorers. These can be split into three groups:

1. Development company with enough resources for a mine.
2. Development company with almost enough resources for a mine.
3. Potential exists.

Early-Stage Explorer: Enough Resources for a Mine

These are the development companies that have found enough resources to build a long life mine, but have not yet reached the late-stage development phase. Thus, they are years away from beginning production. They have not yet released a PEA (preliminary economic assessment), so it will likely be at least five years until production, and perhaps as many as ten. This long time frame makes them a very high-risk investment, and very long term as well.

Some people consider these optionality plays, which is the opportunity to buy gold in the ground cheap that will eventually get revalued higher. However, I have come to the conclusion that the timeline risk (the time it takes until production) is probably not worth it, unless they have a lot of gold/silver in ground. Also, unless a project has a path to production, investors tend to ignore it. I'm not so sure that will change as gold prices rise.

Another red flag for projects that do not yet have a PEA or production guidance is that these companies could, in fact, be Project Generators. Often a company will claim to be a development company, but has no intention of building and operating the mine.

From experience, I have learned that most of the stocks in this category will not achieve high returns. The number one reason why is because of either a JV deal or a takeover. The biggest disappointment for me as a gold mining investor has been how easy it is for large companies to acquire smaller companies for low premiums. It doesn't seem to matter how much gold the smaller company has in the ground. For instance, Andina Minerals was purchased for less than $10 per ounce of gold in the ground. They found 11 million ounces M&I at .7 grams per ton and were acquired for less than $100 million.

These are companies that have already found a significant amount of gold/silver, so they aren't really exploration stocks. However, the only time these stocks seem to make sense as an investment is if they have additional exploration potential and enough insiders own the stock to prevent a cheap takeover. In my opinion, because the risk/reward profile is usually poor for these stocks, they should rarely (if ever) appear in your portfolio. Instead, wait until they become at least Late Stage Development stocks with a path to production.

My one caveat for this category are potential optionality plays. But most of the best optionality plays have large resources and are somewhat advanced, with at least a PEA. Also, it's possible one of these stocks has significant exploration potential and could be a drill story. Other than those two situations, they stocks tend to have a poor risk-reward profile.

Early-Stage Explorer: Almost Enough Resources for a Mine

I've been warning you that investing in Juniors is like gambling and is quite risky. Well, that's not completely true. The previous Junior categories I have discussed in this chapter represent actual investing, although sometimes at high risk. However, these last two groups truly are speculating. If a company does not have enough resources (large enough deposit) for a mine, you are gambling that they will find enough. Early investors in a company are often gambling, but once a mine is found, you then become an investor.

I normally have companies in this category listed as Project Generators in my database. If a company lists themselves as a development company, but are in the early exploration phase, then I am leery of them actually building the mine. Sometimes they make a convincing argument, and I will give them the benefit of doubt that they are a development company.

The only time a stock in this category makes sense as an investment is if their deposit is growing in size and has good exploration potential. I would treat companies in this category as a high-risk exploration stock. If they end up developing the mine, consider that as a bonus.

Enticing Valuations

From an investor/speculator viewpoint, the key is not investing a dime until you do your homework. (In the investment community this is called due diligence or DD.) Exploration stocks can be very enticing and has sucked me in a few times. You look at the drill results and the very low market cap, and you think you have found a possible winner. So you pull the trigger and buy the stock. Then you sit back and wait … and wait ... and nothing happens.

This waiting process can be very long. You can wait for years before the stock makes a jump. Very often it heads south and stays there, while you continue to wait for the company to release exciting drill results that pushes the stock higher.

Some analysts recommend these stocks because of good drill results. Their expectation is that the deposit is going to grow in size. There is a common belief that the best time to make big profits is the discovery phase. That can be true, but the risk level is immense. I've lost enough money chasing drill results to know that it's usually not worth it. My suggestion from experience is to wait until a company has found a large deposit and is aggressively pursuing production. I explained this in the previous category.

Sometimes these stocks are too enticing to pass up. If the early drill results are solid and the strike length and geology point to a very large deposit, sometimes you have to gamble. This is especially true if you think it is a potential 10 bagger and you can buy it very cheaply. Just make sure that if you pursue this strategy to only allocate a very small portion of your portfolio cost basis to these stocks.

If you buy a lot of mining stocks, then you will probably chase drill results for a few companies. It is very enticing because it may appear that a company has found a mine. However, after you do this a few times, you will find that the odds are against you. You may get lucky once or twice, but usually, the initial drill results will not lead to a large mine. It is much smarter to bet on companies that already have the goods.

I do think it can make sense to allocate about 5% of your portfolio to exploration drill stories. While these stocks will have high risk, they also have the potential for stunning returns. Also, it can be fun. The key to your success will be chasing good drill stories. This means that you buy stocks because they release good drill results and it's still cheap. Ideally, you want to make sure that the deposit you are chasing had an excellent discovery hole. Go back to my definitions for what is an excellent drill hole.

Chasing Cash Flow

There are really only two main ways to invest in gold/silver mining stocks. The first way is chasing drill results in the near term, and the second way is to chase cash flow in the long term. On occasion, I have chased drill results, but I have learned that this is a very risky pursuit. Instead, my main investment strategy is to chase future cash flow. This is why I am always looking for mining companies that can provide very large potential future free cash flow.

In my opinion, the best predictor of a higher share price is increased free cash flow. If free cash flow increases substantially, the share price will likely also increase substantially. To prove this, all you need to do is look at the increase in free cash flow in Kirkland Lake Gold in 2018, which translated into a higher share price. Kirkland Lake found a high-grade deposit that decreased their costs and exploded their free cash flow. Subsequently, their share price rose from $2 to $50.

While drill results are very difficult to predict, future free cash flow is much easier to estimate. All you need is an economic project, large producing ounces, and higher gold/silver prices. As you will learn in the last chapter, you can predict the upside potential of a stock using this long-term method of chasing cash flow.

Early-Stage Explorer: Potential Exists

Okay, this is the last group. What do you think that means? Yep, lots of risk. This last group are the Juniors that don't fit into any of the previous Junior categories we have discussed already:

- Near-Term Producer
- Late-Stage Development
- Emerging Mid-Tier Producer
- Small Producer
- Project Generator
- Early-Stage Explorer: Developer with Enough Reserves for a Mine
- Early-Stage Explorer: Developer with Almost Enough Reserves for a Mine

You won't find this list of categories in any other book, although you will find some of the terms. I created these categories specifically to understand and manage risk. I gave them my own definitions so that I would clearly understand where a company stands with regard to risk.

This last category has the highest risk because in this group you can't predict the outcome with any accuracy. Most of these stocks go nowhere after you buy them, except down. Remember when I told you that only 1 in 100 drilling targets hit pay dirt? These are the stocks that hit those dry holes.

Always remember that gold and silver mines are very hard to find and that you should invest in companies who have already found at least a potential mine.

I do not own any stocks in this category. In my opinion, this last category should be avoided due to risk severity. It is nearly impossible to find winners in these small micro-cap companies unless you get extremely lucky.

Most exploration stocks will be listed in the Project Generator category. I use this final category as a catch-all for stocks that are not currently exploring. This can be a milling operator or a company that has lost their mine and is looking for another one. I have very few stocks listed with this category.

Most of Your Mistakes

Many of you are going to be tempted by some of these micro-cap exploration stocks because they can be incredibly lucrative if you guess right. Most of them have market caps under $50 million, and many of them are under $10 million. Some investors like to trade these stocks. You can double or triple your money in a few weeks with some of these penny stocks if they are trending. It's inevitable that you will be exposed to people who are trading these stocks. They are chasing momentum, and it can be very lucrative if you guess right. I consider this to be more gambling than investing.

Exploration stocks are where you will make most of your mistakes. The other categories allow you to somewhat alleviate risk because you know they have already found a mine or a potential mine. With exploration stocks, you are pretty much out on a limb. If I were starting over, I would largely avoid this group, and keep my exposure to 5% or less of my cost basis.

Exploration stocks are for speculating. Ironically, most people are going to think you are speculating by investing in any gold/silver mining company. Little do they realize that you have found one of the best investments of a lifetime and that it can be done in a smart, systematic, and methodical way.

Yes, most gold/silver mining companies are high-risk speculation stocks. However, there are different levels of speculation. Understanding those levels is what makes a good investor. For exploration stocks, I have found that it is a level of speculation that is much higher than companies that already have the goods.

Flagship Property

One of the most important things I have learned, perhaps the most important thing, is the existence of a flagship property. Most of the stocks I have owned that became losers were companies without flagship properties. I have come to believe that focusing on flagship properties, or potential flagship properties, is the smartest thing I can do as an investor.

I define a flagship property in terms of resources. For gold properties, the magic number is 2 million ounces. For silver properties, it is 40 million ounces. Again, these are my definitions, which I have learned through experience. If a company has this many resources (preferably excluding inferred), or if the drilling results seem to indicate the company will accumulate this quantity, then the risk level is substantially lower than it would be with a company with much fewer resources.

If a company does not have these resource levels, but the drill results and strike length point to achieving these levels, then consider it a potential flagship, and a possible investment. I will sometimes go lower than these totals for small producers with exploration potential, but these are usually unique situations that have a good potential return.

If you invest in a company that finds twice the resource level of a flagship property, you have likely just made a lot of money. I am always on the hunt for a company that is going to find more than 4 million ounces of gold or 100 million ounces of silver. This is where you find your home runs. You buy the gold or silver super cheap in the ground, and then eventually it gets revalued higher.

Recently, someone on a blog recommended a Junior gold stock with 1 million ounces of resources. I did some research, and the mineralization on the property had been drilled out. Thus, there was a low probability they were going to add more resources. In the past, I might have bought it because it was very cheap (the market cap was around $25 million). However, because it lacked a flagship property, I passed. If you focus on flagship properties, you will do much better and lower your risk.

When I do my initial analysis, I check three things first: 1) Is there a flagship property, or a potential flagship in a good location? 2) Does the company have a low valuation? I prefer a 500% return. 3) Does the company have a tight share structure? I prefer fully diluted shares to be less than 150 million. Of course, there are many other factors, but these are the first three I check, and by far the most important. If a company has those three, I have to find a reason not to buy it.

Note that part of the first thing I look at is the location. I can't overstate the importance of the location. Ideally, I like properties in Canada and Australia. All other countries are a bit of a crapshoot. I'll either consider these other country locations as too risky, or lower my cost basis somewhat based on the location risk.

The Home Run

I am always looking for home run stocks (1,000% return). It is my goal to find at least ten home runs during this bull market. And usually, the only place to find home runs is with Juniors (also undervalued Mid-Tier Producers). There are many companies today with solid properties that look like potential home runs. Because of the current poor sentiment in mining stocks, with the HUI index under 300, I could list several stocks that are potential home runs.

Potential 20+ Baggers

I currently own about ten stocks that I consider potential 20+ baggers. My goal is for at least one of them to become a 50 bagger. If that occurs, then my junior strategy will have paid off, because the others could be losers and I would still make money. I consider this a highly risky strategy, and perhaps not the best risk/reward approach. In hindsight, I should have focused more on Mid-Tier Producers.

In a previous edition, I listed five stocks as potential 20+ baggers and three of them were taken over by larger companies for very low premiums. My point is that even if you find a potential 20+ bagger, the odds are not always in your favor. The chance of a buyout or JV is very high for stocks with very low valuations. If you can spot a highly undervalued company, so can companies that are looking to grow.

I have come to realize that the best strategy is to find quality producers with 5 to 10 bagger upside potential. Then wait and see if these companies can grow through acquisitions and exploration. Trying to find a 20+ bagger has a poor risk/reward profile. Not because the company can become a 20+ bagger, but because they probably won't. The reason why is because a company with 20+ bagger potential has an uphill battle of becoming a large company.

Good Properties and Good Drill Results

All companies that are potential home runs have one thing in common, and that is exciting properties. As an investor looking for big plays, you are on the lookout for good properties and good drill results. These are never sure things, just a possible opportunity.

The key is recognizing potential. A smart investor would choose wisely and look for an increase in odds and reduced risk. Some of my stocks are high risk and might not pay off. I could have put some of these on my watch list (explained in the next chapter) and waited for the project to advance. This would have reduced my risk substantially, but it would also have required a lot of patience and hard work to keep an eye on these stocks.

Many companies with high upside potential are valued under $50 million and are tempting to buy. However, if you wait until $50 million, the risk level drops, and if you wait until $100 million, it drops substantially. Often, the only reason to buy a stock under the $50 million market cap level is greed and trying to get the best entry price. It is often smarter to wait for the "proof" and the justification as to why a company has made it to the $50 million mark.

Many gold/silver analysts say that the sweet spot of investing is $100 to $300 million market caps. But I think it is lower, perhaps $50 million to $150. I think this is where you get the most value. You take on more risk, but I think it is worth it. A company valued under $50 million has a lot of risk, and a company over $150 million has likely become expensive (if you are looking for big gains). If you are only interested in making 300% returns, then I would agree that you should focus on market caps higher than $150 million.

Mining Life Cycle

The mining life cycle is important to understand as an investor. This cycle is nearly the same for every new mine. The cycle is a series of steps that are required to bring a mine into production. The steps are as follows: stake a claim or purchase a property, preliminary exploration, create a drilling plan, drill, obtain drilling results, 43-101 resource estimate, preliminary economic assessment, pre-feasibility study, final feasibility study, permitting, financing, construction, and finally production. By understanding the mining life cycle, you can know where a company's mine currently fits into the cycle.

Typically, until a preliminary economic assessment is issued, there can't be a feasibility study. And until a final feasibility study is completed, final financing cannot be obtained. Everything follows in a slow, systematic process. The most important thing to understand is that the true value of a company cannot be realized until production begins.

Note: Refer to Appendix C for the steps in the mining life cycle.

Special Categories

In addition to the mining stocks that you can value using the methods and factors I have outlined, there are other investment opportunities for precious metals. These are royalty companies, mill operators, and investment companies. Below I explain how royalty companies work.

Mill operators own mills and make a profit on each ounce that they mill, which is then sent to a refiner. Some investors like mill operators because they have good margins, but I find their upside to be limited.

There are some companies that focus on investing in gold/silver related assets. These are similar to ETFs. So far, none of these companies has captured my interest.

Royalty Companies

Royalty companies usually sign long-term contracts to purchase gold/silver at fixed prices from mining companies. These contracts are called streaming deals because a gold/silver production stream goes to the royalty companies.

To obtain these contracts, they usually pay a lump sum, although sometimes these payments are made both before the mine is built and then during or after it is completed. The royalty company can then resell their purchased gold/silver at market rates. Thus, they are not mining companies and do not own any mines.

When I first wrote this book, there were only about five royalty companies. However, because this model has been so successful, there are now 16 in the GSD database. The successful ones have very high margins and are valued at around 30x free cash flow.

There are some companies that call themselves royalty companies because they have royalty streams from NSR (net smelter royalty) agreements. However, these companies are usually also exploration and development companies. What I consider to be true royalty companies only purchase gold or silver streams using long-term contracts at fixed rates.

These contracts come into being usually because of two needs. The first need is from a base metals company that decides to sell their precious metals production to a royalty company. It's an easy way to monetize an income stream. For instance, a copper mining company would sell a stream of their gold production to a royalty company. The royalty company will pay a lump sum for the right to receive a percentage of the gold production (sometimes all of it). Then, each year, the royalty company will receive their stream. In exchange for receiving the gold each year, the royalty company will pay a fixed rate for each ounce of gold, usually around $400 per ounce.

The royalty company pays the initial lump sum, which is usually large amount of money into the tens of millions of dollars. Basically, they are pre-paying for the gold/silver that they will receive annually. In addition to the lump sum, they also have to pay a fixed amount for each ounce of gold/silver they receive. This amount is supposed to help with the company's cost of mining the gold/silver. Usually, this fixed amount is well below the cost of production.

What happens with these contracts is that royalty company pays a lot of money to obtain the contract and then pays well below the spot price to acquire the gold/silver stream each year. These deals are written so that it is almost impossible for the royalty companies to lose money, unless the mine closes for an unexpected reason. And if the price of gold/silver rises, the royalty company benefits dramatically because their costs are essentially fixed.

The second need is when gold/silver miners need money to build a mine. Royalty companies essentially become bankers. They loan gold/silver miners the money to build their mine. In exchange, they receive a gold/silver stream. The deals are basically the same as explained with the base metal producer. They are contracts to receive a percentage of production each year, and then the royalty company pays a fixed price per ounce, which is a fraction of the spot price.

What amazes me about this business model is how one-sided these contracts are written. Because the contracts have a fixed price, the only party who benefits if gold/silver prices rise is the royalty company. There are many mines today with royalty contracts, yet there are no stipulations if gold and silver prices explode in value. This means the royalty companies will have huge potential windfalls. Will these contracts hold in such an event? If they do, then the royalty companies will be incredibly profitable.

I think there is a good chance that this model will break, or at least go through a transformation, as gold/silver prices rise. I say this because it inevitable that a company will simply stop delivering the stream. Instead, they will demand that the contract be re-written on more equitable terms. Once one company does it, many will follow.

For example, if silver reaches $50 an ounce and a company is delivering 5 million ounces for $4 per ounce (the standard price for most of these contracts), then the royalty company is getting $230 million in profit. This contract was probably obtained for an initial payment under $50 million. That discrepancy is too wide not to cause a problem. Plus, the producer will have a lot of leverage with that much money that can be withheld. Going to court could take many months to resolve, and the court might just side with the producer and say the contract is not fair and reasonable. What would you do if you were the producer under this scenario? I know one thing that is going to happen and that is a lot of phone calls requesting a more fair deal.

CHAPTER 9

How to Make Money

This chapter is about making money using a balanced portfolio, with a focus on finding undervalued mining stocks. For those of you who merely want to maintain your wealth, your focus should be on bullion, coins, ETFs, and perhaps gold mutual funds.

Before I begin this chapter, I want to mention one last time that investing in gold/silver mining stocks is incredibly risky. So, don't go into this thinking that this is easy or guaranteed. Here is a post that I read on ZeroHedge.com that sums up why most investors avoid gold/silver mining stocks:[64]

> *Gold stocks are just another form of paper to be inflated away. Or the mines will be confiscated; or the management team will dilute shareholders to nothing; or fuel and operating costs will more than eat up any profits; or any gains will be taxed away as a windfall profit; or the staff will steal a good part of the gold; or bandits will rob the gold shipments from the mine; or environmental rules will shut down the mine; or 10+ other reasons why paper stocks are just paper...*

While this quote does have relevance, the potential for making substantial returns in gold/silver mining stocks is also true. In fact, I think that the returns could be stunning. We can either ignore this opportunity (higher gold prices, leading to higher mining share prices), or invest for that possible outcome.

Three Main Factors

The unique thing about investing in gold/silver mining stocks is that their valuation is based on three main factors: production ounces, resources in the ground, and the value of the metal. And because we are likely in a gold bull market, with the price of gold potentially heading north of $2,500, this provides an incredible opportunity.

The stock market refuses to anticipate rising prices, but we can. If you position yourself early with a portfolio of gold/silver assets, then when gold reaches $2,500, your stocks will rise dramatically. (I'm being conservative here. I think we will see $3,000 gold or higher in the next few years.)

The key to making money in gold or silver is simply to get in the game. Nearly every gold/silver asset is likely going to do well over the next few years. But the key to making substantial returns and getting the most out of this bull market is finding companies with low valuations versus their upside potential. Investing in these companies positions you to take advantage of these three main factors. In the previous chapters, I have given you enough information to do just that.

The Missing Pieces

I've given you most of what you need to know. However, there are still a few missing pieces if you are going to be systematic and do this right. In fact, without this information, you will be somewhat restricted. For that reason, this is probably the most important chapter.

I have already described in detail how to diversify risk, and how to understand the risk level of each gold/silver asset that you select for your portfolio. Risk is one of those important pieces of information that most amateurs do not understand. After reading the previous chapters, you should now be able to break down your portfolio by risk level quite easily. You should know which stocks are risky bets and which ones should pay off.

Here are the remaining missing pieces that you need to know: building your portfolio, timing the market, watching stocks, research, and an exit strategy. I will explain them, one at a time.

Building Your Portfolio

I think everyone needs to have a core level of lower-risk investments: bullion, coins, bullion ETFs, gold/silver mining ETFs, gold mutual funds, or gold/silver Majors. Without these lower-risk categories, you are going to end up with an unbalanced portfolio that is weighted with too much risk. When you begin building your portfolio, the percentage allocated to these lower-risk investments should be

100%. And until you build it up to a substantial amount, I would ignore the other, riskier asset classes.

> Note: Many of you with only a small amount to invest will likely take on more risk and focus on mining companies with market caps under $1 billion. There is nothing wrong with this strategy, but recognize the additional risk that you are taking.

After you complete this low-risk phase of building your portfolio, all you will have are lower-risk investments. You will have hedged your wealth, and transferred a portion of your current wealth into lower risk gold/silver related assets.

At this point, you should feel good about the choices you have made. If you have any second thoughts, and think that trading your dollars or other assets for gold/silver was a risky idea, then you should stop right here and go no further. But if you are feeling good about getting rid of those fiat dollars and dollar-related assets, let's move on.

Investing to Make Money

Now we have arrived at the point of trying to invest to make money. We are going to start looking at gold/silver mining stocks with market caps from $20 million to $3 billion (we might buy a few stocks outside this range, but those will be outliers). I have given you the tools and knowledge of what to look for. Now, go for it! Pick winners and build a balanced portfolio. Just don't pick too many below $50 million or too many over $500 million. Those stocks will either be too risky or will have less upside potential.

When you analyze a stock, ask yourself, is this a good stock? Does it have those things he said to look for? Does it pass the smell test on all of those valuation factors? Is it a slam dunk, with excellent upside potential? Does it have any red flags?

Begin the second phase of building your portfolio with Mid-Tier Producers. This category has the best risk-reward profile. Mid-Tier Producers can have relatively low risk and high return. You're going to want to load up on these, picking several stocks. How many you choose is your preference.

Then steadily work your way up the risk pyramid. It's smart to compare stocks that are in the same category to find the best ones. With experience, you will learn which stocks are comparable. This is the best way to identify which stocks have the best value within a particular category. The good ones will stand out.

I would suggest that you scour each category (except the extreme risk Juniors) using my database to find your favorite stocks. You can also create your own criteria using the search engine. For instance, you can look for all Silver producers with cash costs under $10 per ounce, and market caps under $1 billion. Just about anything you can think of can be queried. And then once you get your search results, you can compare stocks side by side.

> Note: When you start buying stocks, recognize that this is a volatile market. If you buy a stock and it drops significantly, remember that this is a long-term investment. Sometimes you have to be very patient and endure paper losses for long periods of time. This is why it is important to keep your cost basis low for your high-risk stocks, because sometimes these stocks do not recover.

Buy List

Once you find a stock you want to buy, you place it on your buy list.[65] I include five pieces of information on my buy list: Stock Name, Stock Symbol, Current Stock Price, Preferred Entry Price, and a Note. I consider the entry price to be very important. I will have more to say about this further down. I use the note to remind myself why I added it to the buy list.

Here is a sample buy list I had in 2010, so you can see the format:

Stock	**Symbol**	**Current**	**Entry**	**Note**
Amarillo Gold	AGCBF	.85	.70	1 mil oz. in Brazil with upside.
Endeavour Silver	EXK	4.00	2.50	Wait for crash.
Rio Alto Mining	RIOAF	.55	.50	4 mil oz!
Timmins Gold	TMGOF	.75	.70	Heading towards Mid-Tier.

Your buy list is how you build your portfolio (I rarely buy a stock that doesn't first get added to my buy list). After it reaches the entry price and your account has funds to purchase it, you can then purchase the stock. Some stocks can sit on my buy list for several years, others only a few days.

Once I have purchased a stock, it gets moved off my buy list and into my portfolio (an Excel spreadsheet), which includes the purchase date, purchase price, stock symbol, and number of shares. I also have a column for current price and profit/ loss percentage.

> Note: My website has a portfolio feature which allows you to track your portfolio online. You can also create a portfolio of stocks to watch. Also, you can view a saved portfolio on the Search screen, and a Search can be turned into a portfolio. These are very handy features for building and monitoring a portfolio.

Watch List

Your watch list is one level below the buy list. This is a list of stocks that you don't want to buy at this time, but that you think have potential. These are the stocks that you want to keep an eye on as you wait for more information. When you learn something new about a company, such as a good drill report, a PEA, or an updated 43-101 resource estimate, you might move them to your buy list.

Here is part of my watch list from 2010:

Stock	Symbol	Mkt Cap	Current	Hi	FD Shares	Entry
Esperanza Silver	ESPZF	$40	.70	2.00	50	.50
Impact Silver	ISVLF	$29	.55	1.50	52	.35
Kootenay Gold	KOOYF	$29	.58	2.29	50	.35
Silvercrest Mines	STVZF	$29	.53	1.40	55	.35

Notice the different columns of information. Once I decide I want to buy a stock, I am no longer concerned with the market cap, the number of fully diluted shares, or its all-time high price. However, when I am watching it, these data points can influence my buying decision.

I can also use the watch columns as trigger points. For example, I can set a trigger if my entry price is met. My watch triggers are set in TD Ameritrade, and I receive an email if they are reached. There are a lot of different ways you can set up triggers. My favorite is the stock price. I want to know if it has jumped significantly.

This watch list only includes low market cap Juniors. They weren't interesting enough to make my buy list. But one good drill result, or some other exciting news, and I might have moved one to my buy list. I normally have a few stocks on each list. When I wrote the first edition of this book, I had seven stocks on my buy list and fifteen on my watch list.

Stocks on your watch list should be researched thoroughly and given a rating (which you learn how to do in the next chapter). You should know their story and all of their factors. Often when you research a company for the first time, instead of being placed on your watch list, it gets placed immediately on your buy list.

Three Things to Build Your Portfolio

To build your portfolio, you have to do three things: 1) Fund your account. 2) Add stocks to your buy list. 3) Purchase your stock at an acceptable entry price.

When I was building my portfolio, I generally funded my account once a month, using cash flow from my payroll check. This allowed funds in my account to build. I bought a stock, on average, every other month. So, I needed to find buy candidates. Sometimes, if I didn't have a buy candidate with a good entry price, I would buy more shares for stocks that I already owned.

Purchasing Strategy

I like to purchase stocks based on my overall portfolio cost basis. For a high-quality Producer, my entry level would be around 1% of my portfolio cost basis. For a quality Late Stage Development stock, my entry level would be around .5%. And for an exploration stock, my entry level would be around .25%.

Some of you may be thinking that my allocations are too low. It is your preference to decide how to do your allocations. I prefer to keep mine low because of the high-risk nature of mining stocks.

In conjunction with my cost basis allocation, I prefer to purchase a minimum of 5,000 shares in a company. Sometimes this isn't feasible if it has a high stock price and it will exceed my cost basis allocation. If I buy a stock that has a share price under .20 cents, then I will usually buy 8,000 or 10,000 shares to start. I currently own a few stocks with share counts over 30,000 shares, but I like to keep my stock share counts from getting too high. This is just a personal preference, because I don't want to have any single stock becoming too important. Ideally, I want to be able to lose any stock in my portfolio and not take a big loss.

Most of my stocks were purchased at 1% or less of my portfolio cost basis, with some at 2%, and very few at 3%. I rarely buy an individual stock at 2% of my portfolio cost basis to start, but I have a few that have increased to 2% or greater.

This happened because they dropped in value and I attempted to reduce their cost basis. Let this be a lesson to you to be careful not to let an individual high-risk stock exceed 2% of your cost basis.

I think it is okay to exceed the 3% cost basis limit for mutual funds, bullion, and ETFs. I feel that these lower risk assets can have much higher cost basis limits. In fact, going as high as 10% is acceptable from my viewpoint.

Investment Goal

Today, I am still building my portfolio, although I'm just about done. I have an investment goal in mind, and once I reach that, I plan to sit back and wait for my exit strategy to be triggered (see Exit Strategy below).

Once I hit my investment goal, I will begin researching what to invest in when I sell my gold and silver shares. You should think about an investment goal, too. It helps you to focus on building your portfolio. This can be an intermediate goal. For instance, when I started investing in gold in 1991, I had a goal of obtaining 5,000 shares in a mutual fund. It took a long time, but I reached my goal. After I achieved my first goal, I set another one. I bought another gold mutual fund and proceeded to accumulate another 5,000 shares. After that, I began investing in individual mining shares which resulted in this book.

Finding the Right Entry Price

Once you add a company to your buy list, you need to set a target entry price. However, if you think the stock is incredibly cheap, then buy it at the current market price and don't fool around chasing the price lower. If you prefer a better entry price, then set the target price lower and wait. You might have to wait several months, but the stock market is volatile over time.

From my experience, it is rare for a stock price to go up and never come back down from the day you buy it. I would say that the stock price for 90% of all of my stock purchases have been lower within twelve months. The reason for this is because there is generally a significant stock market correction in mining stocks of at least 20% every year. You will find that this is a very volatile sector. If you use patience and wait for a good entry price, you will be a much better investor.

This is where discipline is needed. You have to be willing to lose those rare stocks that never come back down. But trust me, you will end up with much better entry prices for those stocks that you do buy.

There are enough undervalued stocks out there to ensure that when you focus on getting a good entry price, you will be rewarded. After you wait several months (or even years) for an entry price to come down, you will understand what I mean. During this long gold bull market, there has nearly always been a 20% correction in silver prices at some point during the year. Gold is not as volatile, but there is usually a 10% correction every year. These corrections usually impact stock prices significantly. This provides an opportunity to buy the dip. Moreover, buying the dip is an excellent strategy for getting a good entry price.

Let's say that you analyze a stock and think it is a least a five bagger. You look at the company's stock chart, and it has increased 25% in value in the past six months. Then you look at the gold chart, and it has not had a significant correction in six months. What do you do? The best move would be to wait for a correction. It will come. Perhaps you will be able to buy it for 25% less than its current stock price. That could turn your five bagger into a 10 bagger.

Additional Entry Price Factors

There are several factors to watch for that can affect the overall market and impact entry prices.

1. **Gold/Silver Prices:** If the price of gold/silver has been trending up and has not had a correction in several months, then it is probably due. If you buy during an uptrend, you are asking to be disappointed. Why? Because you could have bought at a lower price if you waited. The reverse is also true. If gold/silver prices are trending down and we have just experienced a correction in gold/silver prices, then it is time to buy before prices head higher.

   Catching the bottom is much more difficult than waiting for an uptrend to correct. To catch a bottom, always wait for the 200 WMA (week moving average) to be broken to the upside. And if you want to be sure the bottom is in, once it is over the 200 WMA, wait another month and see if it holds.

You won't catch the very bottom using this method, but you likely won't catch a falling knife either.

2. **Currency Movements:** The U.S. dollar has a huge impact on the price of gold/silver. While you are waiting for your entry price, watch the trend of the dollar. If the dollar is getting weaker, then gold and silver should rise until that reverses. Conversely, a strong dollar tends to force gold prices lower.

   I generally watch the dollar index on a daily or weekly basis, so that I know the trend. Most of the time it gets stuck in a range, and you have to guess which way it will go. But when it is trending, it will be clear: up or down.

3. **Oil Prices:** When oil prices head higher, gold usually follows. Oil tends to follow U.S. dollar weakness, but not necessarily. If there are price spikes in oil, look for gold to go along for the ride.

4. **Interest Rate Changes:** Lately, interest rates have been very, very low. So they haven't had much of an impact on gold prices. But once they start heading higher, keep a close eye on the trend. Higher interest rates will likely help gold/silver because they are an indicator of inflation.

   Ironically, gold can also be hurt by rising rates due to investors focus on real interest rates. When real rates are negative, it tends to help gold. But when interest rates rise, that tends to raise real rates and thereby hurt gold. So, if interest rates rise, you also want to see inflation rise, otherwise it's not good for gold.

5. **Economic Events:** Any instability is good for gold. Keep an eye on Europe and Japan for their debt problems. This could easily impact the rest of the world and create a global recession and add more instability.

6. **Gold Demand:** Keep an eye on Asia. This region is likely going to drive the gold price higher because they don't have as much as the West.

Already, China, India, and Russia have been accumulating gold. If other countries begin accumulating, then look for a big price jump.

7. **Inflation / Deflation:** Both of these are good for gold because they both create a crisis. What economies desire is low inflation, say 1-3%. Anything that deviates from that norm causes problems.

I monitor the price of gold, silver, oil, natural gas, food commodities, the dollar index, economic news, and political events on a daily or weekly basis. You should, too, if you want to be a gold/silver investor and pick good entry prices.

Selling Stocks

On certain occasions, I have sold some of my existing shares to fund my account. I do this when I see a really good buy that I should not miss, and I don't have the cash.

I recently had a stock with 10,000 shares that had significant profit, but I was concerned that most of the upside was gone. I also had three stocks on my buy list with low entry prices that I wanted to own. I sold 5,000 shares and bought 15,000 shares in these three new companies. I felt good about the trade. I rarely do that, but sometimes it makes sense.

Another reason I sell is if one of my stocks is purchased by a larger company. I generally sell the stock and use the proceeds to invest in another stock. I do this because the upside is usually limited with the merged companies.

I don't like to sell shares and prefer to hold long-term until I reach my exit strategy. However, in the mining business, this is not always possible. Sometimes you make mistakes, and your stocks crash and do not recover. After a while, you get tired of looking at them languishing, and you sell, usually during tax selling season.

Every December (tax selling season), you might decide to sell one of your losers and write them off. I've done that several times. In the U.S., you can write off $3,000 per year for investment losses, although you can offset losses with as many gains as you have in a single year. Also, losses can be rolled over into future years and potentially offset future gains.

> Note: If you sell a stock to obtain a tax loss, you can repurchase it thirty days later. This can make a lot of sense for stocks that are underwater, but you still want to own. You can sell in December and then buy it back after

the thirty day waiting period. This is very handy if you have a lot of capital gains.

Trading Stops

I don't suggest using trading stops unless a strategy calls for it.[66] That's not something you will hear from most professionals, but in my opinion, these stocks are too volatile. It's possible for many of your stocks to drop 50% or more during a large correction. If you use stops, you could be forced to sell many of your stocks at a loss.

I am confident that my portfolio will come back if it goes down significantly in value. Using my pyramid approach for diversification, it should come back. I have seen my portfolio go up and down like a yo-yo. So far, it has always come back, and gone higher.[67] If I were using trailing stops, I would have been stopped out in most of my stocks and forced to pay large capital gains taxes. That is not something I find attractive. I want my investments to ride for the long term.

Yes, there will be stocks that drop dramatically and stay there. But that is the exception and not the rule. Overall, you should be quite happy with your portfolio over the long term, unless all you pick are risky stocks. We have already looked at the risk levels of each stock category, and I have cautioned you about assuming too much risk.

Trading stops could have wiped out most of my portfolio and made me start over. No, thank you. I'll take the huge swings, and then ride the bull market higher. Yes, it is risky not using stops. But I believe we will see $2,500 gold, and I'm willing to take the chance that I'm right.

If by chance, gold drops to $1,000 and stays there, I won't be broke, but I will no longer be looking at early retirement. I put the odds of that happening at 1 in a million. But if it should happen, I don't think I would sell. I would probably just keep waiting for the bull market to return.

Even though I do not suggest using trading stops, most professionals believe the key to investing is cutting losses. Jim Slater, a successful gold stock investor, and author of The Zulu Principle, says the secret of his success is to cut losses and run profits. Moreover, he likes to start with a small investment in a stock and then add to it as the stock goes up in price (once he finds a winner, he likes to load up). He is not unique, as this is a common strategy among gold stock investors. Your job will be to determine when to cut losses.

As I stated, many investors use systems similar to the Zulu Principle. It is quite common for investors to use trailing stops. This locks in their profits and prevents losses. Investors who use these trailing stops also tend to take profits instead of letting their investments ride. It is quite common for investors to sell half their investment after it increases significantly in value. The combination of trailing stops and taking profits works great in non-volatile investments, but for mining stocks, this method can be challenging to use.

Because I invest in so many highly undervalued stocks, which are typically long-term investments, I tend to let them ride. This is perhaps a weakness in my investment strategy. However, I usually learn important lessons from the stocks that go down and do not recover. Education isn't always free. One of the things I have learned is to stay away from stocks in the category Potential Exists. I would also avoid Project Generators that have not yet found a significant discovery. If a company does not have the goods, then stay away.

I have found that most analysts recommend investing in only 10 to 30 stocks. A big reason why they recommend keeping your portfolio to a limited number of stocks is because of volatility. Who wants to get stopped out of 50 stocks? I've heard them say that there aren't 50 good stocks out there, and to only focus on the best. But I disagree. If you only invest in 30 stocks, you are going to miss a lot of opportunities for some very large returns if gold prices reach $2,500. For instance, if you only invest in 30 or fewer stocks, are you going to pick many high risk / high return stocks? Unlikely.

I can't argue that a portfolio of the 30 high-quality mining stocks could do extraordinarily well at higher gold prices. But to capture the value of many high performing stocks in this limited portfolio, would require a lot of trading and nimbleness. And that's not something I enjoy. I like to buy and hold. A portfolio with a limited number of stocks forces you to constantly monitor your portfolio and swap out underperforming stocks. In essence, you need to be a good trader.

There are two situations where using stops make sense. The first is when you chase hot stocks (described below). At some point, these hot stocks will correct and perhaps dramatically. By using a stop loss, you can lock-in profits or limit your losses.

The other is when you want to sell a stock. Once you decide to sell a stock, you can place a stop, which essentially locks-in your profit. Then you can watch and see if it goes higher. If it does, then it becomes a trailing stop-loss. As the stock goes higher, you move the stop-loss higher.

Watching Stocks

Watching stocks is crucial for building your portfolio. Once a stock goes on your watch list, it should be there because you think it has potential. Generally, these stocks have good company websites, and they allow you to be on their email lists. This way, you get all of the company news releases: the latest drilling results, PEAs, resource updates, etc.

Building your watch list allows you to create an information stream. You want information to come to you, especially drill results and 43-101 resource updates. You can also get emails from your Internet brokerage account when a stock price rises to a certain threshold. When the stock price rises, it is proof that something is happening with that stock. You can then research the company to understand why it increased. I generally set my price threshold for a 50% increase. If a company moves that much, something made it happen. A more aggressive investor might look for a 25% increase, to keep a closer watch on things.

Another way to watch stock price movements is to create a portfolio on my website. That way you can watch price changes on a frequent basis. It will provide you with a percentage change from the time a stock was added to the portfolio.

When you are building your portfolio, you should have 25-50 companies that you are watching. As information filters in, you can see how they are progressing. You can get a feel for these companies and decide whether they are going to pan out. After about a year of doing this, you will begin to know which are the good stocks, based on the information stream. You will also learn that exploration and developing mines is a slow process. It can take months to get drill results back from the lab and then analyzed for a press release. It can take more than a year for PEA (preliminary economic analysis), and PFS (pre-feasibility study) reports to be completed.

If you are lucky, several of these stocks will get moved to your buy list, and then you can set an entry price and get your irons hot. As my dad used to say, if you don't have any irons in the fire, nothing is going to happen. If your luck continues, you will get your entry price. And voila, your portfolio starts building.

Research

So, where do those stocks come from that make it to your watch list, or better yet, your buy list? My favorite way to find stocks is to research what smart people already own. These are the experienced investment analysts who would learn very little from reading this book.

I would recommend purchasing a gold/silver investment newsletter for getting tips about companies to research. These will give you a few leads. I tried a few newsletters, and it was worth the experience. The odds are you will not renew, but you will learn something because each newsletter writer has their own approach.

My next favorite is Twitter. There are a lot of good people to follow who provide a steady stream of information.

Another favorite website for gold/silver mining stock information is *www.CEO.ca*. It's a Canadian based website where users share information about mining stocks. I like its popularity, and there is a lot of information shared. If a stock price jumps or dumps, you can usually find out why on this website.

The other two websites that I currently use are the Bullboards on *www.Stockhouse.com* and *www.Hotcopper.com.au*, which has posts for Australian mining companies. These are both similar CEO.ca.

The *www.StateSideReport.com* website has a weekly podcast that covers the hot stocks. This can be a good place to find stocks. Allan Barry has a website called *www.AllanBarryReports.com.* He currently follows a lot of hot junior precious metal stocks.

The *www.TheAUReport.com* is an excellent source for finding stocks. They usually have at least one good interview every week. I used to check it every day when I was building my portfolio.

Another popular site is *www.seekingalpha.com*. They do not focus on gold and silver stocks, but have many articles on this sector. I have posted quite a few articles, which you can read. Just search by my name.

For daily news, *www.Kitco.com* is a great source for news releases. It is a bit difficult to use because they include base metal companies. I wish they would split the news releases into company type, but it is still very useful. I used to check the mining news releases on a daily basis.I used to check *www.321Gold.com* at least once a week. It has a lot of good articles, especially those written by the website's creator, Bob Moriarty. Also, check out Bob's archives.[68] Bob is a great analyst, and he constantly travels to company mine sites and posts his write-ups. I own several stocks because of his posts.

Three other guys you can trust are Al Korelin (*www.kereport.com*), Mickey Fulp (*www.mercenarygeologist.com*), and Jay Taylor (*www.miningstocks.com*). They have a lot of excellent information on their websites. Korelin and Taylor both have Internet radio shows that are very good for finding stocks. Between these sources, you should have a nice list of companies to research. Many of these analysts tend to be aggressive and follow the Junior market closely.

I have posted a few articles on *www.gold-eagle.com*, which has is a good website to checkout for gold/silver articles.

And don't forget my website: *www.goldstockdata.com*. I provide an easy way to find stocks with potential with my rating system and extensive database. I also have a newsletter that includes stock lists.

Next, join the blog of a popular mining company and read it daily. If you aren't getting any fresh information, then look for another company blog. It won't take long to find a company forum that is not a waste of time. The best company forums are on Agoracom.com, Stockhouse.com, Yahoo Finance, and Google Finance. Find a popular stock and then join the blog. You don't have to post. Instead, you can be a lurker. People love to post about their favorite stocks, and you will learn a lot. The GoldStockData forum has become an excellent source of information. It's only available to subscribers.

I have found that the best way to find a good blog is to follow the hot stocks. As you are surfing the web looking for mining stocks, when you find a stock that has been red hot (up over 100% in a short time frame), check its blog. By reading these blogs, you can get a lot of leads on what the smart money is doing.

If you spend time reading or listening to these sources, plus a newsletter, plus a company blog/forum, you should acquire an excellent watch and buy list.

Another excellent source of information are the company presentations that are provided on each company's web page. They nearly all post presentations. This is where you really learn about companies. Keep in mind that they are going to present themselves in the best light possible. So, if you are not impressed, don't put them on your watch list.

A nice benefit from reading these presentations is that they tend to compare themselves to their competitors. Thus, they do the research for you, teaching you about other companies.

The last places where I find information are Internet podcasts. My favorite is Bill Powers website and YouTube channel (*www.miningstockeducation.com*). Next is Jim Puplava's Financial Sense News Hour (*www.financialsense.com*). The other is Chris Waltzek's GoldSeek Radio (*www. Goldseek.com*). If you listen to these shows, you will stay informed on the precious metals scene, as well as the overall health of the economy. Al Korelin (*www.Kereport.com*) and Jay Taylor (*www.miningstocks.com*) also have excellent free Internet radio shows.

Final comments on doing research. Always check the last year's news releases on a company's website. Make sure that you know the company's story. Plus, always read the last quarter's financial report. This is not difficult and becomes easier with practice. You are looking for their cash and cash equivalent totals, plus current and long term debt. Plus, if they are a producer, you are looking for their costs and free cash flow. The best place to find financial reports is at *www.sedar.com* (Canadian listed) or *www.sec.gov/edgar* (USA listed). You can find Australian listed at *www.asx.com.au*.

Hot Stocks

One trend that I have noticed with mining investors is buying hot stocks. These are stocks that have risen 50% or more in a short period. Generally, these are low market cap exploration stocks, but not always. I often find people making posts of the stocks they own, and they tend to be all of the hot stocks. I almost laugh sometimes when I see this, but then I realize this strategy has a good risk/reward profile.

If a stock rises 50% or more, the odds are good that it will trend higher. You can buy it with a 10% stop-loss and then ride it higher using a trailing stop-loss. One thing that is fun about this strategy is that you can follow these hot stocks relatively easily since everyone is talking about them.

To find the hot stocks, all you need to do is frequent *www.CEO.ca* and look for the stocks that are trending. CEO.ca makes it easy to find them. They have a link called Companies on the home page. Click on that one, then click Trending. Then you can read the boards of those stocks that are trending. It won't take long to find out the stocks that people are talking about.

Trading Stocks

I don't like to do a lot of stock trading. Instead, I'm a buy and hold investor. However, due to the volatility of the market, sometimes it makes sense to trade.

If you own a stock that is up significantly and you have a strong feeling that the stock is going to drop, it might be a good time to sell and sit on the sidelines. Then, when it falls, you can buy it back and get some free shares. I know people who do this repeatedly and get a lot of free shares. For instance, let's look at Newmont Mining's one-year chart from February 2010.[69]

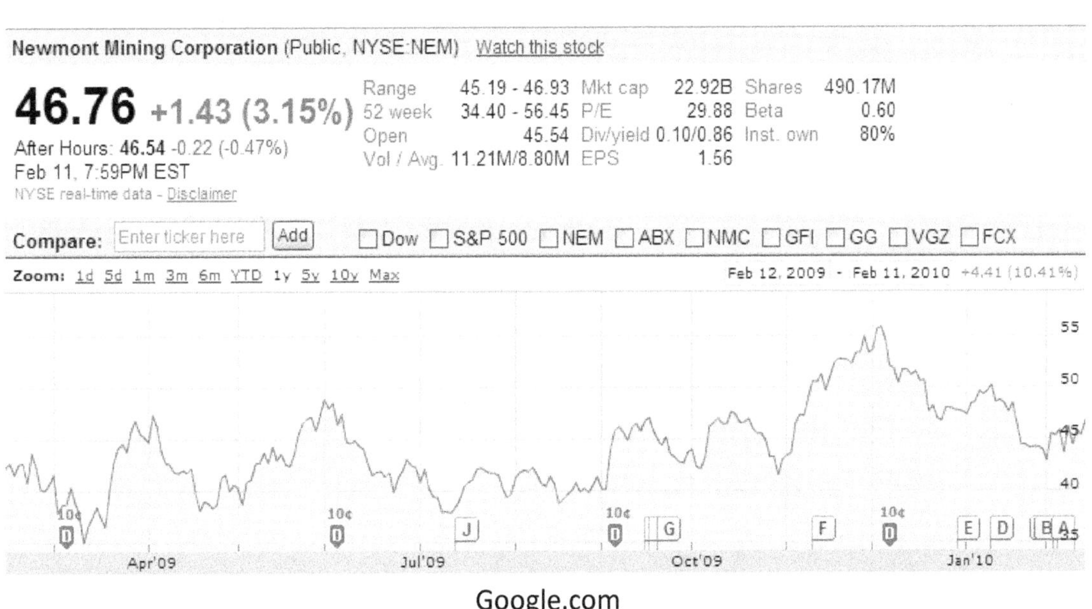

Google.com

Look at all of those peaks and valleys! All you had to do was sell at a few of those peaks, and buy back after it fell. You could have done this several times. The key to this type of trading is waiting until you are substantially ahead before you make your first sell. Also, it is smart to be conservative when you buy back. In this example, an investor could have waited for a 10% or more drop before buying back. However, you could use 5%, which is more conservative.

This type of trading is strictly following the trends up and down. You don't care about anything else but the trend. It goes up to a peak, you sell. It goes down, you buy back. The key is making sure that your first sell point is very profitable. I suggest doing this after at least a 50% return. Once you have locked in a nice return, then you can play this game of adding free shares. It's quite easily done, and you can reduce your overall cost significantly. As long as the trend of the stock is up, you can add a lot of free shares.

> Note: Trading requires that you pay capital gains tax on any gains in the year they were realized.
>
> Note: If you do get involved in trading, make sure to read a book on technical trading (reading charts). The more you understand technical trading, the better the trader you will become. I highly recommend following Mitch Ray on his YouTube channel. It's free and you will learn a lot.

When Not to Trade

This type of trading strategy is dangerous for a strong stock that you want to own long term. For instance, if you sell out of a stock and then it jumps in value, you may sit on the sidelines while it continues to appreciate in value. So, if you are going to trade to get some free shares, use these three criteria:

1. You already have a substantial profit.
2. It is not a strong stock that is likely to run straight up.
3. You are not going to be disappointed if you can't buy back in for a lower price.

Trading stocks for peaks and valleys is only one way to do this, and there are many different strategies. Another way is to trade ETFs, such as SLV or GLD (or a leveraged bullion ETF). Because gold and silver are volatile, and unlikely to head straight up, you can apply your trading strategy to an ETF to catch the peaks and valleys.

If you use this strategy, make sure you do not invest all of your cash! Always leave a significant cushion, which you will need for defending against price drops. Let me explain how this works:

1. Fund your account.
2. Wait for a good entry point.
3. Purchase the ETF to start a position. (Make sure you are very satisfied with the entry price.)
4. Wait for a strong peak in the chart and sell half of your position (which adds profit into your account). Ideally, this should be a 50% profit, which could take some time to materialize.
5. Wait for the next trough and buy more shares, using 50% to 100% of your

profits.

6. Wait for another peak and sell half of your investment (adding more profit into your account).
7. Repeat. If you don't get a peak, but instead another trough, take another position, perhaps 10% of your profits.
8. Always keep plenty of funds in your account in case the ETF keeps dropping and you have to keep adding to your positions.
9. Always take profits at the peaks, thereby adding profits to your bankroll.
10. You are trading on the peaks and valleys. You are buying the troughs and selling the peaks. Or, in other terms, you are selling into strength and buying weakness.

The key to this trading strategy is discipline (following the rules) and having faith that the trend is higher. It's a simple strategy, and it works like a charm in a bull market. You keep selling into strength and buying into weakness, and your account will keep growing.

This can be a lot of fun, although I prefer to simply load up on highly undervalued stocks and let them perform. If you want to play with a small bankroll and try to build it up, go for it. It can be as much fun as gambling in Las Vegas. It's even better, because the odds are in your favor, as long as this bull market marches onward.

While this simple trading system can work, a more professional system is one followed by a TA (technical analyst). You can read many books on TA and follow some professional traders on YouTube to learn how they trade. My favorite is Mitch Ray.

Another Trading System

Another system I learned came from Mickey Fulp (*www.mercenarygeologist.com*). He recommends selling half of your shares after your stock appreciates 100%. This will take your cost basis for that stock to zero, and leave you with zero risk of a loss. Then you take your original investment (actually less, because of capital gains) and find another stock. If that stock rises 100%, you do it again. With a little bit of luck, you will have several stocks with a zero cost basis and zero risk of a loss!

Of course, there is some risk with this method, because if your original stock continues to rise in value, you will have given up 50% of that profit. Moreover, if the next stock you invest in does not rise, the overall investment was a mistake. In other words, this system works if you are very good at picking stocks, and they *all* rise. This system makes sense and can be very profitable for good stock pickers.

Rolling Stocks

You're going to like this one when you get the opportunity to do it. When a stock explodes in value, and you are sitting on a boatload of profit, it is a good idea to roll the profits into new investments. After a stock makes a huge run, the upside potential diminishes. You will have to pay capital gains taxes on these sales, but the rest can be reinvested. You can take the profits and buy more stocks or other investments.

The question arises, when do you do this? It will be different for each stock. There will be a point when you recognize that it is time to get out of some stocks (or at least sell a portion). The profits will be huge, and the upside will be constrained or at risk. This can happen for a variety of reasons: growth could slow, costs could rise, or perhaps the company enters into a merger that you don't like.

Rolling stocks can also be used to raise cash to invest in another stock. If you are up 100% or more and you no longer like a stock's upside potential versus another stock, you might decide to sell one and buy the other. I generally let my stocks ride for the long term, but some investors like to roll out of them when they sense opportunities.

Once you have a stock with significant profit, you have to think of your exit strategy for that stock. At some point, you are going to roll out of the stock and into something else. Some investors do this more frequently than others. You have to find what works best for you.

Exit Strategy

It's important to define your exit strategy. You need to decide what you are trying to do with your investments. Are you going to take profits along the way? Are you going to hold until we reach the magical $2,500 mark for gold? Are you going to take some profits at $2,000? If so, what are you going to do with the money? These are decisions you should think about.

My final exit strategy is to wait for the DOW/gold ratio to reach two. Let me explain. I believe there is a high likelihood that the DOW/gold ratio will reach two. During the last gold bull market that ended in 1980, the ratio reached one (850 DOW / $850 gold price). This takes the emotion out of my decision. I simply wait for the ratio to reach two. My guess is that it will be something like 10,000 DOW / $5,000 gold price. Once it gets close to this ratio, it's time to get completely out of the miners.

Once the DOW/gold ratio reaches two, the odds are that the gold bull market is just about over. In my opinion, that will be a good time to move into other assets. I probably will keep some gold bullion, but most of my assets will be in other areas, such as property, food production, or new technology.

In addition to my DOW/gold final exit strategy, I will steadily sell a few gold stocks as gold rises. There will inevitably be some gold stocks that are simply ready to be sold. This will happen for a variety of reasons, but mostly just to lock-in profits for stocks that do extremely well. I would expect to sell at various price points, such as $2,000, $2,200, etc. Once gold reaches $2,000, I plan to check my portfolio for stocks that have exploded in value.

I may not sell all of a stock at each price point, but I will take substantial profits. I learned an important lesson in 2011 when I did not take profits after gold reached $1,900. Some stocks that I owned in 2011 went bankrupt a few years later. If I had taken profits in 2011, it would have been extremely beneficial. That was a mistake that I won't make this time around.

So, my first exit point is $2,000. By the time gold reaches $2,500, I would expect to have sold at least half of gold mining stocks. By the time gold reaches $3,500, I would expect to have sold at least 80%. After that, I'll probably wait for the DOW/gold ratio to signal the final exit.

I have a separate exit strategy for silver. I plan to begin selling my silver stocks when silver reaches $50. That is my first sell point. I already have two stocks that I plan to sell at that level. My next sell points are $75, $100, and $125, where I will sell a few more at each level. Finally, at $150 silver, I plan to be out of nearly all of my silver stocks. I have not yet decided what to do with my physical silver bullion, but I likely won't sell it before $150 silver.

You may be wondering why I have a separate strategy for silver stocks and gold stocks. In a word: risk. In Chapter 1, I explained why silver investing is much riskier than gold investing. For this reason, I want to cash out as the risk increases. I'm confident silver will reach $100, but beyond that, the risk increases. So I am going to begin getting out as the price rises.

Because I got into silver investing early, I can get out early and still reach my investment goals. At $100 silver, I want to cash out a significant amount of my silver profits. In other words, I want to lock-in my profits before the risk gets too high.

While these are my exit strategies, try to come up with your own. Think about them and even write them down. It is going to be very tempting to roll out of your stocks and take profits. But if we get a mania in stocks, you could be leaving a lot of money on the table. The question to ask is when is it too early to exit? While I will likely be leaving a lot of potential profit on the table for my silver stocks, I am going to keep some of my gold stocks until the DOW/gold ratio reaches close to two. If gold goes to $5,000, then I want to own a few gold miners. If silver goes to $300, hopefully, I will have been smart enough to keep my silver bullion.

One other strategy that I will likely use it keeping 25% of my best performing stocks. Instead of selling all of a stock, I will keep 25%, and let the rest ride. Then for this final 25%, I will use a trailing stop of 20% and let it ride until it stops out. If I get lucky, this final 25% could ride the bull market to the top.

CHAPTER 10

HOW TO VALUE MINING STOCKS

Note: A lot of this chapter is review and has been covered in previous chapters. However, for anyone new to investing in mining stocks, this material will be beneficial.

The difficulty investing in gold and silver stocks is understanding how to value a mining company. I know, because when I started out, I didn't have a clue and made many investment mistakes. Now I make fewer mistakes and I am much more confident that I am making the right choices. Moreover, my understanding of risk has increased dramatically, which is an important component in valuing a stock.

The starting point for valuing a stock is collecting and analyzing data. You need a checklist of information that you are interested in knowing. This is how you find the red flags which nearly every company has to some extent. A short list of these data points includes the stock price, market cap, share structure, location, amount of resources, ore grade, recovery rate, management, the timeline to production, company guidance, growth potential, cash/debt situation, cash costs, and valuation. You need these data points and information to utilize a systematic approach to valuing a company. Moreover, you need to look at all of the data points before you understand the valuation of a company.

There are only two things to do when you analyze a company. First, you want to identify any red flags, and second, you want to determine its future upside potential. For me, the red flags become a risk-reward rating, and the future upside potential become an upside rating. You don't have to use these ratings and can simply go through the analysis process.

The purpose of looking for red flags is two-fold. First, you will use them to adjust down the upside rating. Second, you will use them to determine the risk-reward rating. The red flags are essentially increased risk.

In this chapter, I will show you how to find the red flags and how to value a stock. I will also show you how to arrive at a rating, which you then use to identify the true value of a stock. I invented this rating system through years of experience, and it works very well at finding undervalued stocks.

My system is a ten-step approach, with the first eight steps analyzing data to find any red flags. The ninth step is to check if a stock is undervalued, and the last step is to give the stock a rating.

When I analyze a stock, I use my systematic approach to determine the true value, which is defined by a rating. If you use this ten-step method, you will have a good way to filter out stocks that you don't want to own. Also, once you use this system, when you analyze a company, you will know what to look for.

This system is aimed at identifying highly undervalued gold and silver mining stocks. My goal is to find highly undervalued stocks with upside ratings of 3 or higher, along with downside ratings of 3 or higher. A 4 rating is currently the highest upside rating that I use. It is for stocks with 10 bagger upside potential. Here is the rating chart that was displayed earlier.

Upside

1	Lowest Rating
1.5	Potential 2 Bagger
2	Potential 3 Bagger
2.5	Likely 3 Bagger
3	Potential 5 Bagger
3.5	Likely 5 Bagger
4	Potential 10 Bagger
4.5	Likely 7-8 Bagger
5	Likely 10 Bagger

Downside

1	Lowest Rating
1.5	Very poor risk/reward
2	Poor risk/reward
2.5	Marginal risk/reward
3	Good risk/reward
3.5	Excellent risk/reward
4	Tremendous risk/reward
4.5	Stellar risk/reward
5	Rare risk/reward

Using this two-factor rating system allows you to identify both upside potential and the associated risk. I avoid producers and development stocks with upside or downside ratings of 2 or lower. Plus, I am very careful with downside ratings of 2.5.

I used to believe that it was better to invest in ETFs, such as SIL for silver miners or GDXJ for gold miners, because they were less risky. However, I have come to believe that I would rather pick my own Mid-Tier Producers using my ratings, than own ETFs. It's okay to also own these ETFs, but I think you can outperform them by picking the best mid-tiers based on these ratings.

I never envision investing in a producer or developer with a 2 or lower upside rating, but you may for high-quality income-producing stocks. I do sometimes invest in exploration stocks with upside ratings of 2, because nearly all of the Project Explorer stocks in my database have a 2 upside rating. This is because it's very difficult to assume that drill results will be successful.

Okay, let's begin.

1) Properties / Ownership

You want a company with at minimum a potential flagship property (2 million oz. gold, or 40 million oz. silver). This is the most important criteria for picking stocks. Most of your mistakes are going to be from companies that do not find flagship (or potential flagship) properties. If you invest in undervalued companies with flagship properties, you will likely be rewarded.

It's okay to invest in a few companies that have small properties if the valuations are attractive and they have exploration potential, but don't make it a habit. Focus on flagships, because you are after growth, and small properties are not generally conducive to growth.

The reason why we look for properties with 2 million oz. of gold or 40 million oz. of silver is for the future cash flow potential. At these levels, the cash flow is sufficient to grow the company. For instance, a 2 million oz. property will likely produce about 80,000 to 120,000 oz. per year for 12-15 years. That is both solid cash flow and a long life mine. Anything less, and the potential for growth is limited.

The other benefit of a flagship property is its potential value. Let's use a hypothetical scenario:

Gold Price: $2,500

Production: 100,000 oz.

All-In Costs: $1,200 per oz.

Cash Flow: $1,300 x 100,000 oz. = $130 Million

Valuation at 10x Cash Flow = $1.3 Billion

Only a high-quality company is going to get valued at 10x cash flow, but the potential exists for flagship properties to have very high valuations. This requires two things: cash flow and higher gold prices.

The first thing I always do is check the properties for cash flow potential. Ideally, you want to find a growth-focused company that will leverage cash flow from a flagship property to expand production. Future cash flow is what we are after, and large properties have the potential to provide high cash flow. Properties that can add production ounces and resource ounces are what create increased cash flow. This is what will drive the stock price higher.

It's okay to invest in a company with only one property if the valuation is attractive. However, for a company to have significant growth potential, it will need to have a pipeline of projects or exploration potential. If you can find a company that is highly undervalued and has several pipeline properties that is usually better than a single property. This gives them a pipeline of potential future mines that are likely not valued into their current stock price. This increases the upside potential of the stock.

When you analyze a company's properties, you want to look at several things. How many ounces are in the ground? What percentage is inferred? What is the ore grade? What is the cash cost of mining the deposit? What is the recovery rate? Where is it located? What is the impact of the location? What is the current exploration program? What is the potential resource size? What is the company's plan for this property? Are they giving guidance of production? What is the size of the mineralization zone (exploration potential)? How much of the property has been explored? Does it have a PEA? If so, what is the after-tax IRR? As you can see, there are a lot of questions to ask, and you need to answer them all to get a clear picture.

In addition to checking out the properties, always check to see if they own them 100%. It's not a requirement that they own 100%, but if it is less, then you need to reduce the valuation. I check their website or regulatory reports to find out their ownership stakes.

It is quite common in the mining business to option properties as joint ventures. Ideally, you want companies that own their properties and can leverage the increasing gold/silver price for substantial profits. I generally am comfortable if they own at least 75% of their properties. Anything less than that and I feel like the upside potential is constrained.

One final comment on properties. You want long life mines because once a mine stops producing, cash flow dries up. This will have a deleterious effect on the stock price. For this reason, you need to check the mine life of each project/deposit. Ideally, you want to have at least a remaining ten-year mine life. This will ensure that the expected future cash flow is not impacted.

2) People / Management Team

There are two types of management teams. The first type is an exploration team. This is a company that only knows how to find gold. These are Project Generators. They are called that because they find mines and generate projects for other companies to develop into a mine.

Exploration companies call themselves different names and use a variety of different mission statements. Often they will call themselves exploration and development companies, but their intent is to either option a discovery or sell it. They usually have no intention of building and operating a mine. In essence, these are Project Generators, but they do not call themselves that.

There are two types of Project Generators, those that have very few properties and those that have many properties. In my opinion, there is no difference between them. The only thing that matters is who finds a large mine. I used to think that a company with more properties had a higher chance of finding a large mine, but I no longer believe that. For this reason, I simply wait for a discovery and then decide if I want to chase the drill results.

Some Project Generators will attempt to acquire a number of properties and then find partners to drill their projects. Some investors like this type of strategy, because share dilution can potentially be minimized. At one time, I found some merit in this strategy, but I have come to the conclusion that the risk/reward is not that good unless there has already been a discovery. Any company without a discovery, no matter how many properties they own, will have a hard time finding a large mine.

The other management type is an exploration *and* development team. These are the management teams that build and operate mines. These teams come in all sizes, from very small to very large. The key is identifying the ability and quality of the management team. A small team can be just as effective at execution as a large team. That said, the larger teams tend to have more experience and better quality teams.

When you look at management teams, you want to check if they have the ability to build a mine and if they have done it before. You want to check the experience of all members on the team. This will often be available on the company's website. One thing I have learned is that teams with a lack of experience tend to sell their projects right before it is time to build the mine. This is a big letdown for investors because instead of a potential 500%+ return, you end up with around 50%, which is about the going premium for takeovers.

I prefer management teams with good reputations and track records, and who are investor friendly. To identify companies that are investor friendly, first check the share structure (I will be discussing this in step 3). Low share dilution is a telltale sign that companies are looking after shareholder interests. Note that if a company is not a producer with cash flow, then they will likely be diluting the share structure to raise cash to fund exploration or development. The second thing to look for is the percentage of ownership in the company that management owns. A percentage of at least five percent will ensure they are shareholder focused.

Management experience isn't as important for exploration companies. For these companies, you just want good drill results and a smart geologist. However, once a company decides to build a mine, or is already a producer, then the management team is vital. The reason why is because it is such a difficult industry. It is very easy to make mistakes in this business. Smart management teams are not easy to come by, and you cannot expect all of your stocks to have one.

One of the most surprising things I have learned about this industry is that even good management teams can get into trouble. It's amazing how many companies with quality projects have either went bankrupt or watched their share price crash from 2012 to 2019. The only thing that really protects a company is the quality of their properties.

It is a good idea to do some research on the management team and CEO before investing in a stock. Listen to an interview with the CEO and see if you get a good feeling. If they have a good management team, they usually will brag about their people. Also, if the CEO is excited about their company's potential (and they should be), it will be apparent in the interview or presentation. I prefer companies that have a CEO who is passionate about their prospects.

Try to find a strong management team to go with excellent projects in an ideal location. Then you have the trifecta. These are the stocks you look for, and when you find them, you invest. People and projects are excellent starting points for analyzing stocks, but not the end all. You still have to look at all of the data points to get a clear picture.

3) Share Structure

The share structure is broken into three parts:

- Outstanding Shares
- Outstanding Options
- Outstanding Warrants

Outstanding Shares are what you see published when you get a stock quote on Google Finance. These are the common shares that have been issued.

Outstanding Options are stock options given to employees, contractors, or others who are affiliated with the company. Each option has a specific price threshold (strike price), along with exercise and expiration dates, which must be met before the stock can be issued. Legally, stock options must be granted at or above the current stock price. If an option exceeds the strike price, they are usually exercised (purchased) by the option holder and become common stock, thereby increasing the number of shares outstanding.

What makes stock options valuable is that you usually get to purchase stock below the current market price. This usually creates instant profit for someone holding an option that is in the money (above the strike price).

Outstanding Warrants are options that investors hold to purchase common stock at a specific price for a certain period of time. These are generally given to investors when they participate in a private financing. These are used to entice investors to participate in a financing. They can be very valuable if the stock price increases because of leverage. If you own a warrant, and the stock price appreciates in value, you have essentially been given money. You can then either sell your warrant for a profit, or buy the stock at the warrant price, and let your profits ride.

Because warrants and options generally turn into common stock, it is suggested to use fully diluted shares (common stock, plus warrants and options) to do your stock valuations. I always use fully diluted shares for stock valuations on my website. One lesson that all mining investors learn is that stock prices drop as the stock becomes diluted. Also, stock prices tend to reflect fully diluted shares, as investors anticipate options and warrants turning into common stock.

Anything that increases the number of Shares Outstanding is called dilution. This can happen by private placements, public share offerings, exercised options, and exercised warrants. You will learn very quickly that in the gold/silver mining business that dilution is quite common, especially for Juniors.

I prefer to own companies that have less than 150 million fully diluted shares, although it is more realistic to average around 250 million fully diluted shares in your portfolio. Note that if you purchase a company with low dilution, that does not mean it will remain that way. A company's current fully diluted shares can only remain static if they have cash flow, a large cash position, or plan to issue debt to obtain cash.

Companies without cash will either have to add debt or issue more shares to raise funds. The reason for this is because the mining business is cash intensive. Exploration, development, and production require cash. For most exploration companies, their only option is usually to issue more shares and dilute the share structure. Investment banks are not going to loan them money unless a project is significantly advanced. There are occasions where exploration companies carry debt, but it is the exception.

Try to avoid companies with over 400 million shares (unless it is a large company), because the share price will not have explosive potential to rise. For instance, if a company has 100 million shares outstanding with a $1 stock price and the market cap rises to $1 billion, then the stock price will rise from $1 to $10. Whereas, if the company has 400 million shares outstanding, the stock price will rise from 25 cents to $2.50. On a percentage basis, the increase will be the same, but psychologically it will appear to be rising faster because of the tighter share structure, and more investors will jump in.

It isn't only psychology that favors tight structures, because each share will be more valuable for tighter structures. For instance, if a company has 100 million ounces of silver in the ground and 100 million shares outstanding, then each share will be worth one ounce of silver. Whereas, if there are 400 million shares, each share will only be worth one-fourth of an ounce. This valuation difference can impact the stock price and is attractive to investors.

While you want to avoid stocks with over 400 million fully diluted shares, it is okay to invest in a few highly diluted stocks, if the valuations are very attractive. Just don't make it a habit. My preferred upper limit is about 400 million, although I do own many stocks above this limit. Sometimes the valuation is extremely attractive, even with high dilution. The key for highly diluted stocks is what happens if they stop diluting. If a company has high dilution but is beginning production, then it might be a good investment.

One thing I have noticed is that with non-producers, dilution can severely impact the share price. If you purchase a non-producer with over 300 million shares, then it could easily become 600 million shares or more before they reach production. The reason for the increase is that it costs money to develop and build mines. For a non-producer, you want to start with low dilution, otherwise you will end up with very high dilution.

Another reason investors loath highly diluted share structures is because of the potential for a reverse stock split. For instance, once stock dilution reaches 500 million shares or higher, companies often do a 5 to 1 or 10 to 1 reverse stock split in order to raise the company's stock price. This happened several years ago with Coeur Mining. If you adjust their stock price for the 10 to 1 reverse split, their all-time high is around $70. That is substantially below their all-time high. From my experience, a reverse stock split never seems to be good for shareholders. Although it is good for investors who purchase after the reverse split, because they get a tighter structure.

Always check to see how many fully diluted shares are outstanding. The market cap is calculated using shares outstanding multiplied by the current stock price. However, if a company has a lot of warrants and options, the true current valuation is much higher when you include fully diluted shares. When you buy a share of stock that has a lot of warrants or options, you are paying closer to the fully diluted price, because those warrants and options eventually dilute the stock price. The invisible hand of the market tends to account for that valuation.

Another invisible hand valuation that can impact the market cap is called the EV, or Enterprise Value. This is the market cap plus net debt. This also known as the true value of the company. I like to think of it as the effective purchase price.

Let me try to explain the EV because it is somewhat confusing. When a gold/silver company is acquired, the selling price is usually the market cap plus a premium of about 50%. Thus, the only thing that comes into play is the equity value, which is the market cap. But what if the company has a lot of debt or a lot of cash?

Often the cash and debt are not reflected in the market cap. Instead, the market cap is usually a reflection of the cash flow or gold/silver in the ground. The EV tries to give an investor or buyer a better picture of what they are buying besides the equity. Let's look at an example.

Let's say a company has $50 million in debt and $100 million in cash. Thus, the net debt is negative $50 million. This cash becomes a valuable asset for the buyer. For this reason, the effective purchase price is the market cap minus the net debt. Make sense? In effect, they are paying an implied discount to receive that cash. As an investor, you want to acquire companies with an effective purchase price below the market cap (with negative net debt). Conversely, you want to avoid buying companies with a lot of net debt, because debt eventually has to be paid.

All the EV does is gives you a better picture of the true value of a company. A company with a lot of net debt is worth less (on a true value basis) than the market cap, and the one with a lot of net cash is worth more. Ironically, in the mining business, I rarely see the EV come into play for acquisitions. I think this is because a company's gold/silver resources play such a dominant role in their valuation, which is reflected in the market cap.

4) Location

I prefer locations that are mining friendly. This can be defined as the ease of obtaining permits; the tax structure; environmental laws; ease of getting claims approved; ability to get infrastructure developed; and overall political resistance.

Ideally, you want to invest in Canada or Australia where existing mines are operating. Why? Because they treat mining as a national priority. Those are the two countries that are likely to support their mining industry in the future. However, if it is a new mine that is being developed, then the risk is much higher (unless it is in an established mining district). Currently, the U.S. and Mexico are mining friendly for established mining districts. But I am not confident that it will remain that way for many more years.

Below is my ranked location risk from safest to extreme:

Safest: Canada, Australia, New Zealand, United States.

Moderately Safe: Brazil, Guyana, Nicaragua, Fiji, Ireland, Finland, Sweden, Norway.

Moderate Risk: Mexico, Argentina, Peru, Chile, Panama, Colombia, Mongolia.

High Risk: East Africa, West Africa, Russia, China, Russian Satellites (e.g., Kazakhstan), Ecuador, Turkey, Eastern Europe, Indonesia, Philippines, Middle East, Spain, Bolivia, Papua New Guinea.

Extreme Risk: Venezuela, South Africa, Central Africa.

As the price of gold rises, it is going to be a lightning rod for political foes of mining. Rising taxes and potential nationalization are real threats for long-term investments in many countries. If economies struggle, gold and silver can be perceived as national resources that belong to the people. If South America turns left politically (and potentially other countries in Africa), this creates more political risk towards mining.

After checking whether the location is in a mining friendly place, the next thing to look for is infrastructure. I prefer to invest in companies that have a project in a mining district that has infrastructure in place. However, if a project is not in an established mining district, that is not a deal breaker, but district projects have significant advantages. Mines in mining districts tend to get built. Moreover, properties with no infrastructure can mean waiting years until production begins, or capital costs that are beyond a small company's means.

If you analyze a small exploration company and they are exploring a project that does not have road access and is in the middle of nowhere, think twice. The capex capital requirement is going to increase dramatically, as will the cost of mining the project. Also, they likely will not be able to get financing for the large capex requirement and will have to either JV the project or sell it.

One of the first things to consider about the location is if there is a mine nearby and if it has had any political issues. If there is a nearby working mine without any political issues, then that is normally a green light another mine can be built. In the United States, this does not necessarily apply because the permitting process can be highly contentious and litigation is common.

Always consider the political and environmental risk of a location. There are many factors that can impact mining: taxation, royalties, potential nationalization, permitting, native issues, worker relations (unions), litigation, ecological resistance, etc.

Do not underestimate the impact of local issues on a mine. There are dozens of examples of mining projects halted or suspended due to local issues. This is happening throughout the world with no country being exempt. Moreover, resistance to mining appears to be increasing. The protests are primarily ecological, although sometimes it is about economics (who gets the money for the natural resources).

There are usually two types of protests. The first type is to prevent a mine from being built, and the second type is halt production. The second type can either be to obtain more money for workers or to halt production permanently. The best way to limit these types of protests is to focus on mines in the safest jurisdictions.

The key to finding a good location is to try to limit your exposure to political risk and avoiding infrastructure issues. Depending on how many stocks you end up with in your portfolio, you can expect to lose money in at least one stock because of political issues. And it is highly likely that infrastructure issues will end up costing you money at some point. This will likely occur when you own a stock with infrastructure issues, and other investors avoid it, leaving you holding the bag.

I do not completely ignore stocks in politically unsafe locations. For instance, in West Africa today there are many Mid-Tier Producers that are highly undervalued. Buying a few of them probably outweighs the risk. And having a few stocks in Peru, Argentina, and Chile does not create huge risk. I am leery of Ecuador, but it seems to be getting a lot of activity. Mexico is a concern of mine, which seems to be moving away from its mine friendly reputation.

5) Projected Growth

Projected growth refers to production growth and resource growth. Without growth in these two areas, we are wasting our time. Why? Because production growth and resource growth are vital for stock appreciation. These are the two most important factors that drive a stock price higher, after the price of gold/silver. For clarification, let me explain resources. Resources are composed of three parts:

> *Inferred Resources*. These are resources that have been identified by drilling. Sometimes they are validated with a 43-101 report (if the stock trades in Canada), and sometimes they are estimated by companies. The bottom line is that inferred resources are not guaranteed to ever be mined and should be looked at as potential reserves. Moreover, these are resource estimates that are considered to be unreliable and can be considered speculative resources.
>
> *Measured and Indicated Resources*. These are resources that have been confirmed to exist. These have been identified with drilling results, and if they are a Canadian traded stock, a 43-101 resource estimate. This is an accredited report by an independent company. These are resources that exist, but cannot necessarily be mined economically.
>
> *Proven and Probable Reserves*. These are resources that not only exist but can be mined economically. This is proven using a feasibility study (or pre-feasibility), which is published publicly. Once a study is completed, mining companies can announce to investors how many reserve ounces they have.

To arrive at total resources, you add up all three parts. However, this is where you have to use your judgment and confidence in the management team. It is not always prudent to rely on inferred resources. You have to use your judgment when you value a company. Sometimes I will count the inferred, and sometimes I will not. One thing that we know is that Measured and Indicated resources, and Proven and Probable reserves exist.

On my website, I use a concept called plausible resources. I count 100% of the P&P, 75% of M&I, and 50% of Inferred to get a total of plausible resources. This is a handy way to get a fairly accurate view of future reserves.

One final point on resources and reserves. Usually, a company will list the proven and probable (P&P) totals separately, but then they will include them with the measured and indicated (M&I) totals. You have to be careful to check if the P&P reserves are included in the M&I totals. Otherwise, you can mistakenly count the P&P reserves twice.

Projecting growth coincides with their properties. What are their projections and guidance for increasing production and resources in the next few years? I like to invest in undervalued companies that are forecasting growth in these two areas. For instance, back in early 2009, First Majestic Silver stated clearly in their company presentation that they were forecasting to produce 10 million ounces of silver by 2012. At the time they were producing about 3 million ounces and were undervalued. I bought it. Why? Because of the forecasted growth. Growth means a higher valuation down the road (as long as gold and silver prices don't drop).

If a company is not giving guidance for future production ounces or resource ounces, then you have to forecast it yourself. For instance, if a company has a 1 million ounce resource and is planning to aggressively drill several known mineralized targets, the odds are good that they will increase their resources. We can make two forecasts from their drilling program: 1) They will likely increase their total resources, and 2) They will likely produce more ounces in the future. If we assume a 50% increase in both, then the upside potential can be huge. As a long-term investment, a small market cap company can have the potential to be a 10+ bagger, if they can grow their resources and make it into production.

Growth is what creates upside potential, and what creates growth (increased production and resources) is often not valued into a stock until production approaches. Currently, investors tend to ignore pipeline projects that are on the horizon. Until these projects get close to production, the production ounces and resource ounces are not valued into the stock price. Generally, there is a spike in the stock price when the final permit is granted to build a mine. Then there is another spike when financing is obtained. Finally, there is a large spike a few months before or when production begins.

There are several factors that can hurt a company's valuation even if a company has potential growth in production and resources. These are the location (perceived political risk), infrastructure issues, hedging, high production costs, high energy prices, financial weakness (debt or cash issues), permit issues, environmental issues, native issues, and unexpected events (flooding, mining accidents, legal issues, etc.).

Note that many of these factors are red flags that you can account for when you do a company's valuation. Be aware that some of the factors are unexpected events that add to the risk of mining company investments. While we can try to project growth, in many respects, it is speculation, because we cannot always account for unexpected events that can occur.

When you are looking at projected growth, you need to consider the FD market cap of the company. Why? Because size matters. A company with a large market cap will not have the same upside potential as a smaller company. For instance, I generally only look at Mid-Tier producers with market caps under $500 million, and preferably closer to $150 million. Why? Because I am looking for big returns and larger cap companies are likely not going to have explosive growth.

You need to determine your own market cap preferences and your investment goals. I suggest avoiding very large companies and very small companies. The question you need to answer is what is too big and too small for your investment goals. These answers will vary with every investor.

I prefer companies with market caps below $3 billion and above $20 million. I have found that companies with market caps below $20 million tend to have extensive risk and are highly dilutive. Ideally, I like to invest in companies with fully diluted market caps between $50 million and $150 million. This is a high-risk range, but there are a lot of high-quality companies in this range with high upside potential. This is where you find companies with significant growth potential and very low valuations.

6) Good Buzz / Good Chart

Always check the chart before you buy a stock. How does it look? Is it trending up or down? Is it flat lined? Is it coiled (ready to breakout)? After reading a few charts by following companies, you will know what to look for. For instance, I watched First Majestic's chart from 2005 to 2009. It was coiled and ready to break out. How did I know that? Because it was undervalued versus its projected production growth and the stock price had not broken out. It continually traded under $3, with a market cap around $200 million. Even the CEO at the time said he was puzzled at the low stock price.

When a stock is undervalued and has not broken out, that is an opportunity. You can either buy it or wait for the breakout. Sometimes it is smart to wait because there is always the possibility of a market correction (which seems to happen every year for mining stocks) and you can get a better entry price. For instance, if you find a stock you like, and the chart is flat-lined, why buy it? Why not be patient and see which direction it goes? If you are going to make a long-term investment, it is smart to be patient for your entry point.

When you look at a chart, you will begin to see a good chart and a bad chart. A good chart is an undervalued stock that has not yet had a parabolic move. You want to catch stocks before they make big moves. If you see a stock that has already made a parabolic move, then you want to wait for a major correction to get a better entry point. Sometimes you have to admit that you missed the move and that most of the value has already been built into the stock price.

Stock charts are a handy way to determine a good entry point. Often the stock will show a series of peaks and valleys and will usually trade back to the trend line. Rarely do stocks go straight up after you buy them. For this reason, it is always smart to be patient and wait for a better entry point than on the day you decided to buy it.

In addition to the chart itself, there are other things to check. Does the stock price rise consistently with the gold price? Has the stock price outperformed its peers reflecting investor interest? Are other investors talking about it? In other words, do other investors like it?

I like to buy stocks that other people are buying and talking about. This confirms my valuation and analysis. If I think a company is highly undervalued, I don't want to be the only person who likes it. I want the stock to be desired and people in chat rooms excited to own it. It makes little sense to invest in a company that is severely undervalued if no one agrees with you (this is one of the reasons I avoid stocks in high-risk locations). There has to be a reason why people want to own it. If you find a highly undervalued stock, the odds are good that other people have already found it (and are shouting it to the world somewhere on the Internet).

My favorite places to find buzz about a stock are Twitter, *www.CEO.ca*, *www.Stockhouse.com* (Bullboards), and *www.Hotcopper.com.au* (Australian stocks). Also, the Stateside Report (*www.StateSideReport.com*), Gold Report (*www.TheAuReport.com*),

Kitco News Releases (*www.kitco.com*), and Bob Moriarty's website (*www.321gold.com*) are good sources.

The Stateside Report is a podcast that covers the hot stocks. The Gold Report has daily interviews with mining analysts. These interviews are read by thousands of mining investors, so what they are recommending is being researched by many people. Kitco News posts the daily news releases by miners. 321Gold has daily posts of gold-related articles. Between these four news outlets, many companies get a lot of buzz, and the good ones get their story out.

Other websites to find buzz are the stock forums on Google Finance and Yahoo Finance.

7) Cost Structure / Financing

The cost structure is the cash cost per ounce and the additional cost per ounce to breakeven. You combine these to arrive at the all-in cost per ounce. To simplify how to calculate cash flow, all you need are four numbers: cash cost per ounce, operating cost per ounce, production ounces, and the gold price.

Simplified Cash Flow Calculation:

Cash Flow = Production Revenue minus All-in Costs

(Production oz. x Current Spot Price) - (Production oz. x All-in Cost Per oz.)

A typical gold mining company today will have an operating cash cost of $800 per oz., plus additional non-operating costs of $400 per oz. Thus, their breakeven point (all-in cost per oz.) would be a $1,200 gold price. A low-cost producer would have a breakeven point below a $1,000 gold price.

I consider the additional non-operating costs as a method of identifying free cash flow. I calculate a company's non-operating costs because the reported AISC (all-in sustaining costs) is always below the breakeven cost per oz. The ASIC excludes many hidden costs, such as depreciation, amortization, taxes, royalties, finance and interest charges, working capital, impairments, reclamation and remediation (not related with current operations), exploration and development and permitting (not related with current operations).

Identifying the non-operating cost per oz. is not always easy and requires experience with reading financial statements. The key is identifying the cost level that produces free cash flow. As long as you can get close, that is all that is important. You don't have to be exact. In Chapter 6, I went into more detail on how to identify all-in costs.

Ideally, you want companies that have a low-cost structure and are highly profitable. However, most companies fall into the moderate cost structure category. The companies you want to avoid are those with high costs (which create low profits and high insolvency risk).

An easy way to determine the cost structure of a gold mining company is to divide their cash cost per ounce by the current price of gold. If it is near 1/3, then it is a low-cost producer. Conversely, if it is near 2/3, then it is a high-cost producer. If we use a gold price of $1,500 (for round numbers), then 1/3 is $500, and 2/3 is $1,000. Any cash cost below or near $500 is a low-cost structure, and any cost near $1,000 or above is a high-cost structure. I consider a cash cost over two-thirds the gold price to be a red flag. Unless the cash cost is forecasted to come down, I will likely avoid a high-cost structure (as will other investors).

Note: This same one-third and two-third method works for silver miners.

Items that can impact non-operating costs include debt payments, exploration (new mine), development (new mine), and permitting, depreciation, royalties, and taxes. Some companies seem to have a hard time accumulating cash, even if they have significant free cash flow. This can happen for a variety of reasons. The two biggest reasons are debt and development costs. If a company has a lot of debt, they might need all of their free cash flow to pay back the bank. This is not good for investors in the near term, but once their balance sheet is cleaned up, their share price will likely jump in value.

We want free cash flow to improve a balance sheet. What makes companies valuable is the combination of free cash flow and a good balance sheet. You need both for the share price to constantly rise with the gold/silver price. The ideal situation for an investor is a clean balance sheet and large free cash flow, in conjunction with rising gold/silver prices.

The second big reason a company has trouble accumulating cash is development costs. This can be frustrating as an investor because as a company builds mines, they not only spend all of their cash on development costs, but they nearly always add debt to the balance sheet. Thus, a company that is constantly growing can have a hard time cleaning up its balance sheet.

I don't mind it when a company is growing, which costs money to achieve, but ideally, I want them to pay attention to their balance sheet. Every company will use a portion of their cash for exploration and expansion, but we want them to do it diligently.

Often companies are more growth-focused than cash focused. When that happens, shareholders are never rewarded. A good example of this is Hecla Mining. They had a stock price of $12 in 2008 and today it is below that level. What happened? They took on debt and focused on expansion instead of cash. Hopefully, their awful performance, as reflected in their share price, will change their strategy toward being more cash-focused (and investor friendly).

How a company finances its mines can impact the cost structure and profitability of the mine. Debt financing, streaming deals, and hedging can impact the cost structure. Often companies are forced to hedge portions of production to receive financing. Another common method is when lenders demand to be paid a portion of production at a set price. These are called streaming deals, whereby the lender receives a stream of production. The lender will get a sweetheart deal where they only have to pay a low fixed price for each ounce. Then the lender can sell the gold/silver at the market rate. These can be considered outstanding debts and will impact the cost structure and reduce profitability.

When I own a development stock, I always worry about how they will finance their mine. I have my fingers crossed that they do not use hedging or streaming deals. I prefer two-thirds debt and one-third equity for initial mines. For subsequent mines, I prefer two-thirds cash (organic growth) and one-third debt. A little bit of debt is good, which can be paid back quickly.

Often a gold or silver mine will produce more than one metal. These extra metals can be counted as cost offsets (lowering the cash costs) when they are sold. These offset metals can have a significant impact on lowering the cost of production. You have to be careful expecting these offsets to be in demand in the future. Often companies rely on offset metals, such as copper, lead, and zinc, to lower their costs. Sometimes these offsets determine if a company is profitable or not. I like to know the percent of revenue from each metal that they produce, but it is not always reported by companies.

When I do my valuations, I do not include the base metals as part of resources and reserves. However, I do reduce the cash costs somewhat when there are significant offsets. I tend to be conservative when adding value for offsets because I'm not sure if base metals will be in high demand in the future due to potential economic issues. If global economic growth decreases, then base metal demand will also decrease.

* * * * *

One factor that needs to be included somewhere in your analysis is the timeline risk. This is the amount of time until production begins. After a company reaches production (or gets close), the risk level for the stock drops dramatically, and simultaneously the stock price increases. I always consider the timeline risk for companies that are non-producers. I try to use a limit of five years until production, although I can be flexible and go to six or seven years on occasion. As a general rule, if I think production is more than five years away, I will not invest.

Ideally, for development stocks, you want to have confidence that there is a path to production within five years, and three years is much better. If a company is not giving guidance of this outcome, then the risk is probably too high versus the reward. I have broken this rule of thumb several times, and so far, it has not paid off. Most of these stocks have languished and still do not have a path to production.

Timeline risk can be different for each investor. How long do you want to wait for your investments to pay off? For me, I don't mind waiting five years, but I don't want to wait much longer than that. You may have a shorter timeframe in mind and want to see returns in three years. If that is the case, then your timeline risk is shorter. Some of you may not mind waiting up to 10 years and thus have a longer timeline risk. Based on your timeline risk horizon, invest accordingly based on when you can expect future cash flow.

Two other factors to pay attention to for non-producers that are building their first mine are the project's NPV (Net Present Value) and IRR (Internal Rate of Return). Ideally, you want the NPV to be significantly higher than the current market cap. A good ratio would be 5 to 1. Secondly, you want the after-tax IRR to be above 25% (at $1,300 gold or $18 silver). If the after-tax IRR is below 20%, then that is a red flag.

There are exceptions to this rule of thumb for large projects, because of the high potential cash flow. I can go as low as 15% if the potential cash flow is very high.

The NPV and the IRR identify the economics of the project. If they are both not solid, then the odds of obtaining financing are not good. Conversely, if they are solid, then the project is likely to get built. The one exception are very small companies. I have found that companies with very low market caps have trouble raising money for the capex. Banks are generally not comfortable lending more money than a company is currently worth.

Another thing to compare is the NPV to the capex. You do not want the first mine to have an NPV that is close to or less than the capex. If they are close, then the project likely won't get financed. You want the ratio to be at least 2 to 1.

All of these variables can seem confusing, but after you analyze a few stocks and buy a few stocks, they become much easier to understand. There is a learning curve, but after some time you will quickly catch on. Knowing if a project is economic; if the grade is good; if the stock is highly undervalued; if it is a good location; if there is a likelihood of financing issues, or some other factors, will become clear to you after spending some time as a gold/silver mining investor.

8) Cash / Debt

Cash is king in the mining business, and there are several reasons why. The first is that cash allows for organic growth, whereby a company can self-finance exploration and expansion programs. This can be highly valuable to investors because gold can be found in the ground for about $25 to $30 per ounce (at an existing discovery) and then sold for $2,500 (in a few years). When a company self-funds its growth, it is like manna from heaven for investors. What happens is that growth in resources leads to growth in production, which leads to an increase in the valuation of the company.

The second reason cash is king because if a company has cash in the bank, this reduces the likelihood of dilution. If a company has a lot of cash, then there is no reason to issue more shares. They can now leverage their cash and issue debt to build another mine. As long as the debt is manageable, then leverage is a wise thing to do. Ideally, you want companies with lots of cash and no debt, or have a plan to pay down their debt quickly after building a mine.

A company that is investor friendly understands what impacts the share price, and understands the value of cash. Often, they will state publicly their desire to pay down existing debt and increase their cash. Watch how companies manage their cash and debt. You will find out quickly if they are investor friendly and cash focused. Moreover, you want a company that always maintains a significant cash position.

A weak financial position of low cash and/or high debt will hurt the stock price. Often a company will use too much debt to build a mine, and the stock price will drop. This is from the near-term focus of investors today. However, once the debt is paid down, the stock will roar back. The thing to understand about debt is the burden. Can the company manage its debt? Is it a problem? How much is it impacting profitability? Using debt to build a mine is not a problem as long as the debt is manageable.

Another thing to be aware of is that mining companies without cash flow will often burn through their cash and constantly have to go back and issue more shares to raise money. The amount of cash that is used on a monthly or annual basis is called the burn rate and can lead to high dilution in the share structure. Companies need cash to fund exploration, development, and expansion. If they can't get a loan, then they are forced to issue more shares and warrants. This is quite common in the mining business.

Today, sentiment in mining stocks is down, and many junior stocks are down 50% or more from their all-time highs. For this reason, many of these stocks are going to require large share dilution to raise money. Keep this in mind when investing in a company with a low share price. If a company has a share price below 20 cents, it will require significant dilution to raise money. It's always painful to own a penny stock when they do an equity financing to raise money. Sometimes the dilution is more than 25 percent of their shares outstanding.

As companies add cash to their bank account using free cash flow, it improves their balance sheet. When they are doing this on a quarterly basis, it tends to steadily increase the value of the stock. There is a strong correlation between increased cash and an increase in the stock price. This is especially true in growing companies. As cash accumulates, it gives them opportunities to purchase other companies and to increase production and add resources.

Today, financing and raising money is becoming a significant issue for small mining companies. There are rumors that hundreds of small mining companies could go bankrupt soon because they won't be able to raise financing to fund exploration projects. This is a significant investment risk and is quite real. This is one of the reasons many small mining/exploration companies are so cheap today. Are they good investments or fool's bets? From my viewpoint, unless a company already has the goods (existing flagships or significant discoveries), then the risk/reward is not worth it.

One question to ask yourself is, when is debt a problem. Most companies with debt problems are producers. They obtained their large debt to go into production. For these companies, you can check their debt coverage. This is a simple calculation of debt to cash flow:

Cash Flow = Production Revenue minus All-in Costs

(Production oz. x Current Spot Price) - (Production oz. x All-in Cost Per oz.)

Debt = Debt - Cash

(Always subtract cash, since it could be used to pay off debt.)

Debt Coverage = Cash Flow / Debt

If the debt coverage is less than 20%, then you could have a problem if gold prices fall or cash costs increase. It's always nice to see a debt coverage over 50%.

While I am showing you a formula, this is mainly to show you the concept. You can easily do this in your head. For instance, what is the ratio of free cash flow to debt? If a company only has a little bit of free cash flow versus their debt, then there is a potential problem.

Another number that investors use to identify debt problems is a company's working capital (current assets minus current liabilities). A company's working capital is also a measure of its liquidity (the ability to pay short-term debts). Large companies try to have at least $100 million in working capital. Medium sized companies are probably okay with at least $50 million. If a company does not have adequate working capital, then its share price will be impacted negatively.

One issue that has been occurring recently is that development companies have been borrowing money before they have financing for production. This is very risky and has caused several companies to go bankrupt. Once a company gets into debt and does not have a path to production, they are at the mercy of investors to help them pay off the debt. If they cannot raise more money, then they are faced with bankruptcy. Be wary of investing in development companies that have any debt. If they are wise, they will wait until construction begins before assuming any debt.

9) Low Valuation

If you did not identify enough red flags in Steps 1 through 8 to reject a stock, then it is time to check for a low valuation. (Note that step 9 is only for producers and Late-Stage Development stocks).

My favorite valuation method for finding undervalued stocks is Market Cap Per Resource Ounce. I like to use the current fully diluted market cap divided by future reserves. I estimate future reserves based on the number of ounces that I think they will produce in the future. My future reserve estimates are usually very close to their current M&I ounces (inclusive of P&P), although this can vary by company. I use future reserves, because I'm more concerned with the future valuation of the stock rather than the current valuation. I want to buy future reserves really cheap *today*. Then I will wait for those reserves to get revalued much higher in a few years.

Low Valuation Formula:

Fully Diluted Market Cap / Future Reserve Ounces.

For gold mining companies, you want future reserves to be valued under $50 per ounce. For silver, under $5 per ounce.

These are general guidelines. For gold mining companies, you can go as high as $100 per ounce (if you think the company is going to grow), although I would only invest in a few over $50. For silver mining companies, you can go as high as $10.

If a gold mining company has a current valuation under $50 per ounce for their future reserves, then there is a good chance that those reserves will get revalued in the future much higher, perhaps more than $250. This, of course, depends on the future price of gold. A solid Mid-Tier gold mining company today can expect their reserves to be valued around $300 to $500 per oz. What will they be valued at if gold reaches $2,500?

Many of my gold investments are in companies with valuations below $50 per oz. However, I am aware that Mid-Tier Producers have an excellent risk/reward profile. For this reason, I have purchased several Mid-Tier Producers above $50 per oz. For development stocks, I tend to always invest below $50 per oz.

Today you can find a lot of gold mining companies with future valuations under $50 per ounce and silver mining companies under $5 per ounce. Once you find these low valuations, check the red flags. Which companies do not have any red flags and have low valuations? Which companies have great properties, are located in safe locations, have good management teams, a nice share structure, growth prospects, low costs, a good chart, and good buzz? As you add up all of the factors, you begin to find your favorite stocks.

Finding stocks with a low valuation is not that difficult. What is more difficult is finding a stock with a low valuation that does not have any red flags and passes all of the checks. This chapter helps you to identify what to look for by using a ten-step systematic approach.

* * * * *

Another low valuation method is the future cash flow multiple. This is the future cash flow versus the current fully diluted market cap. If a company is undervalued, then the future cash flow should be more than 1x the current fully diluted market cap.

Example:

Current Fully Diluted Market Cap: $20 Million

Future Cash Flow:

Future Production oz. x (Future Gold Price - Future All-In Cost Per oz.)

100,000 x ($2,500 - $1,500) = $100 Million

In this example, the future cash flow is above the current fully diluted market cap. That is what you are looking for. In this example, the multiple is 5x, which could lead to a potential 10+ bagger. If the projected $100 million in cash flow occurs, the company could get valued between $500 million to $1 billion (5x or 10x cash flow).

10) High Rating

The final ratings (upside and downside) are a combination of a formula and a final analysis. The analysis is a judgment call on your part and will decide how much you like a company. Generally, a low valuation (step 9) and relatively few red flags (steps 1-8) should lead to a high rating.

You can use this ten-step system to rate all of the companies that you analyze. However, if you cannot estimate future reserves, then you have to use a different method for obtaining a rating. I have devised my own method using my experience. For companies for which I cannot estimate future reserves, I do not use any valuation formulas. Instead, I use steps 1-8 and estimate their ratings. These ratings are nearly always below a 3 for companies without future reserves.

Ratings are a snapshot in time, reflecting the moment when an analysis is performed. They should be updated at least annually, or when a significant event occurs, such as an updated resource estimate, a feasibility study is released, production begins, or an unexpected event that impacts that value of the stock.

Theoretical Market Cap Growth:

Future Market Cap Method #1 (Resources)

Future Reserves x Future Gold Price x Resource Multiplier = Future Market Cap

Future Market Cap Method #2 (Cash Flow)

Future Cash Flow x Cash Flow Multiplier = Future Market Cap

Cash Flow = (Future Production Oz. x Gold Price) - (Future Production Oz. x All-in Cost Per Oz.)

(Future Market Cap - Current Market Cap) / Current Market Cap = Future Market Cap Growth

For the future market cap, I use two methods and compare them (see formulas above). If they are both similar values, then I have more confidence. I tend to trust the cash flow method as being more accurate. I usually use 5 for the cash flow multiplier, unless it is a large company, then I will use 10. Future production is my expectation for production in 3 to 5 years. All-in costs are my estimates for future costs in 3 to 5 years.

For the resource multiplier, I normally use 15. Future reserves are estimated based on current resources unless a company provides guidance for future resources.

I divide the current fully diluted market cap by the future market cap and arrive at potential market cap growth as a percentage.

> Note: While I currently use a future gold price of $2,500, a future silver price of $100, a resource multiplier of 15%, and a cash flow multiplier of 5 (or 10 for larger companies), you can be more conservative or more aggressive. It's easy to do these calculations with other defaults based on your expectations. There is a cash flow calculator on the GSD website that is very handy.

Using this theoretical market cap growth, I combine it with my analysis to give it an upside and downside rating. The rating definitions were listed earlier in this chapter.

My future time horizon is 3-5 years. Thus, I am expecting the theoretical growth to occur during this time horizon. However, there are many factors (red flags) that can impact this potential growth target. For instance, some of the red flags include location issues (such as a lack of infrastructure, political risk, permitting, native issues, etc.), weak management, legal issues, timelines issues, financing issues, production costs, debt/cash issues, hedging, share dilution, and a lack of growth potential.

One part of the final analysis is to reduce the upside potential by using red flags. If a company has a potential growth of 500%, but has a few red flags, then you can't give it a 3 or 3.5 upside rating as a potential five-bagger. The question becomes, how much are you going to reduce the rating? Are you comfortable that it will become a three-bagger? If so, then you can give it a 2.5 rating. Otherwise, give it a 2 rating. After you begin rating companies, it becomes fairly easy to determine what they should have.

After you have a list of companies with ratings, you will have to decide which companies you like the best. Sometimes you will prefer a company with a 2.5 upside rating and 3 downside rating over a company with a 3 upside rating and 2.5 downside rating because of a better risk/reward profile.

Let's do an example:

Current Market Cap Fully Diluted: $50 Million

Projected Future Reserves: 3 Million oz.

Projected Future Production: 200,000 oz.

Projected Future All-in Cost Per Oz.: $1,200

Projected Price of Gold: $2,500

Future Market Cap Method #1 (Resources)
3,000,000 oz. x $2,500 x 15% = $1.1 Billion (Projected Future Market Cap)

Future Market Cap Method #2 (Cash Flow)

$260 Million = (200,000 x $2,500) - (200,000 x $1,200)

$260 Million x 5 = $1.3 Billion (Projected Future Market Cap)

($1.1 Billion - $50 Million) / $50 Million = 2,100% (Projected Market Cap Growth)

Final Analysis:

The theoretical market cap growth target is 2,100% or a potential 21 bagger. That is well above a five-bagger, so the next step is to decide if it deserves to have an upside rating of 3, 3.5 or 4? It's likely at least a 3 rated stock, or else you would have kicked it out before step 10. The upside rating is highly impacted by the risk level and the number of red flags. The key here is the path to production. Unless they have a clear path to production, including financing, then you should give it a 3 rating. Without financing, a company will not make it into production and reward you with the high return you are expecting. A rating of 3 means a potential five bagger, whereas a 3.5 rating means a likely five bagger.

When I rate stock, a potential 20 bagger can have an upside rating from 2 to 4 depending on its risk level and the number of red flags. It's rare for a stock with that much potential to be rated below a 2 rating. If it has a strong path to production, then it will get either a 3.5 or 4 upside rating, depending on my confidence that it will make it to production.

The downside rating is completely based on the number of red flags. If a company is solid, then the downside rating will be at least a 3. The better I like the project and management team, the higher the downside rating. The quality of project also is a factor. If the project is excellent, with very few red flags, then the downside rating will likely be a 3.5. It's rare for me to give an upside rating of 4, but I gave one to MAG Silver when its share price was under $10. Even with the project in Mexico. Why? It's the best silver project on the world. The risk-reward was amazing when its share price was under $10. Once their share price reached $20, I dropped the downside rating to 3.5.

Well, that's it, except for a few appendixes that include handy reference information, such as a glossary and formulas. If you would like a two-week free trial, send me an email. You can use the Contact Us link on the GSD website. Thanks for reading, and good luck with your gold and silver investments. I hope that you become a subscriber at *www.goldstockdata.com*.

Appendix A - Glossary

43-101 Resource Estimate: This is the Canadian national standard report required for mining companies to trade on a Canadian Exchange. It defines the Measured and Indicated Resources, as well as the Inferred Resources. When a company reports resource estimates, they are usually based on this report. Because most mining companies trade in Canada, it is essentially an industry standard.

All-in Costs: I consider all-in costs to be the cost per ounce that results in free cash flow. Unless a company provides its free cash flow, this can be difficult to calculate. The most conservative number to use for free cash flow is net profit. However, net profit can understate free cash flow because it does not remove intermittent costs.

All-In Sustainable Costs (AISC): AISC is the reported all-in cost per ounce excluding depreciation, amortization, taxes, royalties, finance and interest charges, working capital, impairments, reclamation and remediation (not related with current operations), exploration and development and permitting (not related with current operations).

American Eagle Coins: Gold and Silver American Eagle coins are minted by the U.S. Mint and are the official gold/silver coins of the U.S. Government. Circulation began in 1986 for the modern version. From 1849 to 1933, Double Eagle gold coins were minted. Beginning in 1795, America began minting gold and silver coins. Paper currency was not issued until the Civil War.

Bagger: This is the term used to indicate a large return of 100% or more. For example, a three bagger would be a 300% return.

Blow-Off Phase: At the end of a gold/silver bull market, there is usually a blow-off phase, where the price of gold/silver explodes in value in a short period of time, and then drops back down to a more normal level.

Capex: This is the capital requirement to build a new mine. Ideally, you want the first mine to have a relatively low capex (below $200 million) so that financing is not an issue and the balance sheet and share dilution will not get severely impacted.

Cash Cost: The cash cost per ounce includes the cost of production. This is primarily the labor, fuel, electricity, transportation, and raw materials needed to produce an ounce of gold. It does not include taxes, depreciation, expansion costs, exploration costs, interest, debt, sustaining capital, or any other miscellaneous costs not associated with operating the mine.

Cash Flow: Defined here as the dollar value of production minus the cost to produce those ounces. Cash flow can be used to service debt and expand the company. I use the projected all-in cash cost per ounce. This creates a more conservative estimate of cash flow.

Cash Flow Multiple: Market Cap / Cash Flow. This shows the cash flow strength of a company. On average, a company is valued (market cap) at approximately 10x cash flow. A company valued at a multiple of 3 would be highly undervalued.

Cubic Meters of Mineralized Ore (Length x Width x Depth): This is generally converted to tons as follows: Cubic Meters x 1.5 = Tons

Cutoff Grade: The cutoff grade is the minimum ore grade that will be mined.

Cutoff Grades (Gold): There are minimum requirements for profitability when mining a ton of ore. The gold cutoff grade is generally .5 grams per ton for surface mining, and much higher for underground mining, approximately 3 grams per ton. If costs are low, you will see cutoffs as low as .3 grams per ton for surface mining.

Cutoff Grades (Silver): The silver cutoff grade is generally 2 grams for surface mining and much higher for underground mining, approximately 3 ounces per ton. If costs are low, you can see cutoff grades that are somewhat lower.

Emerging Major: These are gold/silver companies with a market cap between $1.5 and $3 billion. They must also have gold production greater than 200,000 oz., or silver production greater than 5 million oz. (my definition).

Emerging Mid-Tier Producer: These are gold/silver companies forecasted to become Mid-Tier producers within three years (my definition). These are usually companies that have given guidance of increased production.

EPS: Earnings Per Share. Computed by dividing Net Profit by the Outstanding Shares.

ETF (Exchange Traded Funds): ETFs have become a major trading vehicle for investors. These funds trade on the major stock markets, using a stock symbol no different than that of a corporation. For instance, the symbol GLD is traded on the

New York Stock Exchange as if it were just another company. However, the symbol GLD is actually a trading vehicle that is managed by a major investment bank - Mellon Bank of New York.

ETF vs. Mutual Funds: The difference between a mutual fund and an ETF is often imperceptible. The one difference is that an ETF attempts to emulate something, such as the current price of gold. Whereas the manager of a traditional mutual fund would invest in gold mining companies and try to make a profit by selecting the best gold stocks, the manager of an ETF would use their investors' money to "track" the price of gold.

ETF (Leveraged): These are ETF funds that attempt to double (or triple) the daily movement in the underlying asset. There are leveraged funds for the price dropping, called short funds, and there are funds for the price rising, called long funds. They were created specifically for short-term traders, and are not recommended for long-term investing. Due to a mathematical anomaly, it is impossible for these leveraged funds to track the underlying asset over an extended period of time.

EV (Enterprise Value): Market cap + net debt. This also known as the takeover price, or true value of the company. Because the debt has to be paid back, the takeover price is actually more than the market cap. Conversely, any excess cash makes the takeover price much cheaper.

Gold Double Eagle Coins: Minted from 1849 until 1933, these coins were the official gold coins of the U.S. Government. They are the ultimate collector item and are highly valuable, based on the quality and rarity of the coin.

Gold/Silver Ratio: The price of gold divided by the price of silver. For example, today (2/8/2012) the ratio is 52 ($1,730 / $33). Historically it has averaged about 30, although when silver was recognized as money in the 18th and 19th centuries, the average was 16. Many are expecting a return to this narrow ratio because the amount of silver mined versus gold is about 10 to 1.

GPT: Gram per ton.

Grade Chart:

Surface Gold		
High Grade	5 gpt	1 million tons = $225 million @ $1,500/oz.
Good Grade	2.5 gpt	1 million tons = $105 million @ $1,500/oz.
Low Grade	1 gpt	1 million tons = $50 million @ $1,500/oz.

Underground Gold		
High Grade	15 gpt	1 million tons = $750 million @ $1,500/oz.
Good Grade	5 gpt	1 million tons = $225 million @ $1,500/oz.
Low Grade	2.5 gpt	1 million tons = $105 million @ $1,500/oz.

Note: The cutoff grade is generally .35 grams for gold surface mining, and much higher for underground mining, approximately 2.5 grams per ton. However, as gold prices rise, it will become the norm to use cutoffs of .3 grams per ton for gold surface mining, and 2 grams per ton for underground mining.

Surface Silver		
High Grade	10 opt	1 million tons = $300 million @ $30/oz.
Good Grade	5 opt	1 million tons = $150 million @ $30/oz.
Low Grade	3 opt	1 million tons = $90 million @ $30/oz.

Underground Silver		
High Grade	20 opt	1 million tons = $60 million @ $30/oz.
Good Grade	10 opt	1 million tons = $300 million @ $30/oz.
Low Grade	5 opt	1 million tons = $150 million @ $30/oz.

Note: The cutoff grade is generally 5 grams for silver surface mining, and much higher for underground mining, approximately 1 ounce per ton. These cutoffs will fall as the price of silver rises.

Hedging: Offsetting the risk of an investment. This is often done by gold and silver producers by selling their future production at a fixed price.

In Situ Value: An estimate of the value of the resources (total ounces not counting inferred) in the ground at today's gold/silver prices. This is generally multiplied by 10% to get a conservative estimate of the company's value. Strong companies are often valued at 20%.

IRR: Internal Rate of Return. You want the pretax IRR to be above 25% at $1,300 gold. If the pretax IRR is below 20%, then that is a significant red flag.

Junior Mining Company: This is any silver/gold mining company that has not yet reached Mid-Tier Production (my definition). I break Juniors into eight categories:

Small Producer: This is the category that is producing, but not enough to be an Emerging Mid-Tier Producer.

Near-Term Producer: This is the category that is planning to begin production within two years.

Emerging Mid-Tier Producer: This is the category where production is forecasted to exceed 80,000 oz. of gold or 3 million oz. of silver in the next three years.

Late-Stage Development: This is the category where production is forecasted to begin within three to six years.

Early-Stage Explorer: Developer with Enough Reserves for a Mine: This is the category that has found enough reserves to build a long-life mine.

Early-Stage Explorer: Developer with Almost Enough Reserves for a Mine: This is the category that has found almost enough reserves to build a long-life mine.

Early-Stage Explorer: Developer where Potential Exists: This is the category for companies that do not apply to any of the other categories. These are the true explorers, and represent the most speculative investments.

Project Generator: The objective of these companies is not to mine gold/silver, but to find it and sell it in the ground (usually keeping a percentage as an equity owner). Thus, they are only concerned with finding gold/silver. These are the true explorers who only have one objective: finding gold/silver. Many investors like this business model because they tend to maintain their share structure and are investor friendly.

Market Cap: Shares outstanding multiplied by the current stock price. The fully diluted market cap is fully diluted shares multiplied by the current stock price.

Major Mining Company: Any gold/silver mining company with a market cap greater than $3 billion (my definition). I categorize a company as a Major differently than the professionals. They define a company as a Major from a production standpoint. To them, a Major must have production that exceeds 500,000 ounces per year. (Generally, this requires a market cap of at least $5 billion.)

Metallurgy: This is the science of determining the recovery rate of a metal from mineralized ore. This is performed by a third party company, and is usually done when the 43-101 resource estimate is produced. Recovery rates are generally around 90%. This will vary depending on the geology, ore type, and mining method. High-grade underground sulfide ore usually has very high recovery rates over 95%. Lower grades tend to have lower recovery rates. Surface oxide ore recovery rates can vary significantly depending on the mining method and ore grades.

Mid-Tier Producer: These are gold/silver companies with a market cap between $150 million and $1.5 billion (my definition). They also must produce significant amounts of gold/silver. For gold producers, this would be more than 80,000-100,000 ounces per year. For silver producers, this would be more than 3 million ounces. At this size, a Mid-Tier Producer would have an approximate minimum gross income of $50 million dollars (assuming current prices of $1,700/oz. gold and $35/oz. silver).

NPV: Net Present Value. Ideally you want the NPV (at a 5% discount rate) to be significantly higher than the current market cap. A good ratio would be at least 5 to 1. Another thing to compare is the NPV to the capex. You do not want the first mine to have an NPV close to the capex. If they are close, then the project likely won't get financed. You want the ratio to be at least 2 to 1.

NSR: Net Smelter Royalty. This is a percentage ownership of the gold/silver that is converted from ore into dore bars. Generally the percentage is quite low, only about 2%. This is a net amount. For instance, if the mine has 100,000 oz. annual production, then the NSR would be 2,000 oz. At $1,500 gold, that is $3 million in annual cash flow.

Numismatic Coins: Any coin that is no longer minted and is considered a collectable.

Numismatic Coins, Grading: The grading for coins is rather complicated, but falls into the following categories. The best grading is a MS-70.

Mint State (MS): MS-70 through MS-60.

Almost Uncirculated (AU): AU-58, AU-55, and AU-50.

Extremely Fine (XF): XF-45 and XF-40.

Very Fine (VF): VF-35, VF-30, VF-25, and VF-20.

Fine (F): F-12.

Very Good (VG): VG-8.

Good (G): No number designations.

Almost Good (AG): No number designations.

Fair: No abbreviation, and no number designations.

Options: These are leveraged trading vehicles (contracts) for betting which way the price of a stock or commodity will go. There are two types of limited liability options, a put and a call. A call is an option bet that the price will rise. A put is betting that the price will fall.

Here are the basic options trading terms:

Ask: The ask price is the amount you have to pay for an option contract. Generally this is the bid price, plus commissions. Each option represents 100 shares of the underlying stock or commodity, so you have to multiply the ask price by 100.

Bid: The bid price. This is the amount an option buyer is willing to pay for an option. It is a combination of the intrinsic value and the time value (See Options, Value - below.)

Chg: This is the change in price between the current bid price and yesterday's closing bid price.

Expiration Date: This is last day that you can sell or exercise an option.

In the Money: This is when the strike price has been exceeded, and therefore the option can be sold or exercised at a profit.

Last: This is the last bid price at which the contract traded. Normally, this is very close to the bid price. However, option prices can be volatile due to changes in the price of the underlying stock, as well as other risk factors, such as time, interest rates, and dividends.

Open Int: Open Interest, or the total number of contracts open.

Premium: The total cost of the option contract (i.e. ask price plus commissions). On TD Ameritrade, the commission is $9.99, plus 75 cents per contract.

Strike: The strike price is also called the exercise price. In the case of a "put" option, this is the price the option must drop below before the expiration date. If it drops below, it is said to be "in the money."

Symbol: Trading symbol assigned to an option (e.g. SLVXX). Every option has its own trading symbol, which is associated with a particular strike price and expiration date, and can be quoted just like any stock symbol.

Vol: Daily Trading Volume, or the number of contracts traded today.

Options, How to Exercise: When an option is "in the money," you have the right to purchase (puts) or sell (calls) the underlying stock at the strike price. But most investors never exercise their options. Instead, they sell them for cash.

Options, Value: An option carries a value related to the underlying asset, as well as a time value, which is correlated to the amount of time until the option expires.

Intrinsic Value: Once your option is "in the money," and has exceeded your strike price, the intrinsic value will be the difference between the strike price and today's actual price.

Extrinsic Value (Time Value): This is the ask price beyond the intrinsic value. It is based on the time remaining before the option expires. Note that the time value of money is always shrinking and reaches zero on the expiration date.

OPT: Ounces Per Ton.

Prove Up: This is a term used to indicate that a company is attempting to prove through drilling that they have enough resources for a mine.

Recovery Rate: This is the percentage of gold/silver that is recovered versus the number of ounces that are mined. A ton of ore might have 10 grams of gold, but you never recover all of it. Ideally you want at least 90% and anything lower than this is a red flag. If a company has a 2 million ounce gold property, but the recovery rate is only 75%, then it is really a 1.5 million ounce property. Metallurgy is the scientific process used to determine the recovery rate.

Reserves/Resources: These are the minerals (gold/silver) in the ground. There are several ways of estimating reserves/resources:

Inferred Resources: These are resource estimates based on drilling results and geology. The better the geology is understood, the more likely the estimate will be accurate. These are generally unreliable without further drilling. Normally these are provided by third party companies who prepare a 43-101 resource estimate using drilling results and geology.

Measured and Indicated Resources (M&I): These are the gold/silver resources that were determined by drilling and a legal 43-101 resource estimate. They are considered to be reliable. A good rule of thumb is to expect about 80% of the M&I to be mined over the long term.

Proven and Probable Reserves (P&P): These are Measured and Indicated Resources that have been validated through a mine plan, usually called a Preliminary Feasibility Study. Thus, the only difference between M&I and P&P is a mine plan. Actually there is a second difference, and that is you can expect 100% of P&P to be mined.

Note: Technically, Inferred Resources and M&I Resources are not reserves, although many people refer to them as reserves.

Share Structure: Share structure is comprised of several elements.

Shares Outstanding: This is the number of shares that have been issued to shareholders, excluding Options and Warrants. These are the common stock shares that trade on stock exchanges.

Options: These are stock options given to employees, contractors, or others who are affiliated with the company. Each option has a specific price threshold, along with exercise and expiration dates, which must be met before the stock can be issued. Legally, stock options must be granted at or above the current stock price. If an option exceeds the strike price, it is usually exercised by the option holder and becomes common stock, thereby increasing the number of shares outstanding. This is called dilution.

Note: If someone is given stock options, normally they have to wait a period. First, they might have to wait for the strike price to be reached. Second, they might have to wait until a vesting period has been reached (vesting periods are generally only used to keep employees from leaving the company). Third, if the expiration date occurs before these dates are reached, then the options expire worthless.

Note: If someone owns options that are at or above the strike price, at or above the vesting date, and before the expiration date, then they have the right to purchase the stock at the strike price (also called the exercise price). Essentially, they will be purchasing the stock at a discount. Once they own the stock, they can either hold it or sell it.

Warrants: These are essentially options owned by private investors that can be used to purchase stock at a fixed price. Private investors can obtain warrants by participating in a private share offering. This is quite common in the mining business. Companies use warrants as an incentive to get investors to participate in a private share offering. Generally, when an investor agrees to participate in a private share offering, they will receive either a half or full warrant for each common share they purchase. Investors can then hold the warrants and purchase the stock directly from the company at a later date at this fixed price (before the warrants expire). If a warrant is exercised and stock is purchased by an investor, these new shares become common stock and increase the number of shares outstanding.

Fully Diluted Shares: These are the combined total of shares outstanding, along with options and warrants that have not expired.

Note: It is a good practice to use this number for calculating valuations instead of the shares outstanding, if you wish to use more conservative numbers. I always use FD (fully diluted) shares in my valuations.

Float: The float is the number of shares that can actually be traded. All shares outstanding are not traded. Normally, there is a small percentage of stock held by company insiders who are long-term investors. Also, there can be shares that are restricted from trading. For these reasons, companies with tight share structures can have a small float. Moreover, a company with a small float can be highly explosive, since there are fewer shares available to be traded.

Dilution: When additional shares are issued, the Outstanding Shares total increases. This is called dilution. This reduces the earnings potential of each share, and reduces the value of each share. This is easy to comprehend. If there are 10,000 shares outstanding and a company is worth $1 million, what happens if they issue another 10,000 shares? The effective worth of each share has dropped by 50%. In all likelihood, the stock will also drop by 50%. Thus, dilution is bad.

Tightly Held: When there are a small number of Fully Diluted shares, a company's share structure is said to be tightly held. I consider anything less than 100 million shares as tight. But some investors prefer to define tight as closer to 50 million shares.

Silver Bars: These come in two standard sizes, 10 ounces and 100 ounces. You can also purchase 1,000 ounce bars, but these are mostly used in industry. While the 100-ounce bars weigh exactly 100 ounces, the 1,000-ounce bars weigh somewhere between 980 and 1,100 ounces - approximately 65 lbs

Spot Price: The current market price for gold or silver, quoted by the ounce.

Strike: Location of found mineralization.

Strike Length: The length of the known deposit.

Strike Width: The width of the known deposit.

Strike Depth: The depth of the known deposit.

Open at Depth: Drilling has not completed exploration at depth.

Open along Strike: Drilling has not completed exploration for the length and width.

Open in all Directions: Drilling has not completed exploration in any direction yet.

Surface Mining: Refers to mining at the surface (also called open pit mining), as opposed to underground mining.

Sweet Spot: The sweet spot for investing in gold/silver mining companies is finding an undervalued company with a market cap between $100 million and $300 million. This is the ideal market cap for finding low-risk, high-return investments.

Tax Rules: Here is some basic tax info to consider.

Purchases: If your purchase is over $10,000, then the seller must report it to the IRS using a 1099B form as a cash transaction. This is actually for a calendar year, per business. If you use two coin shops, you can spend $9,999 in each and have no 1099B forms. Out-of-state Internet sales can be taxable, so do your own due diligence. In California, purchases over $1,500 are not taxable. Taxes vary by state.

Sales: If you sell your gold coins to a dealer, they do not have to fill out an IRS form, unless the sale was for more than 24 gold coins. Gold bullion and silver appear to be exempt from sales reporting by dealers. But do your own due diligence.

Capital Gains: You have to report any capital gain. Sadly, bullion and coins are considered collectables and long-term gains are taxed at 28% for Federal taxes. State tax rules for capital gains will vary. Again, do your own due diligence.

Troy Ounce: 31.1 grams. An ounce as we are used to it weighs 28.3 grams, but precious metals are measured in troy ounces. This dates back to the time of Rome.

Upside: This is a term used to indicate how much a company's stock price can potentially increase. A company with a lot of upside is said to be highly undervalued. However, often this potential upside comes with risk and is not always a sure thing.

APPENDIX B - FORMULAS

Note: This is meant to be a Quick Reference Guide. Please refer to the Table of Contents for additional info on each formula.

Formula Variables

Cash Flow = (Production oz. x Current Metal Price) - (Production oz. x Cost Per oz.)

Note: It is a good idea to use the all-in cost per ounce to get a more conservative cash flow amount.

Debt = Debt - Cash

Note: Always subtract cash, since it could be used to pay off debt.

Market Cap = Fully Diluted Shares x Stock Price

Resource Ounces = Include Proven or Probable Reserves and Measured and Indicated Resources. Exclude Inferred Resources unless you are confident they will become Measured and Indicated.

Valuation Formulas

% Return:

Investment Profit / Original Investment

Cash Flow Multiple:

Market Cap / Cash Flow

Debt Coverage:

Cash Flow / Debt

EPS or Earnings Per Share:

Net Profit / Shares Outstanding

Market Cap Valuation Per Resource Ounce:

Market Cap / Resource Ounces

PE or Price Earnings Ratio:

Stock Price / EPS

Quick and Dirty Market Cap Valuation:

Resource Ounces x Gold/Silver Price x 10%

Resource Valuation as a Percentage of Market Cap:

Market Cap / (Resource Ounces x Gold/Silver Price)

Share Price Valuation by Resources in the Ground:

Resources / Shares Outstanding

Future Market Cap (Reserves):

Future Reserves x Future Gold Price x 15% = Future Market Cap

Future Market Cap (Cash Flow):

Future Cash Flow x Cash Flow Multiplier = Future Market Cap

Future Market Cap Growth:

(Future Market Cap - Current Market Cap) / Current Market Cap = Future Market Cap Growth

Note: This is the projected market cap increase divided by the current fully diluted market cap.

APPENDIX C - MINING LIFE CYCLE

Initial Public Offering (IPO): This is when the company offers stock market shares to the public to obtain their initial funding. Normally, the initial offering is very small, perhaps $5-10 million dollars.

Small Team of Geologists / Managers: An initial team is formed. This is a very small group of people, perhaps less than 10.

Property Search: Geologists search for mining opportunities.

Property is Obtained: Generally the purpose of the IPO is to fund the purchase of land, obtain mining rights, or purchase an existing mine.

Drilling Plan Generated: Once a company has obtained mining rights, they carefully analyze the geology and determine the prospective drilling opportunities. Then a drilling plan is generated, which is often released to the public to generate interest in the stock.

Drilling Begins: This is what it is all about for exploration companies - finding gold/ silver. Nearly all mining companies have drilling programs, and they are always searching for more gold/silver. These programs can be extremely expensive, and can bankrupt a Junior very quickly. The burn rates for drilling can be more than $1 million per month. Even with a shoestring budget, it can easily cost a few hundred thousand a month.

Assays Returned (Drill Results): This is what we are interested in. We want to see the results, and see how many ounces (or grams per ton) were found. Remember, the value of a mining company is directly related to how many ounces they own in the ground. It all comes down to ounces (resources and production).

New Round of Financing: Those lucky companies that find gold/silver can go back for another round of financing and raise more money for more drilling. They do this by issuing more shares and diluting the share structure. This is why mining companies tend to have millions of shares outstanding.

More Drilling: With cash in the treasury, an exploration company will drill. That's what they do. You want to be invested in companies that are "proving up" a mine. In other words, each drill result adds more ounces to their resources.

More Assays: More drill results for us! These are the results that you want to receive by email, just as soon as news is released.

The Company Begins to Grow: As results come in and more money is raised, the company begins to add employees. In the mining business, this tends to be a slow process. Note that this will only happen if the company has found significant resources.

43-101 Resource Estimate: Once the assays have shown that there are significant resources on the property, a 43-101 report is generated. This report authenticates the estimated resources on the property. The 43-101 is the foundation for an accurate valuation of the company. It normally takes more than two years from the time the first hole is discovered until this report is released.

Preliminary Economic Assessment: Once the 43-101 has authenticated the resources, the company will pay for a PEA by a third party company. This assessment will show viability of a mine and an estimated ROI (return on investment). Once there is a positive PEA, the company can then get serious about permitting and developing the mine.

Pre-Feasibility Study: If the PEA is satisfactory, the company will pay for a pre-feasibility study. This study will detail how the mine will be built, including timelines for permits, the length of time for development, along with all of the details about the mine. This document is what converts M&I resources into reserves. It is the mine plan.

Note: Both the PEA and the pre-feasibility Study can be completed in about a year each, although it often takes longer.

Feasibility Study: If the pre-feasibility Study reveals an economic mine, then a company will usually proceed to a final feasibility study. This can often be done in less than a year because it is based on the pre-feasibility study.

Development Stage: Once the feasibility study is completed, all that is left is to obtain the necessary permits, raise the money, and build the mine. This is by far the longest stage in the mining life cycle, and it can take 3-8 years. Obtaining licenses, permits, and environmental impact studies can take a long time. Furthermore, some countries are much more mining friendly than others.

Note: During this development phase, it is not uncommon for small Junior companies to enter into joint ventures with larger companies to acquire funding and expertise. This will limit the upside of the stock. Also, banks can demand gold/silver hedging (production sold at fixed prices) for a few years, so that they ensure they will get paid back. This can also limit the upside of the stock.

Note: Sometimes a company will wait to complete permitting before initiating a final feasibility study. If they wait, this will delay the mine by at least a year. Most companies will do permitting and the final feasibility study concurrently. Then once permitting is completed they will raise financing to build the mine.

Note: Quite often companies will begin building their mines without final financing. This can add risk to investors if they get partially through construction and then have financing difficulties. This recently happened to both Allied Nevada and Colossus Minerals in 2013.

Production Begins: The Holy Grail! A company takes a mine into production. The stock will generally begin to soar a few months prior to actual production - if it is an economic project. As production ramps up over the first few years, the stock price will steadily rise.

A couple of final comments about how a stock's valuation is effected by the mining lifecycle. When a company first finds a mine, and releases excellent drill results, the stock tends to take off. This is the initial lift off, and can be the most lucrative phase, depending on investors' demand for the stock.

Once the size of the mine is known, the stock tends to drop in value and languish for a period of time. Then the stock will get another boost once a final feasibility study is released, along with a timeline for building the mine. Then when financing is obtained and construction begins, the stock will begin to take off. Then another boost occurs once production begins. If all goes well, the stock will continue to rise as production ramps up during the first year of mining.

END NOTES

[1] *http://www.silver-info.com/resources-and-stocks.htm*

[2] *http://digg.com/business_finance/Silver_in_Clothing_Keeps_Odors_Away*

[3] *http://www.silverwheaton.com/Theme/SilverWheaton/files/docs_company%20fact%20sheet/World_Silver_Survey_2011_Summary_72011.pdf*

[4] Ibid.

[5] Ibid.

[6] *http://www.silver-info.com/resources-and-stocks.htm*

[7] *http://www.sprott.com/news-centre/press-releases/sprott-physical-silver-trust-updates-investors-on-the-delivery-status-of-its-silver-bullion-purchases/*

[8] The totals for the COMEX Silver Exchange and Silver ETFs are from *http://www.silveraxis.com/*. The other totals are the author's estimates. There is no definitive known inventory. Any estimate is simply that. The above ground silver inventory is likely somewhere between 800 million and 1 billion ounces.

[9] *http://www.gotgoldreport.com/2010/06/endeavours-report-on-silver.html*

[10] *http://www.coinnews.net/2013/11/12/us-mint-silver-eagle-sales-reach-record-40175000/*

[11] *http://www.24hgold.com/english/interactive_chart.aspx?title=COMEX%20WAREHOUSES%20REGISTERED%20SILVER&etfcode=COMEX%20WAREHOUSES%20REGISTERED&etfcodecom=SILVER*

[12] *www.kitco.com*

[13] Peak Oil is the point in time when global oil production reaches peak production and then begins to decline.

[14] *http://www.dani2989.com/gold/worldagprod208gb.htm*

[15] *http://silverprice.org/silver-price-history.html*

[16] *http://www.gold.org/investment/why_how_and_where/why_invest/demand_and_supply*

[17] *http://www.gold-eagle.com/editorials_05/zurbuchen011506.html*

[18] *http://goldprice.org/*

[19] *http://www.usgovernmentdebt.us/debt_deficit_history*

[20] *http://www.concordcoalition.org/*

[21] *http://www.treasurydirect.gov/govt/reports/ir/ir_expense.htm/*

[22] *http://www.rasmussen.com/*

[23] *http://goldsilverworlds.com/gold-silver-general/china-accelerates-gold-accumulation/*

[24] *http://ww2.dowtheoryletters.com/*

[25] *http://www.itulip.com/forums/showthread.php?t=507*

[26] *http:/en.wikipedia.org/wiki/Gold_reserve#Officially_reported_gold_holdings*

[27] *http://www.barchart.com/articles/etf/gold*

[28] *http://www.kitco.com*

[29] *http://paperempire.net/wp-content/uploads/2010/11/exters-pyramid.png*

[30] *http://www.silverdoctors.com/gold-run-43-tonnes-of-gold-stand-for-february-delivery-on-1st-notice-day*

[31] *http://www.24hgold.com/*

[32] *http://thecoinologist.com/sales-tax-state-by-state-breakdown/*

[33] The gold withdrawal fee is 2.5% for 400 oz. bars, and 7.5% for non-full bars, plus VAT taxes in Europe. For withdrawing silver it is 10% for less than one ton, plus VAT taxes in Europe. I would consider storing the gold in New York to avoid VAT taxes if you plan to take delivery.

[34] *http://www.newworldeconomics.com/archives/2009/012509.html*

[35] Ibid.

[36] *http://www.coinfacts.com/historical_notes/history_of_the_eagle.htm*

[37] *http://www.coinfacts.com/historical_notes/history_of_the_silver_dollar.htm*

[38] *http://americanhistory.si.edu/collections/numismatics/doubleea/doubleea.htm*

[39] *http://www.thenewamerican.com/usnews/item/12813-judge-govt-can-keep-10-confiscated-double-eagles-worth-$80-million*

[40] The following information was found at www.acoin.com/ grading.htm, although I rewrote it using my own words.

[41] *http://www.google.com/finance?q=NYSE%3AUNG*

[42] *www.ishares.com*

[43] Ibid.

[44] *http://us.ishares.com/library/kits/slv_vault_inspection_certificates.htm*

[45] *http://us.ishares.com/content/stream.jsp?url=/content/en_us/repository/resource/slv_vault_inspection.pdf*

[46] *http://www.etfsecurities.com/msl/etfs_physical_silver_us.asp*

[47] *http://www.sec.gov/investor/pubs/leveragedetfs-alert.htm*

[48] *http://en.wikipedia.org/wiki/Nick_Leeson*

[49] These are also listed in the Glossary in the back of the book.

[50] Profit divided by Original Investment = % Return. $27,000 / $3,000 = 900%.

[51] *http://www.eaglewing.com/compare.html* *http://www.vaneck.com*

[52] *http://www.vaneck.com*

[53] *http://www.silverstandard.com/assets/pdfs/SSR_in_Brief_January_2010.pdf*

[54] *http://www.cpmgroup.com*

[55] *http://finance.yahoo.com/*

[56] *http://www.finance.yahoo.com/*

[57] This is only an estimate, as solid data does not exist. However, it is actually worse than this, when you consider how many drilling exploration programs turn into producing mines.

[58] *http://www.canadianzinc.com/content/mine/permitting.php*

[59] *http://www.google.com/finance*

[60] Flagship projects are defined later on in this chapter.

[61] The best is probably Stockhouse.com, but also check Google Finance, and Yahoo Finance.

[62] Refer to Cutoff Grades in the Glossary at the back of the book.

[63] *http://www.rubiconminerals.com/i/pdf/2010Jan-CorpPres.pdf*

[64] *http://www.zerohedge.com/contributed/2013-12-14/has-tide-turned-precious-metal-stocks#comment-4247659*

[65] I use a MS Word file, which I constantly update. Any similar file will work.

[66] Trading stops are price points at which the stock is automatically sold. They are used as protection from stocks dropping too much in value. A typical stop price would be 10% or 20% below the current price.

[67] As I have stated repeatedly, my forecasts are all based on this gold bull market continuing. Once it ends, many people will lose money.

[68] *http://www.321gold.com/archives/archives_authors.php?author=Bob+Moriarty*

[69] *http://www.google.com*

End Notes

CPSIA information can be obtained
at www.ICGtesting.com
Printed in the USA
LVHW101023250521
688444LV00005B/75